D0609164

MAPPING AMERICAN CULTURE

The American Land & Life Series

EDITED BY WAYNE FRANKLIN

MAPPING
AMERICAN
CULTURE

Edited by Wayne Franklin and

Michael Steiner

University of Iowa Press Ψ *Iowa City*

University of Iowa Press, Iowa City 52242

Copyright © 1992 by the University of Iowa Press

Printed in the United States of America

Design by Richard Hendel

Printed on acid-free paper

96   95   94   93   92   C   5   4   3   2   1

Library of Congress Cataloging-in-Publication Data

Mapping American culture/edited by Wayne Franklin and Michael

    Steiner.

        p.   cm. — (American land and life series)

    Includes bibliographical references and index.

    ISBN 0-87745-379-9

        1. United States—Civilization.   2. Human geography—United

    States.   I. Franklin, Wayne.   II. Steiner, Michael (Michael C.).

    III. Series.

    E169.1.M257   1992   92-10421

    973—dc20   CIP

CONTENTS

ACKNOWLEDGMENTS

Many people and places have shaped this book. The California American Studies Association deserves special thanks for vigorously supporting a conference at San Luis Obispo on "Place in American Culture" in May 1990. George Cotkin, Wayne Hobson, Sheila McCoy, and Damaris Palmer helped guide the conference to completion; David Scofield Wilson, Sarah Emily Newton, Michael Cowan, and many other CASA members provided intellectual encouragement and practical advice for the meeting and this book that has grown out of it.

We also are very grateful to those participants at the meeting whose revised and expanded papers were submitted for possible inclusion in the book. Making the choices we made proved difficult, which was both gratifying and distressing. It would have been easy, had funds allowed, to make the volume twice the size it is or to publish a sequel containing the other excellent essays we were fortunate to be able to consider.

On the more personal level, we both are especially grateful to our respective academic homes. Michael Steiner wishes to thank the American Studies Department at California State University, Fullerton, a valued community of scholars, teachers, and friends who have always found a place for his work and have nurtured his enthusiasms. Wayne Franklin wants to pay sincere tribute to his colleagues in American Studies and in English at Iowa, where spaciousness of thought and free inquiry have long been prized.

Introduction

I take SPACE to be the central fact to man born in America, from Folsom Cave to now. I spell it large because it comes large here. Large and without mercy. It is geography at bottom, a hell of a wide land from the beginning. . . . PLUS a harshness we still perpetuate, a sun like a tomahawk, small earthquakes but large tornadoes and hurrikans, a river running north and south in the middle of the land running out the blood. . . . Some men ride on such space, others have to fasten themselves like a tent stake to survive. – Charles Olson[1] When everything else has gone from my brain – the President's name, the state capitals, neighborhoods where I lived, and then my own name and what it was on earth I sought, and then at length the faces of my friends, and finally the faces of my family – when all has dissolved, what will be left, I believe, is topology: the dreaming memory of the land as it lay this way and that. – Annie Dillard[2]

Taking Place: Toward the Regrounding of American Studies

WAYNE FRANKLIN & MICHAEL STEINER

Charles Olson and Annie Dillard evoke the purpose of this book: to illuminate the taken-for-granted groundwork of American culture, to grasp how space and place permeate the grand acts as well as the ordinary events of American life. Space comes large and rough-hewn in America, where sprawling, unfinished vistas are both exhilarating and daunting, beckoning a fresh start for some, bringing emptiness for others. If some "ride on such space, others have to fasten themselves like a tent stake to survive," and in fastening themselves and dwelling on the land Americans pay tribute to the power of place as well as space in their lives. Open space is a driving force in American culture, but the closer attachments of place—the valued environments and "dreaming memory of the land as it lay this way and that"—may be more influential. American spaciousness engenders a counterdesire for placefulness; perpetually striking out for new territory, we are equally anxious to inhabit the land and make it home.

As suggested in the first essays in this book, space and place are distinct but closely related: one begets the other and both are needed for a full life. "Place is security, space is freedom; we are attached to one and long for the other," geographer Yi-Fu Tuan has written. "What begins as undifferentiated space becomes place as we get to know it better and endow it with values," he argues. "Enclosed and humanized space is place." For artist Alan Gussow, "A place is a piece of the whole environment that has been claimed by human feelings," while for novelist Eudora Welty, place is the "gathering spot of all that has been felt," a still point in the flux of life, where the spirit is enshrined and the imagination is focused.[3]

Paradoxically enough, the need to stand still and claim space with feeling results in flight when emotions gather too thickly. If we can be lost in space, we also can be stuck in place. A complex interplay between space and place, the thrill of the open road and the certainty of home, westering and dwelling, migration and habitation, innovation and tradition, weaves its way throughout our collective and personal histories. Space and place mean different things to different people at various stages in their lives. From the inner geographies of migrants and inhabitants to the imposed topographies of shopping malls and power projects, from a Massachusetts swamp to Minnesota's Lake Wobegon to Brooklyn neighborhoods and beyond, *Mapping American Culture* explores the teeming implications of this cultural dialectic in American life.

Beyond tracing this primal pulse beat, these essays emphasize an even more basic truth: the simple fact that things take place. With startling clarity, D. W. Meinig has stressed that "history and geography are bound together by the very nature of things: history takes place, and places are created by history." Place is a powerful though often unacknowledged condition of experience. Life does not exist in a vacuum: everything takes place, from sweeping historical events (the "birth of the Republic," for instance, in the solemn confines of "Independence Hall") to the most private occurrences (the birth of a child, for example, in a seventeenth-century bedchamber, with its warm but rough wood surfaces, or in a twentieth-century hospital ward, with its smooth white sterility). Natural and built settings do not determine our lives or the course of history, but they do establish boundaries and supply possibilities. Although human beings have an insatiable yearning to shape space and live within built environments, they are still influenced by the places they create and natural forces they will never transcend. Winston Churchill's famous declaration that "at first we shape our buildings and afterwards our buildings shape us" applies to our reciprocal relationship with the physical environment in general.[4]

As an all-encompassing condition of life, place informs our identity. Our very sense of the world is colored by the physical environment; the landscapes and settings and things of our lives influence our attitudes and values, penetrate our thought and behavior. As Annie Dillard and several contributors to this book suggest, early memories of the land are lodged in our minds, deeply influencing the course of our lives. The terrain of late childhood is especially potent, nurturing the developing intellect and dwelling in adult memory as a guiding image of coherence. "Expose a child to a particular environment at his susceptible time," Wallace Stegner argues, "and he will perceive in the shapes of that environment until he dies." Indeed, clinical psychologists have argued that memory itself exists only as it is anchored to remembered places and that mental health requires continual interaction with diversified environments. Analyzing the "strange and necessary relationship between place and mind," how children soak up the spirit of a particular place, and how this osmosis continues across a lifetime, Paul Shepard concludes that "knowing who you are is impossible without knowing where you are."[5]

To appreciate where we are and to know that everything takes place is not as easy as might be expected. Of the ubiquitous yet hidden spatial dimension of culture, Edward Hall has noted that ". . . virtually everything man is or does is associated with the experience of space." Elsewhere he adds, "man has developed his territoriality to an almost unbelievable extent. Yet we treat space somewhat as we treat sex. It is there but we don't talk about it." The power of place may be so pervasive as to be ineffable, so intrinsic as to be invisible—"no more noticed," Tuan writes, "than is circumambient air on which we absolutely depend." More often than not, it is immediately lived rather than deliberately known: unreflective immersion in or movement through the landscape is far more common than deliberate sense of place. "We soon cease to see what we are accustomed to seeing," William Gass shrewdly observes. "The sightless, who bump along on Braille, don't care to count what their fingers read. That would be twice blind."[6]

A degree of environmental blindness may be necessary in order to be at ease and function smoothly in the world. Yet there are times when it is important to *see* the land and how we've changed it before its true character is lost. The need for such awareness has been variously expressed. English poet Alexander Pope counsels, "To build, to plant, whatever you intend, /. . . / Consult the genius of the place in all." On our own soil, Henry Thoreau's call for us "To rear [our] lives to an unexpected height, / And meet the expectation of the land" finds more recent echoes in Aldo Leopold's reminder that the land is a community to which we belong rather than a commodity which belongs to us, or in Gary Snyder's plea that we recover our "first ground," the *where* of who we are. We need to know such things because, as Wendell Berry has eloquently reminded us, "A human community, . . . if it is to last long, must exert a sort of centripetal force, holding local soil and local memory in place."[7]

It has been especially difficult for Euro-Americans to meet the expectations of the land and to know the where of who they are. As Berry himself acknowledges in *The Unsettling of America* (1977), the dispersing, centrifugal forces have been powerful indeed. Mobilized by the challenge of an immense continent and gripped by visions of a profitable future, migratory Euro-Americans—"the wearers out and movers on," John Graves calls them—have often been too busy to think about where they are at any given moment. From the agrarian frontier to the postmodern landscape, movement through space has been more appealing than cultivating a sense of place. "Action," according to David Lowenthal, "became so strong a component of the American character that landscapes were often hardly seen at all: they were only acted upon." As early as the 1830s, Alexis de Tocqueville observed that Americans "are insensible to the wonders of inanimate Nature, and they may be said not to perceive the mighty forests which surround them till they fall beneath the hatchet. Their eyes are fixed upon another sight: the American people views its own march across these wilds—drying swamps, turning the course of rivers, peopling solitudes, and subduing nature."[8]

The Argentinian traveler Domingo Faustino Sarmiento made a similar point with more humor in his *Travels* of 1847. "In the United States," he joked, "you will see evidence everywhere of the religious cult which has grown up around that nation's noble and worthy instruments of its wealth: its feet." No wonder that simply sitting still has not been allowable in America, where the Old World chair itself, fitted with runners for its feet, has taken to "rocking." Thornton Wilder traced the American's unwillingness to stay put and "unrelatedness to place" to the fact that "place and environment are but decor to his journey. He lives not on the treasure that lies about him but on the promise of his imagination." Echoing D. H. Lawrence's notion that "the American landscape has never been at one with the white man," psychoanalyst Erik Erikson argues more probingly still that "this country is loved almost bitterly and in a remarkably unromantic and realistic way. Oratory may emphasize localities; deeper loyalties are attached to voluntary associations and opportunities, signifying level of achievement rather than local belonging." John Graves is more direct: "pride of destruction has marked us as a breed," he writes in his 1960 farewell to the soon-to-be-dammed, and damned, Brazos River of Texas.[9]

Mobility and the profit motive blunt our sense of place, allowing the land to be bulldozed into a vast commercial way station. With poetic hyperbole, Berry has argued that most Americans are "moving about on the face of this continent with a mindless destructiveness . . . that makes Sherman's march to the sea look like a prank." In an equally acerbic tone, Meinig has described Americans as a people whose "response to landscape and history seems almost pathologically crippled: a people unable to discern, or care about, the difference between a theme park and the real thing—and ready to turn the real thing into a theme park at the slightest prospect of profit." Surveying the forlorn stretches of Holiday Inns and Wal-Marts and McDonald's, or Levittown, Las Vegas, and much of Los Angeles, Dolores Hayden has concluded that "despair about placelessness is as much a part of American experience as pleasure in the sense of place." British poet Charles Tomlinson finds in a commercial oasis of the Mojave only the "execrable conjunction / of gasoline and desert air":

> Nervy with neons, the main drag
> was all there was. A placeless place.
> A faint flavour of Mexico in the tacos
> tasting of gasoline. Trucks refueled
> before taking off through space. . . .

(As if to balance accounts, his compatriot W. G. Hoskins inveighs against the Americanized "England of the arterial by-pass, treeless and stinking of diesel oil, murderous with lorries.") [10]

Many commentators on the modern American scene stress the ingenuity with which people still contrive to make place in the most unlikely places. Residents personalize Levittown's faceless houses, for instance, as Herbert Gans has found. Or they fabricate, as on Robert Venturi's Las Vegas strip, a vast landscape of communication that organizes space and meets the wanderer's needs with intriguing allure. So, too, the "other-directed houses" of J. B. Jackson's roadside zone, with their quaint forms, garish lights, and decided modernity, have evoked a whole library of worshipful and celebratory books. But such locales are largely expedients that cannot really supply the more substantial solace fostered by abiding attachments. A deep love of place eludes most urban, nomadic Americans. In our relation to place, we are profoundly absent-minded. [11]

SCHOLARS ARE NOT immune to the spatial amnesia of the culture at large, and at times their rootlessness can even be deliberate. Michel Foucault has described a stubborn "devaluation of space" that has afflicted several generations of historians for whom "space was treated as the dead, the fixed, the undialectical, the immobile. Time, on the contrary, was richness, fecundity, life. . . . If one started to talk in terms of space that meant one was hostile to time." Surveying recent American historical scholarship, geographer John Jakle has noted "the lack of spatial orientation . . . in all but a few historical works." Rare is the scholar like John Stilgoe, for whom history *is* space. Much more typical is a complete neglect of space, a state of affairs that is understandable if one agrees with Daniel Boorstin and others that modern history represents the conquest of space. If "the fulfillment of modern America would be its power to level times and places, to erase differences between here and there," as Boorstin asserts, then place ought to wither away as an academic concern. [12]

Other disciplines reflect this antispatial bias. Literary critics announce the extinction of regionalism, declaring it "as dead as the carrier pigeon," and they welcome in its place the rise of free-floating, "extraterritorial" art. At the same time, sociologists praise the "overthrow of the tyranny of geography" and the advent of increasingly placeless life styles. In the grip of this transcendent spirit, an influential economist asserts that "the central event of the twentieth century is the overthrow of matter," and even a geographer cheerfully predicts that "we will witness increasing negation of the significance of place—we will overcome the tyranny of place" by the middle of the next century. In instance after instance, the place of place seems to have been shrinking of late as more fashionable topics implicated in the apparently placeless, transnational culture of the modern and post-modern eras—the media, consumerism, issues of social relations involving power, gender, race, and class—have come to dominate the journals and the professional meetings. In the "global village," the current wisdom seems to hold, there really are no villages as such.[13]

Yet we believe that this waning of interest in geocultural issues is in fact only apparent. We see a number of signs that suggest a new grounding of cultural inquiry, in America and elsewhere, in issues of land, place, and space: the rise of a sophisticated new rural history stressing the detailed explication of local economies and cultures;[14] the powerful reemergence of regionalism and regional studies;[15] the resuscitation of historical and cultural geography;[16] the evolution of new scholarly fields concerned with landscape and material culture, with a concomitant expansion of archeology to include, more ambitiously than in the past, literate, historical communities;[17] and, finally, burgeoning interest in nature writing as a cultural practice linked to environmental issues and concern with "eco-criticism" in literary circles.[18]

However these various ventures may develop, it remains true that almost every issue on earth is deeply implicated in actual places. We experience issues such as consumerism, colonialism, and patriarchy in concrete locales, whether those locales be the high-toned architecture of a department store, the partitions imposed on a countryside by a foreign power, or the domestic sphere as a material—not just an ideological—construct. It is the rare human issue that is truly placeless. Peter Bacon Hales demonstrates just this point in his essay on the built environments engendered by that keystone of modernism, the Manhattan Project: although ironically it had nothing to do with the island of Manhattan, that undertaking still took place in several large, particular settings, which it powerfully altered. The dreadful condition of Hanford, Washington, at present underscores exactly how much effect the project and its progeny have had on the American landscape. And this is to overlook the non-American sites of Hiroshima and Nagasaki.

Such devastated places in Japan and the United States raise an allied issue. We believe with Don Scheese in his essay here, and with such other scholars as Carolyn Merchant, Donald Worster, Patricia Limerick, Roderick Nash, and William Cronon, that the environmental crisis facing the world today should direct our attention to the groundwork of American culture and to the wider global culture it has been so instrumental in creating. Scheese's attention to how the solitary Thoreau explored the meanings of a gemlike swamp near his home in Concord in the 1850s forms a neat contrast to the transcontinental story Hales tells, a story involving enormous bureaucracies and thousands of individuals almost a century later. Yet beyond the contrast in their scale, the two essays share the conviction that when attentively read place can tell us volumes about our own behavior, values, and history. Both testify to the need William Cronon has articulated lately, the need to investigate "the human place in nature" in order to illuminate "all the many places that give shape to the modern world."[19]

Place can tell us a good deal, as well, about issues of gender. This is especially true of the work of the ecofeminists, on which Kinereth Meyer draws in her essay on landscape, language, and history in *Paterson*. Engaging the fruitful links between exploitation of natural resources and exploitation of women, the ecofeminists remind us that gender is not a neatly separable category of experience or belief. Material practices and ideology always interpenetrate, so that what white male Americans have done to the landscape and how they have talked about it may also disclose what they have done to and said about—or wanted to do to and say about—women as well. Meyer details how Williams excavates the history and language of Paterson, reenacting and hence sharing the responsibility for America's "primal scene," Myra Jehlen's term for the Columbian discovery. The mastery of the Other engages both Columbus and Williams, so that land, gender, and race are intertwined in Williams's modernist epic.

Other current issues likewise have profound connections with place. Consumerism, for instance, needs to be understood in terms of the psychology of the marketplace, as Roland Marchand demonstrates in *Advertising the American Dream*,[20] but also in terms of the environmental costs of production and disposal. And, as with gender, it requires attention to the attitudes toward the natural world that underpin it. Consumerism also has a history that in some respects long antedates the rise of modern industrial society, a history that attention to place can help us appreciate. Richard Keller Simon's essay on the shopping mall thus traces intriguing connections between that seemingly placeless site of modern consumerism and the venerable gardens of Western tradition, where design and dalliance and display have for long been equally, if also quite differently, practiced. Simon supports the need to see how current paradigms may merely repackage quite old ones; we must unwrap the surfaces if we are to understand the underlying substance.

As if in response to this last warning, Steven Marx takes us on a delightful but sobering tour of the Diablo Canyon nuclear plant, improbably built a few miles from an offshore fault line near San Luis Obispo, California. Marx tears open some of the public relations packaging of this site and of its complex media image, showing us the unnerving technical and social and political realities that are the infrastructure of modern America. His deft attention to the meaning of the Diablo site for the Chumash inhabitants long ago and today adds poignancy to his narrative. Diablo Canyon has always, it seems, been a place of "power."

ALL ELEVEN of the essays published here originated as brief papers presented in San Luis Obispo at the 1990 meeting of the California American Studies Association, a conference devoted to "Place in American Culture." Given their lively engagement with this topic, the papers found an appropriate setting in that old Spanish mission town with its nearby Chumash sites and, of course, its nuclear reactor. And a regional gathering of American studies scholars provided an especially appropriate occasion for such a topic. As an academic inquiry into the nature of national culture, American studies has had a long attachment to the spatial dimensions of American experience. Many of the definitive books in the American studies movement, from Henry Nash Smith's *Virgin Land* of 1950 to Annette Kolodny's *The Lay of the Land* of just a quarter-century later, have sought to understand the larger dimensions of national life by reference to the geocultural conditions of the New World. These and many other books that form the original "canon" of American studies as a movement sprang from the benign nativism of the era stretching from the Depression to Vietnam, as expressed, say, in Alfred Kazin's *On Native Grounds* of 1942. Arising in the 1920s and 1930s, when thinkers such as Lewis Mumford and Van Wyck

Brooks and Constance Rourke were calling for renewed attention to space and place and region, and artists as diverse as Walker Evans and William Faulkner, Josephine Herbst and Jean Toomer, Grant Wood and John Steinbeck, or Georgia O'Keeffe and Aaron Copland rooted their practice firmly in the regional landscape, American studies has remained absorbed with the topic ever since.[21]

The San Luis Obispo CASA meeting was also a fitting venue because American studies has always engaged a polyvocal community of scholars with questions that transcend and therefore elude the concerns of a single discipline. Place is a surprisingly spacious concept that is well served by such a transdisciplinary approach. As the eleven essays here demonstrate, it can invoke and interrelate insights from traditional fields as diverse as geography, ethnic studies, social history, musicology, regional studies, literary criticism, environmental studies and ecology, folklore, art history, urban and regional planning, political science, photography, and landscape architecture—even nuclear physics, at least in its more institutional and applied facets.

Concerned as it is with malls and nuclear plants, the tiny Massachusetts swamp studied by Thoreau, and Williams's industrial city, *Mapping American Culture* challenges us to reground American studies, to see national culture as profoundly situated, placed, and materialized. We have arranged the essays in topical groupings, to emphasize the local patterns of coherence and dialogue below their common concern with place. Yi-Fu Tuan, the distinguished geographer at Wisconsin, provides a magisterial overview that explores place as a fundamental basis for understanding human behavior and human nature. His probing philosophical essay stands alone at the head of this collection not only because so many of the other essayists here have been heartened by Tuan's seminal work as a geographer attentive to the humanistic dimensions of his field, but also because he reminds us that intellectual inquiry serves ends more lasting and rewarding than fashion. Tuan describes here how two fundamental principles of organization—spatial and behavioral—serve to assuage the individual's alienation in the modern world.

We have followed his piece with a group of three essays ("Cultures: Migration, Place, and Placelessness in America") that center on the experience of alienation among American migrants. For these individuals and groups, finding their new place entailed losing old ground, with all the resulting conflicts of feeling and idea that we might expect. Clarence Mondale uncovers those conflicts with telling detail in the oral history of immigrant groups, both those moving from the rural South to the urban North and those entering the country from abroad. His focus is on the "inner geography" of their experience (a term he borrows from Tuan), and his particular concern is with how migrants and immigrants order their lives by means of ingenious expedients. They remake their homes in their new surroundings by material, social, or psychological means, persisting as much as adapting—inhabiting "place-on-the-move."

April Schultz traces out just this contrast between persistence and innovation, but in a single piece of immigrant fiction, Rolvaag's *Giants in the Earth*. Focusing on the divergence between Per Hansa and his wife, Beret, and paying particularly close attention to the folkloristic elements of the novel and to Rolvaag's sensitive use of the Dakota landscape, Schultz offers a reading that situates the novel firmly in the context of immigration history. Likewise, Ray Allen's insightful study of black gospel quartets in the urban North and their ties with their homeland in the South traces both institutional and aesthetic ties between the two regions. And his attention to the way this gospel music encompasses a mythical Southland shows how at least three different disciplinary perspectives—folklore, musicology, and social history—can intersect to illuminate a complex cultural world.

The next group of essays in the book ("Texts: Language and the Making of American Place") shifts from the places that migrants experience and create to those evoked by writers. Mondale's use of oral history narrative and Schultz's concern with Rolvaag's novel already have suggested how such texts may inform historical inquiry. In the latter case, Rolvaag's "novel" is at least as much a document of his people's experience as it is a work of belles lettres invented by its author. In this next group of essays, literariness is likewise seen in a broad frame of reference. Thus, Don Scheese's reading of Thoreau's *Journal* as a document of landscape, recording its keeper's ecological ramblings and speculations, helps to recover from the hermetic world of literary criticism the messier entanglements of texts in the "real" world. Scheese uses Thoreau as an exemplum for the American studies scholar, promoting the idea of an integrative method by emphasizing Thoreau's standing as America's premier nature writer.

Kinereth Meyer likewise historicizes William Carlos Williams's epic by reading *Paterson* against the Americanist topology or topography—nature-writing, place-writing—of his era. Williams's attempt to get Paterson down on paper was also, Meyer argues, an attempt to uncover that "fresh, green breast of the new world" at which so many writers of the time, Fitzgerald most famously, leered. It was an attempt not just to see the place that America once had been but also to participate in its theft, to ravish as much as be ravished by it. And, as Kathleen Wallace reminds us in her essay on the place of the Midwest in women's autobiographies, that kind of ravishment may displace other people with legitimate historical, cultural, imaginative claims on the land. Studying how women writers of Minnesota have articulated their sense of place, Wallace concludes that the Minnesota of Garrison Keillor, the "10,000-Lakes" license plate slogan, and the popular tourist rhetoric (we are back to packaging here, too) is subtly racist and sexist, excluding those who do not fit or do not want to fit its ready-made plottings. The imagination of place in literary texts thus is seen as a complex cultural and political act.

The final group of essays ("Topographies: The Built Environment and Modern American Culture") moves our focus from the inner geography of migrants and from the topology of verbal texts to the spatial texts of outer geography, of "real places." Timothy Davis offers a sweeping overview of cultural landscape photography in America from the 1930s to the 1990s, emphasizing three main periods—the "sacred" era of Walker Evans, the "iconoclastic" interlude of Robert Frank, and the "profane" era of the "New Topographics." Davis makes many powerful connections between images and the places they frame, but also between image-making and the cultural and personal contexts that it involves. His essay has added significance in this collection because its starting date coincides with the academic rise of American studies, and the photographers he discusses in his first section shared in that rediscovery of the American scene that helped feed the movement.

Davis offers compelling testimony for the importance of place-imagery in modern America, and as such his essay also serves well to introduce the remaining pieces in the book. For these three essays—Simon's on the mall, Hales's on the Manhattan Project, and Marx's on Diablo Canyon—both individually and as a group are rich in images and in their meditation on how and why these powerful and seemingly universal places have come to typify so much of modern American life, visually and materially and indeed politically.

Simon performs a valuable service in dissecting what we might call the iconography of one such place, the mall, and he shows in the process the ways in which such a characteristically modern site in fact is an anthology of older topoi and spaces. Hales enriches this "intertextual" sense of the modern scene by probing how the federal government sought to replicate "normal" (in fact, normative) models in providing shelter for the scientists and workers at three Manhattan Project sites, Hanford, Los Alamos, and Oak Ridge. His analysis isolates general principles that guided or rather misguided the enormous undertaking and provides telling interpretations of individual policies and their conflict with presumed American values, political and otherwise.

In the final essay, Steven Marx offers none of the sweeping, continent-sized narrative that Hales does. He gives us instead the narrative of two personal visits, under escort, to the Diablo Canyon nuclear plant. As one of the legacies of Hanford and Los Alamos and Oak Ridge, such plants have their own insistently authoritarian design. And of course they are packaged (is that elevator music playing on the tour bus?) and officially lied about. In short, they are massively engineered nonbombs (so far) that sit like sores on too many American places, threatening all of us. Not that they look like sores; not that we're supposed to say it even if they do; surely it's better to live electrically. Marx's piece has in its very modesty a kind of Swiftian, almost Kafkaesque power, with an odd bit of James Thurber and Joseph Heller thrown in. It makes you want to turn off your computer, shut down the lights, evacuate.

IT IS on the level of personal, bodily experience of the kind Marx presents that all of us know, each day, the many places that compose our American world. Perhaps it is because of the obviousness of the ground on which we stand that we do not examine it as much as we might and should. But now that nature itself is becoming an artifact of our industrial culture, as Bill McKibben among others has argued, it is time to examine the maps that have guided us to this point, the maps in our hands and our minds, and ask exactly what it is that we have wrought. With Thoreau, we well might begin by asking, "*Who* are we? *where* are we?" for the questions in fact are versions of each other.[22]

Many have labored hard, recently, to disjoin those questions. We believe that it indeed is crucial to see how culture forms us, the insight that lies at the center of much recent American studies scholarship. But it may be one of the deepest ironies of this era that, for all our passion to discover how culture constructs groups and individuals to suit ulterior purposes, few have yet perceived the greatest construction of all—the one that makes us accept without question the premise that we are, inescapably, children of the hearth rather than of the land. This assumption, which fixes our allegiance to human culture even as we inveigh against its injustices, diverts our attention from what our culture is doing, quite tangibly, to our earth. Thus, it is an assumption capable of producing yet more harm to the ground beneath our feet. We may not have pushed the questions far enough. How does culture construct our bodies? Of some of the means we have heard much recently. But there are also others: by dictating what food we are to eat, for instance; and by determining how that food is processed and grown and what is done to the earth in the course of its way to us; and by interposing, between each of us and the ground from whose stuff our earthen bodies spring, the manifold poisons that by design or accident have made their way from our minds through our hands and out into the world at large. Cancer may be a fact of life; it is also an artifact of how we live. In more ways than we have admitted, our culture acts on us by first shaping the world and then positioning us in it. Too many of our environments resemble large, complex, often sinister behavioral boxes. They are three-dimensional ideology masquerading as "simple" shelter.

We would close this introduction with a final shift of perspective. One of the more touching moments in the history of our industrial culture came in 1969, when television viewers worldwide were transfixed with wonder as human feet first touched down on the moon. Seen from that alien ground in the sky, the earth showed its glowing beauty and its irrefragable yet fragile substance to all who cared to see. Without it, we not only would be nowhere—we never would have been. And if we keep on altering that fragile globe beyond real melioration, we shall be placeless in a quite final sense. Only then will place cease to matter vitally to all of us. As the meeting point of cultural pattern and the order of the earth, place may be the place to start building a new vision of our common fate. How ironic that so modern a device as a disembodied camera planted a quarter million miles away should call us home. How fitting that the exploration of nonhuman space should remind us of the precious value of this one irreplaceable human place.

NOTES

1. Charles Olson, *Call Me Ishmael* (San Francisco: City Lights, 1947), 11–12.

2. Annie Dillard, *An American Childhood* (New York: Harper and Row, 1987), 3.

3. Yi-Fu Tuan, *Space and Place: The Perspective of Experience* (Minneapolis: University of Minnesota Press, 1977), 3, 6, 54; Alan Gussow, *A Sense of Place: The Artist and the American Land* (San Francisco: Friends of the Earth, 1971), 27; Eudora Welty, "Place in Fiction," in *The Eye of the Story: Selected Essays and Reviews* (New York: Random House, 1978), 122.

4. D. W. Meinig, "The Continuous Shaping of America: A Prospectus for Geographers and Historians," *American Historical Review* 83 (1978): 1205; Winston Churchill, cited by René Dubos, "A Theology of the Earth," in *Western Man and Environmental Ethics*, ed. Ian Barbour (Menlo Park, Cal.: Addison-Wesley, 1973), 54. See also Meinig's *The Shaping of America: A Geographical Perspective on 500 Years of History*, vol. 1, *Atlantic America, 1492–1800* (New Haven: Yale University Press, 1986).

5. Wallace Stegner, *Wolf Willow* (New York: Macmillan, 1962), 21; Paul Shepard, "Place in American Culture," *North American Review* 262 (1977): 23, 32. Important studies on the necessary relationships among mind, memory, and place include Edith Cobb, *The Ecology of Imagination in Childhood* (New York: Columbia University Press, 1977); Maurice Halbwachs, "Space and the Collective Memory," in his *The Collective Memory* (New York: Harper and Row, 1980), 128–57; Harold F. Searles, *The Nonhuman Environment: Its Normal Development and Schizophrenia* (New York: International Universities Press, 1960); and Robert Coles, *Migrants and Sharecroppers: Mountaineers* (Boston: Little, Brown, 1971), 47–116 and passim.

6. Edward Hall, *The Hidden Dimension* (New York: Anchor Books, 1969), 181, and *The Silent Language* (New York: Doubleday, 1959), 188; Yi-Fu Tuan, "In Place, Out of Place," *Geoscience and Man* 24 (1984): 4; William H. Gass, "The Face of the City," *Harpers* 272 (1986): 37.

7. Alexander Pope, "Epistle to Burlington" (1731) in *The Poems of Alexander Pope*, ed. John Butt (New Haven: Yale University Press, 1963), 590; Henry Thoreau, "Our Country" (1841?), in *The Collected Poems of Henry Thoreau*, enlarged ed., ed. Carl Bode (Baltimore: Johns Hopkins University Press, 1964), 135; Gary

Snyder, *The Old Ways* (San Francisco: City Lights, 1977), 59; Wendell Berry, *The Work of Local Culture* (n.p.: Iowa Humanities Board, 1989), 4.

8. Wendell Berry, *The Unsettling of America: Culture and Agriculture* (New York: Avon Books, 1978); John Graves, *Goodbye to a River* (New York: Knopf, 1960), 176; David Lowenthal, "The American Scene," *Geographical Review* 58 (1968): 72; Alexis de Tocqueville, *Democracy in America*, trans. Henry Reeve (New York: Random House, 1946), 343–44.

9. Domingo Faustino Sarmiento, *Travels in the United States in 1847*, trans. and ed. Michael Aaron Rockland (Princeton: Princeton University Press, 1970), 149; Thornton Wilder, *American Characteristics and Other Essays* (New York: Harper and Row, 1979), 15, 17; D. H. Lawrence, *Studies in Classic American Literature* (1923; rpt. New York: Viking Press, 1961), 56; Erik Erikson, "Reflections on the American Identity," in his *Childhood and Society* (New York: W. W. Norton, 1963), 305; Graves, *Goodbye to a River*, 29.

10. Wendell Berry, *A Continuous Harmony: Essays Cultural and Agricultural* (New York: Harcourt, Brace, Jovanovich, 1970), 68; D. W. Meinig, "Foreword" to *The Making of the American Landscape*, ed. Michael P. Conzen (London: Unwin Hyman, 1990), xvi; Dolores Hayden, "The American Sense of Place and the Politics of Space," in *American Architecture: Innovation and Tradition*, ed. David G. DeLong et al. (New York: Rizzoli, 1986), 185; Charles Tomlinson, "At Barstow," in *American Scenes and Other Poems* (London: Oxford University Press, 1966), 34; W. G. Hoskins, *The Making of the English Landscape* (1955; rpt. Baltimore: Penguin, 1970), 299.

11. Herbert J. Gans, *The Levittowners: Ways of Life and Politics in a New Suburban Community* (New York: Pantheon, 1967); Robert Venturi, Denise Scott-Brown, and Steven Izenour, *Learning from Las Vegas: The Forgotten Symbolism of Architectural Form* (Cambridge, Mass.: MIT Press, 1972); J. B. Jackson, "Other-Directed Houses," in *Landscapes: Selected Writings of J. B. Jackson*, ed. Ervin H. Zube (Amherst: University of Massachusetts Press, 1970), 55–72; for an example of the many recent enthusiastic books on the roadside, see John Baeder, *Gas, Food, and Lodging* (New York: Abbeville Press, 1982); for a more scholarly treatment, see Chester H. Liebs, *Main Street to Miracle Mile: American Roadside Architecture* (Boston: Little, Brown, 1985), with an excellent bibliography. A final word here about J. B. Jackson, who has been a crucial figure in the development of academic interest in the American landscape and in the human need to organize space into place: his curiosity has been broad and populist and insightful and we do not wish to understate his importance by citing just this one brief essay in this one, partly negative, context. Readers should consult D. W. Meinig's appreciative essay on Jackson and his (less populist) English counterpart, W. G. Hoskins, in D. W. Mei-

nig, ed., *The Interpretation of Ordinary Landscapes* (New York: Oxford University Press, 1979), 195–244. See also J. B. Jackson, *American Space: The Centennial Years: 1865–1876* (New York: W. W. Norton, 1972), and *The Necessity for Ruins, and Other Topics* (Amherst: University of Massachusetts Press, 1980), as well as Jackson's essays in Ervin H. Zube and Margaret J. Zube, eds., *Changing Rural Landscapes* (Amherst: University of Massachusetts Press, 1977), and in *Landscape* magazine during the years of Jackson's editorship (1951–1968).

12. Michel Foucault, "Questions of Geography," in *Power / Knowledge*, ed. Colin Gordon (New York: Pantheon, 1980), 70; John A. Jakle, "Time, Space, and the Geographic Past: A Prospectus for Historical Geography," *American Historical Review* 75 (1971): 1087; John R. Stilgoe, *Common Landscape of America, 1580 to 1845* (New Haven: Yale University Press, 1982), *Metropolitan Corridor: Railroads and the American Scene* (New Haven: Yale University Press, 1983), and *Borderland: Origins of the American Suburb, 1820–1939* (New Haven: Yale University Press, 1988); Daniel Boorstin, *The Americans: The Democratic Experience* (New York: Vintage Books, 1973), 307.

13. Kenneth O. Hanson, in John R. Milton, ed., "The Writer's Sense of Place: A Symposium and Commentaries," *South Dakota Review* 13 (1975): 21 (apparently Hanson meant to refer to the *passenger* pigeon; we would argue in any case that, like his *carrier* pigeon, regionalism is in fact still quite alive); George Steiner, *Extraterritorial* (New York: Antheneum, 1971); Alvin Toffler, *Future Shock* (New York: Random House, 1970), 70; George Gilder, *Microcosm: The Quantum Revolution in Economics and Technology* (New York: Simon and Schuster, 1989), 17; Allen K. Philbrick, "Perceptions and Technologies as Determinants of Predictions about Earth, 2050," in *Human Geography in a Shrinking World*, ed. Roland Abler et al. (North Scituate, Mass.: Duxbury Press, 1975), 33; Marshall McLuhan, *The Global Village: Transformations in World Life and Media in the 21st Century* (New York: Oxford University Press, 1989). See also Joshua Meyerowitz, *No Sense of Place: The Impact of Electronic Media on Social Behavior* (New York: Oxford University Press, 1985).

14. On the new rural history, consider the books and articles listed and discussed in Robert P. Swierenga, "The New Rural History: Defining the Parameters," *Great Plains Quarterly* 1 (1981): 211–23; and Hal S. Barron, "Rediscovering the Majority: The New Rural History of the Nineteenth-Century North," *Historical Methods* 19 (1986): 141–52; also, these representative recent books: Hal S. Barron, *Those Who Stayed Behind: Rural Society in Nineteenth-Century New England* (New York: Cambridge University Press, 1984); DeWitt Historical Society of Tompkins County [New York], *Images of Rural Life: Photographs of Verne Morton* (Syracuse: Syracuse University Press, 1984); Steven Hahn and Jonathan Prude, eds., *The Countryside in the Age of Capitalist Transformation: Essays in the Social History of Rural America*

(Chapel Hill: University of North Carolina Press, 1985); Deborah Fink, *Open Country, Iowa: Rural Women, Tradition and Change* (Albany: SUNY Press, 1986); Joan M. Jensen, *Loosening the Bonds: Mid-Atlantic Farm Women, 1750–1850* (New Haven: Yale University Press, 1986); Sally McMurry, *Families and Farmhouses in Nineteenth-Century America: Vernacular Design and Social Change* (New York: Oxford University Press, 1988); Sarah Burns, *Pastoral Inventions: Rural Life in Nineteenth-Century American Art and Culture* (Philadelphia: Temple University Press, 1989); and Wayne Franklin, *A Rural Carpenter's World: The Craft in a Nineteenth-Century New York Township* (Iowa City: University of Iowa Press, 1990).

15. On the new regionalism in history, see David R. Goldfield, "The New Regionalism," *Journal of Urban History* 10 (1984): 171–86; for a folklorist's perspective, see Archie Green, "Regionalism Is a Forever Agenda," *Appalachian Journal* 9 (1982): 172–80. An overview of regional studies is provided by Jim Wayne Miller's "Any Time the Ground Is Uneven: The Outlook for Regional Studies—and What to Look Out For," in *Geography and Literature: A Meeting of Disciplines*, ed. William Mallory and Paul Simpson-Housley (Syracuse, N.Y.: Syracuse University Press, 1987), 1–20. Michael Steiner and Clarence Mondale, eds., *Region and Regionalism in the United States: A Source Book for the Humanities and Social Sciences* (New York: Garland Press, 1988), provide a thorough multidisciplinary guide to the subject. The special issue of *Architectural Review* 180 (November 1986), "Anatomy of Regionalism," considers the subject in terms of the built environment, while Leonard Lutwack, *The Role of Place in Literature* (Syracuse, N.Y.: Syracuse University Press, 1984), treats some of its textual implications.

Among the more interesting developments in American literature in the 1980s has been the resuscitation of the regional novel, as suggested by the following groups of books written by authors deeply rooted in the locales they deal with: William Kennedy's Albany trilogy, the "Northeast Kingdom" books of Vermont writer Howard Frank Mosher, John Edgar Wideman's Homewood novels, and the "Rocksburg" detective novels of K. C. Constantine. For poetry, see the illuminating anthology *Handspan of Red Earth: An Anthology of American Farm Poems*, ed. Catherine Lewallen Marconi (Iowa City: University of Iowa Press, 1991).

16. D. W. Meinig's work typifies the revival of historical geography, especially his magisterial *The Shaping of America* (see note 4 above); but on a more local level, see John C. Hudson, *Plains Country Towns* (Minneapolis: University of Minnesota Press, 1985); for a volume of essays aimed at encouraging historians to employ maps as evidence, and illustrating the great variety of maps available for use, see David Buissert, ed., *From Sea Charts to Satellite Images: Interpreting North American History through Maps* (Chicago: University of Chicago Press, 1990). The resuscitation of cultural geography may be represented by John A. Jakle, Robert W. Bastian, and

Douglas K. Meyer, *Common Houses in America's Small Towns: The Atlantic Seaboard to the Mississippi Valley* (Athens: University of Georgia Press, 1989); Terry G. Jordan and Matti Kaups, *The American Backwoods Frontier: An Ethnic and Ecological Interpretation* (Baltimore: Johns Hopkins University Press, 1989); Philip Lord, Jr., *War over Walloomscoick: Land Use and Settlement Pattern on the Bennington Battlefield, 1777*, New York State Museum Bulletin, no. 473 (Albany: State Education Dept., 1989); Michael P. Conzen, ed., *The Making of the American Landscape* (see note 10 above); and Richard V. Francaviglia, *Hard Places: Reading the Landscape of America's Historic Mining Districts* (Iowa City: University of Iowa Press, 1991).

17. On landscape and material culture, see many of the titles given in note 16, plus the writings of J. B. Jackson (note 11 above); Henry Glassie, *Pattern in the Material Folk Culture of the Eastern United States* (Philadelphia: University of Pennsylvania Press, 1968), and *Folk Housing in Middle Virginia* (Knoxville: University of Tennessee Press, 1975); the *Annual Proceedings* of the Dublin Seminar for New England Folklife (published by Boston University, 1976–); the writings of John R. Stilgoe (see note 12 above); Rhys Isaac, *The Transformation of Virginia, 1740 to 1790* (Chapel Hill: University of North Carolina Press, 1982); Mark Klett et al., *Second View: The Rephotographic Survey Project* (Albuquerque: University of New Mexico Press, 1984); Allen G. Noble, *Wood, Brick, and Stone: The North American Settlement Landscape*, 2 vols. (Amherst: University of Massachusetts Press, 1984); Dell Upton and John Michael Vlatch, eds., *Common Places: Readings in American Vernacular Architecture* (Athens: University of Georgia Press, 1986); Robert Blair St. George, ed., *Material Life in America, 1600–1860* (Boston: Northeastern University Press, 1988); Catherine Grier, *Culture and Comfort: People, Parlors, and Upholstery, 1850–1930* (Amherst: University of Massachusetts Press for the Strong Museum, 1989); Lois Green Carr, Russell R. Menard, and Lorena S. Walsh, *Robert Cole's World: Agriculture and Society in Early Maryland* (Chapel Hill: University of North Carolina Press, 1991); and J. Ritchie Garrison, *Landscape and Material Culture in Franklin County, Massachusetts* (Knoxville: University of Tennessee Press, 1991). Thomas Schlereth's *Material Culture Studies in America* (Nashville: American Association for State and Local History, 1983), and a volume he edited, *Material Culture: A Research Guide* (Lawrence: University Press of Kansas, 1985), provide good guidance on the subject.

On the significant influence of historical archaeology, in addition to several titles given in the previous paragraph, see James Deetz, *In Small Things Forgotten: The Archaeology of Early American Life* (New York: Doubleday, 1977); and Ivor Noël Hume, *Martin's Hundred: The Discovery of a Lost Colonial Virginia Settlement* (New York: Knopf, 1982).

18. For the interest in nature writing, see the review essay by Don Scheese, "Nature Writing: A Wilderness of Books," *Forest and Conservation History* 34 (1990): 204–8. A number of anthologies have appeared recently: for instance, the special issue of *Antaeus* 57 (Fall 1986), "On Nature"; Thomas J. Lyon, ed., *This Incomparable Lande: A Book of American Nature Writing* (Boston: Houghton Mifflin, 1989); and Robert Finch and John Elder, eds., *The Norton Book of Nature Writing* (New York: W. W. Norton, 1990). Writers like Annie Dillard, Ann Zwinger, Barry Lopez, John Hanson Mitchell, Edward Hoagland, Edward Abbey, Robert Finch, John Hay, John Graves, and David Rains Wallace, among many others active from the 1960s on, suggest the emergence of a rich new tradition centered on the revaluation of nature and the human presence in it. For secondary works on American nature writing, see Peter A. Fritzell, *Nature Writing and America: Essays upon a Cultural Type* (Ames: Iowa State University Press, 1990), especially chap. 2, "The History and Criticism of Nature Writing," 37–88; and *The American Nature Writing Newsletter*, established in 1988 and edited by Alicia Nitecki of Bentley College. The special issue of *North Dakota Quarterly* edited by Sherman Paul and Don Scheese, 59:2 (Spring 1991), contains both essays on nature writing and new examples of the form. For "eco-criticism," consult the tentative bibliography by Cheryll Burgess, in *American Nature Writing Newsletter* 3:1 (Spring 1991): 8–22.

19. Carolyn Merchant, *The Death of Nature: Women, Ecology, and the Scientific Revolution* (1980; rpt. New York: Harper and Row, 1990), and *Ecological Revolutions: Nature, Gender, and Science in New England* (Chapel Hill: University of North Carolina Press, 1989); Donald Worster, *Nature's Economy: A History of Ecological Ideas* (1977; rpt. New York: Cambridge University Press, 1985), *Dust Bowl: The Southern Plains in the 1930s* (New York: Oxford University Press, 1979), *Rivers of Empire: Water, Aridity, and the Growth of the American West* (New York: Pantheon, 1985), plus Worster, ed., *The Ends of the Earth: Perspectives on Modern Environmental History* (New York: Cambridge University Press, 1988), and Worster, ed., "A Round Table: Environmental History," *Journal of American History* 76 (1990): 1087–1147, with contributions by Carolyn Merchant, William Cronon, Stephen J. Pyne, Alfred Crosby, and Richard White; Patricia Nelson Limerick, *Desert Passages: Encounters with the American Deserts* (Albuquerque: University of New Mexico Press, 1985), and, especially, *The Legacy of Conquest: The Unbroken Past of the American West* (New York: W. W. Norton, 1987); Roderick Nash, *Wilderness and the American Mind*, 3rd ed. (New Haven: Yale University Press, 1982), and *The Rights of Nature: A History of Environmental Ethics* (Madison: University of Wisconsin Press, 1989); William Cronon, *Changes in the Land: Indians, Colonists, and the Ecology of New England* (New York: Hill and Wang, 1983), and *Nature's Metropolis: Chicago and the Great West* (New York: W. W. Norton, 1991).

Also, Richard White, *Land Use, Environment, and Social Change: The Shaping of Island County, Washington* (Seattle: University of Washington Press, 1980); Alfred W. Crosby, *The Columbian Exchange: Biological and Cultural Consequences of 1492* (Westport, Conn.: Greenwood Press, 1972), and *Ecological Imperialism: The Biological Expansion of Europe, 900–1900* (New York: Cambridge University Press, 1986); Timothy Silver, *A New Face on the Countryside: Indians, Colonists, and Slaves in South Atlantic Forests, 1500–1800* (New York: Cambridge University Press, 1990); and Stephen J. Pyne, *Fire in America: A Cultural History of Wildland and Rural Fire* (Princeton: Princeton University Press, 1982). The quotation from William Cronon is taken from "Modes of Prophecy and Production: Placing Nature in History," *American Historical Review* 76 (1990): 1131.

20. Roland Marchand, *Advertising the American Dream: Making Way for Modernity, 1920–1940* (Berkeley: University of California Press, 1985); also, Dolores Hayden, *Redesigning the American Dream: The Future of Housing, Work, and Family Life* (New York: W. W. Norton, 1984).

21. Henry Nash Smith, *Virgin Land: The American West as Symbol and Myth* (Cambridge, Mass.: Harvard University Press, 1950); Annette Kolodny, *The Lay of the Land: Metaphor as Experience and History in American Life and Letters* (Chapel Hill: University of North Carolina Press, 1975); and Alfred Kazin, *On Native Grounds: An Interpretation of Modern American Prose Literature* (New York: Harcourt Brace, 1942). For a survey of American studies scholarship from the viewpoint of regionalism, see Steiner and Mondale, "American Studies," in *Region and Regionalism*, 3–25; also, Clarence Mondale, "Concepts and Trends in Regional Studies," *American Studies International* 27 (1989): 13–37.

22. Bill McKibben, *The End of Nature* (New York: Doubleday, 1990): "we live in a postnatural world" (60). The final pair of questions climaxes Thoreau's rush of language in his account of his frustrated ascent of Mt. Katahdin; see *The Maine Woods*, ed. Joseph J. Moldenhauer (Princeton: Princeton University Press, 1972), 71.

Place and Culture

A Theoretical Perspective

Place and Culture:

Analeptic for Individuality

and the World's Indifference

YI-FU TUAN

"Place" is a key word and concept for geographers. "Culture" occupies a similar position in anthropology. I should like to explore the meaning of these words as a way of showing what these two disciplines have in common and how they differ.[1] Here I offer capsule histories of ideas, but I hope to do more. Geography and anthropology are only two of a number of formal approaches to understanding the human scene. History, sociology, and literary studies are others that come to mind. In addition, novelists and artists have shown deep concern for place and culture, and, indeed, the same kind—if not the same intensity—of interest occurs in inquiring people in all walks of life. Generally speaking, professional as well as lay people tend to see place and culture from two perspectives: as techniques of adaptation and survival and as manifestations of human creativity. To these two I wish to add a third, which sees place and culture as a salve or analeptic for our ineluctable separateness (a consequence of our individuality) and the world's indifference. This third perspective falls somewhere between the first two: it takes the position that place and culture are an adaptive device, as the word "salve" suggests, but that the adaptation goes far beyond urgently felt needs—it is creative.

AN ILLUSTRATIVE CASE

My thesis may be introduced with a simple illustrative case. Not long ago, I attended a baby girl's birthday party. Her father, whom I know well, was a graduate student in the university at which I teach. The apartment was packed with people: the little girl and her older brother, their parents and grandparents, other graduate students, and a few family friends like myself. The single candle on the cake was extinguished with parental help, the cake was cut and distributed, and then we dispersed. Some went to the kitchen to do the washing up, while others stood about in the living room or found comfortable chairs in which to sit. The grandparents looked relaxed and drowsy; the graduate students were engaged in a vigorous debate; the little boy rushed around on his tricycle, almost banging into his sister, who was beginning to act up and clearly needed her afternoon nap.

At first I thought, as most people would, "Here is community and place, family ritual and belongingness." But then the idea occurred to me that I could have drawn a different conclusion. We at the party were isolated individuals who were barely able to communicate with one another. The little boy nearly rammed into his baby sister but established no contact otherwise: their difference in age made mutual understanding nearly impossible. The grandfather woke up to make a comment on the weather to which no one listened; our host was drying dishes with his wife, but his mind was elsewhere; the other graduate students were, as I have noted, arguing. Each member of the party was a unique being locked into his or her separate reality, and yet we were also together, part of a community, keeping in touch somehow, though nonverbally.

Place and culture gave us a sense of communal oneness. The material place itself provided coherence. If the party had taken place outdoors, buffeted by wind and other distractions, we could not have held together so well. The familiarity of the rooms, the furniture, the location of the apartment helped: they were what anyone would have expected of a graduate student and his young family. Everything one perceived resonated reassuringly, and this resonance was a deep kind of nonverbal communication. Every thing and every person belonged. We did not have to talk, just as the pieces of furniture, though mute, could project an aura of relational integrity such that to walk between the armchair and its ottoman would seem an offense, as though one had interposed between friends engaged in conversation.

Culture, to use the anthropologist's key word and concept, provided coherence. The celebration of a one-year-old's birthday by proud parents was normal in middle-class America, as was also that informal gathering of kith and kin and of friends belonging to different age groups. We were all there because we were invited, and we felt at ease with one another because we were all related to our host by readily identified, socially accepted categories. We knew now to act—we knew how to make the proper sounds of amusement and mock distress when the baby smeared her face with cake icing. We knew when to leave and how to take our leave.

Place and culture, as this simple example shows, are inextricably intertwined. Whether one attends primarily to the one rather than the other is a matter of disciplinary convention. Geographers prefer to let place come to the foreground and to load on its material structures the weight and meaning of social relations and other values. By contrast, anthropologists tend to go directly to customs and social relations, as these are manifest in gesture, informal and formal modes of behavior, and the smaller articles of tools, dress, and ornaments, some of which have high symbolic import. Larger units such as houses and streets, their spatial arrangements and location, may also receive close study, but usually only to the extent that they reveal important cultural traits and social relations. In practice, needless to say, lines of professional focus are not so sharply drawn. A cultural geographer may take the American custom of celebrating Christmas as his point of departure; an anthropologist, for his part, may argue that place and geographical propinquity, rather than webs of kinship, play the greater role in traditional communal life.[2]

LITERARY WORKS AND PAINTING

I have noted some similarities and differences in the works of geographers and anthropologists. One more similarity may well be that neither group is likely to show much interest in my account of the birthday celebration. Geographers turn a deaf ear if only because it is too microscale. Anthropologists, for their part, have traditionally labored over exotic cultures; an ordinary, nonproblematical contemporary American scene has little appeal.

Who, then, is interested in my story? People at the party may welcome a replay of what has happened, but even for them the event is soon forgotten. So the answer has to be that no one is really interested; and yet, potentially, everyone is. Much depends on how well the story is told. Many writers and artists, after all, count on the human ability to see significance in the seemingly inconsequential. Any warm domestic scene has the potential power to carry resonance. One reason why even a very ordinary event can catch our attention is that, in the artist's depiction of it, the assumption of unified place and culture is subtly transgressed. In a short story, the simple fact that people have individual names ruffles the image of communal homogeneity and coherence. People with the same name, it is easy to assume, will see place and culture in roughly the same way. Family members do indeed share a name, thus culturally reinforcing the illusion of a common view, but in the work of a novelist the emphasis is, of course, on their differentiating given names—on their existence as individuals. The result is a comedy or tragicomedy of understanding and misunderstanding, communion and aloneness, that, despite variations in detail, people throughout the world can recognize as their own.[3]

Discontinuity and isolation within a warm human place and culture are a common theme in literary works. Their occurrence in painting is less well known, although W. H. Auden has drawn our attention to it in a famous poem called "Musée des Beaux Arts." In the poem Auden pays homage to the Old Masters. Like geographers, the Old Masters depict scenes and landscapes in which the separate elements of tree, rock, and human figure are arranged artistically to create a harmonious whole. But unlike geographers, the Old Masters may in the same carefully composed whole reveal human discontinuities—the lack of communication between people and even their fundamental indifference toward each other. A masterpiece may show, as its central theme, adults waiting reverently for the miraculous birth of Christ, but another part of the picture may show children skating on a pond at the edge of the wood who "did not specially want it to happen." In Pieter Breughel's *Icarus*, which illustrates the story of the brash youth falling out of the sky, the poet Auden asks us to note "how everything turns away / Quite leisurely from the disaster; the ploughman may / Have heard the splash, the forsaken cry, / But for him it was not an important failure. . . ."[4]

EXTERNAL UNITIES OR WHOLES

Geography and anthropology, as cultural enterprises, are part of a larger culture and society. The geographers' objects of interest overlap with those of their fellow humans. What places are like, where churches and shopping centers are located, are not questions restricted to any occupation or group. Similarly, the questions that anthropologists have often raised, such as kinship networking, the rules of gift exchange, the proprieties of ceremonials and rites, are also the stuff of common human interest and gossip. Besides these specific concerns, geographers and anthropologists share two more general traits with other people. One is the tendency to focus on what lies beyond the self and its immediate environs, and the other is the tendency to attend to organized entities or wholes and overlook the fissures and chasms that may crisscross a seemingly unified group.

The first trait is manifest in a variety of ways. Children's interest in and knowledge of the external world, for instance, precede self-knowledge. Objects at the horizon have more magical appeal than have familiar objects close at hand. By the time children in the West are six to eight years old, they are far more likely to be drawn to pageantry in the Middle Ages and to China than to their own period of history and hometown.[5] As for a true understanding of the self and of the subtle human relationships without their own family, such knowledge usually comes late in life and may not come at all. The attraction and prestige of the distant appear to be retained in adulthood. Thus, geographers have traditionally studied distant places. Indeed, for many years, the public's image of a geographer was that of an explorer.[6] As for anthropologists, the name of their profession has come to connote the remote and the exotic.

True, in recent decades both geographers and anthropologists have shifted their gaze closer to home, and among the more avant-garde practitioners the gaze has turned in on themselves, so that studies of place or culture are also the researchers' probes into their own manner of work and thinking.[7] But if this is true, my point is strengthened: we look critically at what is closest and most familiar to us *last*—and often not at all. To the obvious question "Why should we examine what we already know?" the answer is that the familiar is not necessarily the known. Furthermore, the familiar may be that which we wish *not* to know. And one reason why we wish not to know is that the familiar, when looked at closely, may turn into its opposite: fissures in understanding and a certain indifference can emerge at what seems a thoroughly genial birthday party.

PLACE AS ORDER

The second trait is the human need to see order, pattern, and relatedness in reality, whether these characteristics exist or not, whether they are necessary to survival or not. Almost all people recognize, for instance, spatial pattern in their physical environment. They may divide their territory into ecological areas, each of which has a distinctive composition of plants and animals of use to them. They may see, more abstractly, hierarchies of place—a market town surrounded by centers of less importance—with exchanges of goods, people, and ideas linking them together into a larger functional whole. They may construct mythical spaces, intellectually and emotionally satisfying, that have no clear link to the pressing needs of economic life.[8] Geographers do the same, only they make careers of identifying, classifying, and trying to understand the nature of, the patterns on, the earth's surface.[9]

In daily life, this human inclination to see and construct wholes is likely to be frustrated by all sorts of unforeseen events and mishaps. However inconsequential individually, in the aggregate they can cause deep-seated anxiety. Two ways to combat them are submerging the self in active group life and attending only to those aspects of reality that encourage a sense of relatedness and order. Academics, who tend to be individualists, favor the second approach: more than other people they seek to escape the world's messiness by withdrawing into a crystalline realm of ideas.[10] Geographers, like most people, see spatial order in towns and cities, plowed fields and landscapes, but they go beyond them to conceive of wholes that may be invisible to those outside the discipline's influence. An example is the Great Plains. This region, which is neither an economic nor a political unit, does not exist as such for its widely scattered inhabitants. It is postulated apparently for no other reason than that geographers derive a certain intellectual satisfaction from discerning spatial order and unity in that sweeping and forbidding space.[11]

Consider another type of space—the city. Faced with the enormously complex city, geographers may try to organize it into areas of uniform appearance and function dominated by commerce, industry, residence, and so on. The result is an urban land-use map which, because it is easily comprehensible, can seduce the casual viewer into thinking that the city itself is as easily understood. The colored units are especially likely to mislead. Each unit, uniformly colored, may suggest a high degree of internal coherence, manifest as neighborly exchange, in the actual place, which does not in fact exist.

If the map has this power to convey coherence and homogeneity, so has—even more powerfully—the concrete, multisensorial presence of built environments. An area that is architecturally homogeneous immediately suggests common function and shared activities. If a residential area has houses that look alike, it is easy to assume that it is a neighborhood—that its people are as little differentiated as their houses and that they communicate with one another in neighborly ways. This may or may not be true. Whether true or not, cultural products such as the map or the built environment encourage us to see reality in terms of simplified wholes. Even when we are presented with visual chaos, as in a disintegrating inner city, we may seek to escape the disturbing implications of the image by training our mind's eye on the underlying invisible causes of disorder—that is, find consolation in the lawful world of the mind. Naturally, the urban geographer or planner is in a better position to do so than are local residents who must struggle with the day-to-day incoherences to survive; nevertheless, they too must rationalize—that is, see some kind of underlying reason or pattern—if they are to retain a foothold on sanity.

SUBMERGENCE IN A WORLD

Thus far I have emphasized place, which is a type of material culture. Geographers tend to focus on cultural products that are also environments, such as a house, a city, or a landscape. Myriads of artifacts are thus left out of account. Culture is, of course, a far more inclusive concept than place: at its broadest, it embraces all those behavior patterns (foremost, speech and the ideas it generates and makes public) and all those manufactured objects that go beyond the instinctual and the given. However, people rarely think of culture in this inclusive sense. An awareness of the distinction between culture and nature itself arises only under special circumstances, such as when parents urge children to abandon their natural behavior for the cultural modes of society, or when individuals, oppressed by society and an artificial environment, seek solace in nature. Most of the time, people simply live in a taken-for-granted world. This taken-for-granted world is a pattern or order experienced at the deepest level.

The self is submerged in the world in recurrent rounds of activity. These rounds may be called economic, social, or ceremonial, although in actual life, especially in premodern times, the boundaries between them are often fuzzy. The degree of awareness that what one does exhibits the values of the group presumably differs with the type of activity. In the midst of physically demanding work, people are unlikely to be aware of its cultural significance. In a social activity, cultural values may well surge to the surface of consciousness: friends who gather under a tree to make merry can suddenly notice the propriety or distinction of what they wear and say—their social standing within the group. In a ritual ceremony, consciousness peaks: the order of the world and the values of society are made dramatically present through formalized gestures, music, and dance.

CULTURE AS ORDER

Culture is manifest not only in the orderly processes of behavior but also as systematized knowledge. In a nonliterate community, a specially endowed individual—a shaman or a medicine man—may on occasion articulate the wisdom of the group. At its most ambitious, such a person presents a worldview in which heterogeneous elements are classified and integrated into an interdependent whole. Anthropologists have concentrated on studying other people's behavior and activity, material artifacts, and systems of thought. The first two categories require them to invent interpretive schemata of their own, for the native population may not have tried to understand them at a conscious level and hence will find it hard to articulate them coherently. The third category—systems of thought—can be obtained, in the ideal case, by simply asking a wise informant, although the ambitious researcher would aspire to go beyond the information thus given by putting it into a broader theoretical context.[12]

I surmise that anthropologists, like most academics and intellectuals, have a greater than normal need to see order. Their concepts of culture contain, historically, presuppositions of order that have blinded them to the more random, atomistic, and messy aspects of reality. An early and influential definition of culture is that of E. B. Taylor, who characterized it as a "complex *whole* which includes knowledge, belief, art, morals, etc. . . ." (my italics).[13] That human need to see patterns and wholes is raised to a higher level among anthropologists. Consider Ruth Benedict's influential work *Patterns of Culture* (1934). Given the central message of the text, the appearance of the word "patterns" in the title is certainly appropriate. What may seem confusion to the uninitiated outsider and ad hoc attempts at making sense and making do to the native are, to the trained ethnographic eye, a pattern. Benedict herself might have gone further. She came to feel, according to Margaret Mead, "that each primitive culture represented something comparable to a great work of art. . . ."[14]

Another distinguished anthropologist who gave impetus to the idea of culture as a pattern in the period 1930 to 1950 is A. L. Kroeber, who wrote: "We must be ready . . . to ignore and suppress the individual, who from the angle of the understanding of culture is perhaps more often irrelevant and distracting than helpful." He went on to say: "The ordering or relating which yields understanding in the study of culture is basically best defined, perhaps, as a process of perceiving significant interrelations of forms as forms."[15] Assuredly, the study of culture as pattern and as the significant interrelations of forms becomes much easier if culture's most fractious element—the human individual—is removed.[16]

MODERN SEGMENTATION AND GROUP UNITY

A widely noted feature of modern life, which distinguishes it from earlier times, is the isolation of the individual and an increasing awareness of this isolation. Many pointers to this change have been observed in European history from the Middle Ages onward: from sitting on benches to sitting on individual chairs; from eating whole animals and mixed grills to eating individualized foods in their separate compartments or dishes; from participation in morality plays of cosmic temporal-spatial scope to seeing, from one's chair in the darkness of the hall, a family drama of interpersonal misunderstanding and conflict.[17]

This awareness, toward which modern men and women appear to feel both pride and alarm, has not, however, got out of hand. It occurs, after all, in familiar social situations of dinner party and theater; and if in such situations a person is surrounded by mere acquaintances and strangers they are still of his or her own kind. While old sociocultural wholes decay, new ones emerge. These may not be as emotionally warm as those of the past, but they are still able to provide some cushioning against the chill of isolation and loneliness. Isolation of a rather severe kind, it has often been said, is common in the large modern city. This is true, though even there a stranger with a modicum of resources can find comfort in place and culture—that is, in the recognizable architectural persona and patterns of behavior of such amenities as movie house, bar, beauty parlor, health center, fast-food restaurant, supermarket, ball park, and city library.[18]

MODERN GEOGRAPHY

The segmented, agonistic, and conflictual character of modern society and consciousness is increasingly noted in, and reflected by, the writings of geographers from the turbulent 1960s to the present. In this period, geographers have tended to pay less attention to the making of places and more to their dysfunction, less to how places and social networks hang together and more to how they suppress or veil discontinuities and conflicts. Struggle and resistance, hegemony and the need to challenge it, entered the vocabulary of academic discourse.[19] However, in all these accounts of social reality the irreducible existential fact of human isolation—the kind of fact noted in my illustrative case and in literature generally—is not the issue. Indeed, by emphasizing group struggle and conflict the individual is more than ever absorbed into the embrace of the group. Thus, in our time, the human need to forget the self in a larger whole has not changed. What is perhaps new is the unstable character of these wholes, both in membership and in ideological content.[20] So, although the loss of the self in group activism is as much an option now as in the past, it lacks the reassuring sense of deep commitment and permanence.

Segmentation is one aspect of modern reality; the other is its opposite—integration. The whole earth has penetrated our consciousness and compensates for the segmentation we also experience. The word "global" is now freely used. We speak of the "global village" and "global climate"; we are aware of multinational companies with a global reach and of environmental problems that are global in impact. Since the 1960s, even as some geographers have painted a harsh picture of difference and division, conflict and struggle, others have chosen to direct their attention to the earth as an interdependent system. The tradition in geography of studying the entire earth and the geographer's natural desire to see the relatedness of parts to the whole now find endorsement in the aspiration and fears of society at large. Modern men and women, even as they feel a painful lack of communication in their own neighborhood and workplace, see themselves at the same time as members of an integrated world community.

MODERN ANTHROPOLOGY

Anthropologists, like geographers, have been influenced by the social and intellectual turmoils of the recent decades. Attempts at impersonal description and understanding are displaced or complemented by other modes of interacting with the other, which may include participatory action of a more or less political thrust,[21] or a self-conscious kind of description that weaves data concerning a native people with the researcher's personal history. In general, a deconstructive frame of mind is unsympathetic to the quest for overarching patterns and metanarratives. To return from the field and produce a work that demonstrates the existence of a "complex whole" (to use Tyler's term) or a finely woven pattern is not so much a triumph of intellect and scholarship as a symptom of suffering from delusions of grandeur.[22] Moreover, contemporary anthropologists no longer assume, as Ruth Benedict has done, that a primitive culture can be compared with "a great work of art," for art or literature entails the intentional mastering of details to produce a composition. Not even ritual needs to be such a composition; each part can have import for its participants, and yet the whole may lack overall meaning.[23] A corollary of this view is that the ethnographic report itself should exhibit the fragmentariness of life. What it should aspire to is not a representation, with its traditional ideals of coherence and accuracy, but a multivocal evocation.[24]

Unlike geographers, anthropologists have studied the small group in detail. They are more concerned with intimate personal matters than are geographers, whose work often depends on official statistics and operates at a regional or global scale.[25] Anthropologists, again unlike geographers, are firmly rooted in the humanities and the literary tradition. Many show a literary flare; a few have written novels.[26] Moreover, an anthropologist's report can itself have the richness and drama of fiction. Oscar Lewis's studies of the poor in Mexico, San Juan, and New York read like novels: the people in them all have personal names and distinctive personalities; they eat, sleep, make love, fight, and suffer like characters in a work of fiction. If Lewis's books still belong to anthropological rather than imaginative literature, the reason lies not only in their firmer adherence to facts but also in their illustration of a thesis. This thesis, popular in the 1960s and early 1970s, argues for the existence of a culture of poverty that transcends the seemingly unique features of any particular case.[27] Thus, novelistic details notwithstanding, the scholar's desire to operate under an overarching concept remains.

UNIQUENESS AND ISOLATION

I have offered the idea that place and culture are a salve or (more positively) an analeptic—a creative solution—for the threatening awareness of being alone in a world that is ultimately unresponsive. By aloneness, I do not have in mind such well-known experiences of our time as the feeling country people may have when they migrate to a city, or what anyone may feel in a gathering of strangers. I have in mind, rather, a more fundamental, "precultural" state with which culture has to cope and on which it builds. This state, which can never be fully overcome, exists as a substratum for the more culture-specific, easily recognized and accepted experiences of dislocation and isolation.

What is this fundamental state? Consider two important aspects of it: the uniqueness of human individuals and the indifference of the world. Uniqueness is a good word in our society. We do not want to be merely a part of the woodwork; most of us like to be seen as having a special quality that differentiates us from others. But the downside of uniqueness is isolation. An exceptionally talented person may feel isolated in the midst of her less gifted fellows, but she (at least) is compensated by the knowledge of her own superiority. Uniqueness, however, may be the result of a concatenation of traits, none of which is in itself especially praiseworthy. One is simply different. We are all sufficiently different so that life in any group (though not to the same degree) is a constant flow of contacts and communications that are seldom right on the mark and may fall wide of the mark even when we are among friends in a familiar place.

An important source of our individuality is our biology. The human species is exceptionally polymorphous. The uniqueness of our fingerprint and of our scent is well known. Body shape and size can vary enormously, as a visit to any large American city will show. But the differences of our "insides" are even greater, according to biochemist Roger Williams.[28] "Stomachs, for example, vary in size, shape and contour far more than do our noses or mouths." The amount of pepsin, an enzyme which plays an important role in digestion, differs greatly from person to person, even among people with no known stomach ailment. How fast people can eat is affected by the size of their esophagus, through which food must pass. Some people have trouble swallowing pills, others have accidentally swallowed whole sets of false teeth. If presiding over ceremonial dinners is an important part of the administrator's job, then clearly good digestion and a large esophagus, enabling one to eat and carry on a social conversation at the same time, are an advantage. Indeed, differences in digestive powers can significantly affect people's outlook on life. Some are bold and sanguine, others are shy and hesitant, perhaps for no other reason.[29]

The senses are our windows to the world, and here again we tend to forget that their power and sensitivity vary in striking ways even among "normal" people. Take hearing: as soon as the organs of hearing are tested for their ability to register specific pitches, differences immediately show up. Ears may be insensitive at certain frequencies and supersensitive at others. When all aspects of hearing are considered, including pitch sensitivity, it becomes clear that we differ from one another in all sorts of ways that matter to our day-to-day sense of well-being, such as tolerance for various kinds of noise and the "ability to hear and appreciate music and to hear and understand words spoken in conversation or in movies, television or on stage."[30]

Finally, there is the mind. If relatively simple internal organs, such as the esophagus, can vary so much, we can expect the exceptionally complex organs—the brain-mind—to vary even more. The greater the care with which the mind is studied, the more its uniqueness becomes apparent.[31] Not only do people differ in such specialized abilities as music, spatial competence, mathematics, verbal skill, interpersonal relations, and intrapersonal understanding, but surprising facilities and blockages can occur with each. A pure mathematician, for instance, may show a genuine flair in one area of highly abstract thought and be something of a plodder in another.[32]

THE WORLD'S INDIFFERENCE

The second aspect of our fundamental state, of which place and culture are a constructive response, is the indifference of the world. Note first that even a comfortable human life is lived against a background awareness of the threat of suffering. Is there an experience which allows us to cover with one word all suffering, including physical pain, fear of a task above one's powers, grief at the death of loved ones, fear of one's own death, rejected love and humiliation, impotence, loneliness, and numerous other situations? The philosopher Leszek Kolakowski's answer is yes: it is indifference—the world's indifference. He believes that "attempts to overcome this indifference constitute the crucial meaning of human struggle with fate, both in its everyday and its extreme form."[33] I agree with the statement, but I would amend and expand it to conform with the point of view taken here. I would say that attempts to overcome this indifference and the isolating uniqueness noted earlier constitute the crucial meaning of human struggle with fate, and that the measure of success in this struggle lies in the creation of human culture in all its myriad forms, both everyday and exceptional.

Consider the world under its two broad aspects of nature and society. Take, first, nature: how is nature indifferent? This may seem a strange question, for nature has hardly ever been judged indifferent. Through most of human history, and in nearly every part of the world, it was deemed a powerful, quasi-personal force, sometimes benevolent, often hostile, that was to be channeled, deflected, or propitiated. True, modern science and technological progress presuppose and encourage the view that the forces and substances of nature are impersonal and neutral, but even scientists and technologists, outside the austere milieu of their laboratories, are rarely able to look at a mountain stream or stars without attributing to them a responding intelligence. In our own time, even as science dominates more and more aspects of nature, the rising tide of concern for the environment throughout the world is not just scientific and pragmatic but also romantic: explicitly or implicitly nature is perceived as sentient, almost human.[34]

Nature has always been and is today an intimate, emotionally charged part of human experience. In earlier times, people have woven nature into myths, legends, and taxonomies of social relationship. Today, animal totems in the shape of stuffed bears, gophers, and badgers remain a notable presence on American college campuses; in a thoroughly urbanized society, pets, animal toys, and stories about speaking animals show little sign of losing their grip on the imagination.[35] These cultural practices and products relate individuals to each other, group to group. humans to nature, and so continue to serve important sociopsychological functions. At a deeper level, I see them as attempts to overcome the half-buried awareness that nature is neither hostile nor loving toward humans, but is simply there, going about its own business.

People are good at repressing what they do not wish to acknowledge. To illustrate, think of our great reluctance to accept the fact that animals, by virtue of their very different sensory capability and body posture, may live in worlds strikingly different from our own. Think of all those casual, vaguely disturbing encounters with nature, which we quickly dismiss, because they catch us offguard, without the protection of our culturally scripted responses. The English diplomat Harold Nicolson notes in a diary entry of 1939: "Nature. Even when someone dies, one is amazed that the poplars should still be standing quite unaware of one's own disaster, so when I walked down to the lake to bathe, I could scarcely believe that the swans were being sincere in their indifference to the Second German War."[36]

The world is also society. If nature is neutral or indifferent, humans are not. With our own species and, in particular, members of our own group we can communicate, and the response we receive from them is not merely an anthropomorphic projection of our urgent needs and desires. Parental and conjugal love, the bonding of comrades, and the deep exchanges of friendship are real, as are, at a more superficial yet nevertheless rewarding level, the multiple webs of social intercourse. Moreover, reciprocal recognition is not confined to amicable exchanges; it is manifest as the various bickerings of buyers and sellers in a traditional market square, as quarrels among neighbors, and even as the clinch of enemies in battle.[37] By comparison with the frequency of all these forms of contact, experiences of isolation and indifference are rare. But, though rare, they play a generative role in culture. The role is paradoxical. Isolation and indifference too often and deeply felt corrode the fabric of culture and society and will discourage even the stouthearted from weaving new links. But in small measure, openings onto the void and meaninglessness can be a goad to action—to the building of worlds that have meaning and are sometimes beautiful, which enable us to forget.[38]

I have noted the indifference of nature. Let us now turn to the indifference of people and society. How is this *human* indifference experienced? On what occasions? In contemporary society, the words "human indifference" are likely to evoke the dramatic image of pedestrians ignoring the cries of a mugger's victim, or such irritations as the unhelpfulness of a large bureaucracy, or the coolness of caretakers toward their charges in public hospitals. Two comments are appropriate here: one is that these experiences are characteristic of a certain kind of society and the other is that they are infrequent enough to be seen as departures from the norm or an ideal. The experiences I have in mind are not so confined: they are those disturbances and shocks, trifling in themselves but able to generate deep anxiety in the aggregate, from which all humans suffer.

An adequate evocation of these dispiriting commonplaces of life would call for the sensitivity and skill of a poet, qualities that society has tended to discourage, for they can expose that which seems better hidden. In any attempt to evoke them, it helps to have at the back of one's mind an awareness of the frailty of the human young, their long period of dependence on other people, the nature of which changes with growing maturity but which remains an ever-present fact throughout life. Note then, as the barest sample, the following occurrences: an infant struggling to find the nipple of a mother who has drifted off to sleep; a room that suddenly elongates when a child realizes that the object of his infatuation has merely played with him;[39] the sense of being out-of-step with one's group, no matter how hard one tries to belong; the hurried telling of a tale through awareness that even a close friend owes one only a few minutes of attention; the tiny acts of betrayal and the fleeting sensations of being betrayed in the daily marketplace of love;[40] the feeling that human relation is ultimately what matters, combined with the chilling knowledge that, as Albert Camus puts it, "it is only our will that keeps these people attached to us (not that they wish us ill but simply because they don't care) and that the others are *always* able to be interested in something else."[41] Lastly, and as a summary, there is the general truth of the cliché "out of sight, out of mind." We strive to remain "in sight," while knowing deep down that death can remove us at any time—once and for all—from sight and, soon, from mind. Culture, with its funeral rites and memorial services, enables us to forget this fate, but it does not always succeed, as the Chinese poet T'ao Yuanming noted more than 1,500 years ago. Taking the viewpoint of the dead, he wrote:

> Those who just now saw me off
> have all gone back, each to his home,
> my kin perhaps with a lingering grief,
> but the others are finished with their funeral songs.[42]

SUMMARY AND CONCLUSION

Place and culture can be viewed as a creative adaptation to the myriad individual human experiences of fragility and transcience, aloneness and indifference. Place supports the human need to belong to a meaningful and reasonably stable world, and it does so at different levels of consciousness, from an almost organic sense of identity that is an effect of habituation to a particular routine and locale, to a more conscious awareness of the values of middle-scale places such as neighborhood, city, and landscape, to an intellectual appreciation of the planet earth itself as home. Consider again the room in which the graduate student celebrates his daughter's birthday. Its cozy, informal order communicates to the people attending the party that they are at the right place. A prickly sense of self dissipates in the familiarity of the group and its physical setting. When a guest rouses herself from this pleasant torpor to look outward at the larger environment, she sees buildings, lamp posts, and pavements made of fitted flagstones, which, even if they are poorly maintained, signify an original human intention for pattern and meaning, and which, even if they are magniloquent or aggressive, carry an indisputable human message. And if, in a reflective mood, she sees the entire earth as homeplace, palpitating with significance both large and small, then a sensitive mind, drawing on the resources of culture, has succeeded momentarily in overcoming the concrete anxieties and defeats of personal experience.

Place helps us to forget our separateness and the world's indifference. More generally speaking, culture makes this amnesia possible. Culture integrates us into the world through shared language and custom, behavior and habits of thought. It supports us at an unconscious level; most of the time, we are unaware of how language and custom give meaning to what we do and to the things around us—how culture constructs and maintains relationships and ties, integrating unique selves into groups, and humans into nonhuman reality. When, for some reason, we depart temporarily from this embeddedness to look at culture "out there," we can still find reassurance and meaning in its perceived regularities, its purpose-guided webs of exchange.

Culture enables us to forget, but this forgetting is seldom total. Reminders of our difference and the world's indifference occur everyday. No society is exempt. To say: "But the Pueblo Indians or the Japanese are very caring and have no consciousness of the isolation of the self and of the world's indifference" is to me unconvincing. Such conclusions derive, I believe, from a failure to look at people close enough—in novelistic specificity rather than through the broad categories of social science. The failure itself is understandable, for I have argued that a major function of culture is to provide generalized frames and scenarios that enable us to gloss over the vexations and wounding details of life.

Although no society is exempt from experience of isolation and indifference, societies do vary in their degree of awareness. Perhaps at no time has this awareness been more keen, widespread, and publicly acknowledged than it is today, as modern literary works and art amply testify. But if such cultural products exist to reveal and encourage the awareness, how can I say that a principal purpose of culture is to repress it? My answer is: just as a culture can admit—even publicly dramatize—raw, disruptive emotions, so it can allow the curtain to part for a glance at human vulnerability. These partings of the curtain are just that: if I plunge into a tough-minded book I do so, after all, in an armchair, and I count on its disturbing message to dissolve as soon as I close the book and rejoin the family in the common tasks and rituals of culture.[43] Moreover, the literary work, by its own art, contains and attenuates the stress of human isolation and conflict.

If human separateness is an ineradicable fact,[44] and if awareness of it has increased in modern times, prompted both by social-material circumstances and by greater psychological knowledge, how will we in modern society respond? Will we use place and culture to muffle the apprehensions of self by a return to some emotional form of group solidarity such as ethnicism or nationalism? Will we, on the contrary, seek self-loss in sensual stimuli and material affluence? Or will we learn to do something very difficult: acknowledge the reality of "islanded" selves and the world's indifference,

peer "beyond" the carapaces of place and culture in all their myriad en-
thralling forms, and, by thus putting a slight distance between us and what
we create, recognize not only their necessity and power to delude but also
their goodness and beauty?

NOTES

1. Both geography and anthropology are very broad fields that range from physical science to the humanities. Needless to say, the focus here is on a narrow band:
in geography, the idea of place, and in anthropology, the idea of culture.

2. Patrick McGreevy, "Place in the American Christmas," *Geographical Review*
80 (1990) [in press]; Peter J. Wilson, *The Domestication of the Human Species* (New
Haven: Yale University Press, 1988).

3. G. G. Chavis, *Family: Stories from the Interior* (St. Paul: Graywolf Press,
1987).

4. W. H. Auden, *A Selection by the Author* (Harmondsworth, U.K.: Penguin
Books, 1958), 61.

5. S. Bruner, *Beyond the Information Given: Studies in the Psychology of Knowing*
(New York: W. W. Norton, 1973).

6. When I was an undergraduate in England (1948–1951), the professor of geography at Oxford was Kenneth Mason, an explorer-surveyor of the Himalayas,
and the professor of geography at Cambridge was famed as a member of the Scott
expedition to Antarctica.

7. The autobiographical turn in geographical writing is evident, for example, in
Anne Buttimer, *Values in Geography* (Washington, D.C.: Association of American
Geographers, 1974), and further encouraged by the 75-Year Anniversary issue of
the *Annals of the Association of American Geographers*, 69 (1979): 1–180, in which
noted geographers describe their perception of the discipline through the lens of
personal history and experience. See also Anne Buttimer, *Creativity and Context*
(Lund Studies in Geography, Human Geography, no. 50, 1983). While it is not
autobiographical, note the high degree of self-consciousness in Dagmar Reichert,
"Writing around Circularity and Self-Reference," in *A Ground for Common Search*,
ed. Reginald G. Golledge, Helen Couclelis, and Peter Gould (Goleta, Cal.: Santa
Barbara Geographical Press, 1988), 101–25. Note, moreover, that the present paper
itself begins with "an illustrative case," in which I, the author, play a part.

In anthropology, the books in the series "New Directions in Anthropological
Writing," edited by George E. Marcus and James Clifford, and published by the
University of Wisconsin Press, illustrate the self-conscious, "autobiographical" ap-

proach to ethnography: for example, Virginia R. Dominguez, *People as Subject, People as Object: Selfhood and Peoplehood in Contemporary Israel* (Madison: University of Wisconsin Press, 1989); and Michael M. J. Fischer and Mehdi Abedi, *Debating Muslim: Cultural Dialogues in Postmodernity and Tradition* (Madison: University of Wisconsin Press, 1990).

8. Robert D. Sack, *Conceptions of Space in Social Thought: A Geographic Perspective* (London: Macmillan, 1980).

9. Richard Szymanski and John Agnew, *Order and Skepticism: Human Geography and the Dialectic of Science* (Washington, D.C.: Association of American Geographers, 1981).

10. To the question "Why are you a scientist?" Einstein's reply is: "I believe with Schopenhauer that one of the strongest motives that lead men to art and science is flight from everyday life with its painful harshness and wretched dreariness, and from the fetters of one's own shifting desires"; quoted in Gerald Holton, "On Trying to Understand Scientific Genius," *American Scholar* 41 (1972): 108.

11. Ruth F. Hale, "A Map of Vernacular Regions in America" (Ph.D. diss., University of Minnesota, 1971); Cotton Mather, "The American Great Plains," *Annals of the Association of American Geographers* 62 (1972): 237.

12. The Colombian anthropologist Geraldo Reichel-Dolmatoff wrote a whole book on the worldview of the Desano Indians based on the knowledge of a single native informant, who, in the course of the interviews, became more his colleague and co-author than mere informant. See his *Amazonian Cosmos: The Sexual and Religious Symbolism of the Tukano Indians* (Chicago: University of Chicago Press, 1971).

13. Edward B. Tylor, *Primitive Culture*, 2 vols. (London: John Murray, 1871), 1:1.

14. Margaret Mead, "Preface," to Ruth Benedict, *Patterns of Culture* (1934; rpt. New York: Mentor Books, 1959), vi.

15. A. L. Kroeber, *The Nature of Culture* (Chicago: University of Chicago Press, 1952), 104, 127.

16. James Duncan, "The Superorganic in American Cultural Geography," *Annals of the Association of American Geographers* 70 (1980): 181–98.

17. Yi-Fu Tuan, *Segmented Worlds and Self: Individual Consciousness and Group Life* (Minneapolis: University of Minnesota Press, 1982).

18. Ray Oldenburg, *The Great Good Place* (New York: Paragon House, 1989).

19. In urban geography, see K. R. Cox and J. J. McCarthy, "Neighborhood Activism as a Politics of Turf: A Critical Analysis," in *Conflict, Politics and the Urban Scene*, ed. K. R. Cox and R. J. Johnston (Harlow, U.K.: Longman, 1982), 196–219; and David Harvey, *Consciousness and the Urban Experience: Studies in the History and Theory of Capitalist Urbanization* (Baltimore: Johns Hopkins University Press, 1985); in cultural geography, see K. F. Olwig and K. Olwig, "Underdevelopment

and the Development of 'Natural' Park Ideology," *Antipode* 11 (1979): 16–25; and Denis Cosgrove and Peter Jackson, "New Directions in Cultural Geography," *Area* 19 (1987): 95–101. In general, *Antipode*, subtitled "A Radical Journal of Geography," accommodates this trend.

20. Robert D. Sack, "The Consumer's World: Place as Context," *Annals of the Association of American Geographers* 78 (1988): 642–64.

21. Robin M. Wright, "Anthropological Presuppositions of Indigenous Advocacy," *Annual Review of Anthropology* 17 (1988): 365–90.

22. Clifford Geertz, *Works and Lives: The Anthropologist as Author* (Stanford: Stanford University Press, 1988), 49–72; Stephen A. Tyler, *The Unspeakable: Discourse, Dialogue, and Rhetoric in the Postmodern World* (Madison: University of Wisconsin Press, 1987).

23. Rodney Needham, *Exemplars* (Berkeley: University of California Press, 1985), 157–58.

24. Tyler, *The Unspeakable*, 199–216.

25. Like geography and the other social sciences, anthropology in the 1970s, under the influence of Marxism and Emmanuel Wallerstein, *The Modern World System* (New York: Academic Press, 1976), has shown an interest in the global economy and world system. By directing attention to the global scale, anthropology appears to be altering its unique approach to knowledge, which rests on detailed examination of particular cultures. See Sherry Ortner, "Theory in Anthropology since the Sixties," *Comparative Studies in Society and History* 26 (1984): 126–66.

26. Adolf Bandelier (1840–1914) drew on his knowledge of the prehistoric Indians of New Mexico to write his novel *The Delight Makers* (1890), 2nd ed. (New York: Dodd, Mead, 1918). Elizabeth Marshall Thomas, author of *Reindeer Moon* (New York: Pocket Books, 1988), is an anthropologist who is also a successful novelist. Clifford Geertz, widely acknowledged doyen of American cultural anthropology, writes with distinction. His book *Works and Lives: The Anthropologist as Author* is an analysis of style in anthropological writing and is itself the winner of the National Book Critics Circle Award for Criticism for 1989.

27. Oscar Lewis, *The Children of Sanchez: Autobiography of a Mexican Family* (New York: Random House, 1961), and *La Vida* (New York: Vintage Books, 1968); Charles A. Valentine, *Culture and Poverty: Critique and Counter-Proposals* (Chicago: University of Chicago Press, 1968).

28. Roger J. Williams, *You Are Extraordinary* (New York: Random House, 1967); "Nutritional Individuality," *Human Nature* 1 (1978): 46–53.

29. Williams, *You Are Extraordinary*, 12–15.

30. Ibid., 43.

31. Howard Gardner, *Frames of Mind: The Theory of Multiple Intelligence* (New York: Basic Books, 1985).

32. Jacques Hadamard, *The Psychology of Invention in the Mathematical Field* (Princeton: Princeton University Press, 1949), 115.

33. Leszek Kolakowski, *The Presence of Myth* (Chicago: University of Chicago Press, 1989), 70.

34. Roderick Nash, *The Rights of Nature: A History of Environmental Ethics* (Madison: University of Wisconsin Press, 1989).

35. John Berger, *About Looking* (New York: Pantheon Books, 1980); James Fernandez, "The Mission of Metaphor in Expressive Culture," *Current Anthropology* 15 (1974): 119–45.

36. Harold Nicolson, *The War Years, 1939–1945* (New York: Atheneum, 1967), 30.

37. Miles Richardson and Robert Dunton, "Culture in Its Places: A Humanistic Presentation," in *The Relevance of Culture*, ed. Morris Freilich (New York: Bergin and Garvey, 1989), 75–89.

38. Eric Klinger, *Meaning & Void: Inner Experience and the Incentives in People's Lives* (Minneapolis: University of Minnesota Press, 1977).

39. Elizabeth Bowen, "Ivy Gripped the Steps," in *Collected Stories* (London: Jonathan Cape, 1980), 707–8.

40. Jules Henry, *Pathways to Madness* (New York: Random House, 1971), 88.

41. Albert Camus, *Carnets 1942–1951* (London: Hamish Hamilton, 1966), 37.

42. Burton Watson, *Chinese Lyricism: Shih Poetry from the Second to the Twelfth Century* (New York: Columbia University Press, 1971), 50.

43. The same fate awaits this paper, if my line of reasoning is correct. A short story or a novel, if it is good, is a brief parting of the curtain that can intensify life. And even though it may also subtly reorient our outlook in reality, it does not tell us what to do; it cleanses the spectacles, but it does not offer a methodology or a course of action, and hence it can be easily put aside as "philosophy" or "entertainment" and dismissed.

44. I. Dilman, *Love and Human Separateness* (Oxford: Blackwell, 1987).

Cultures

Migration, Place, and

Placelessness in America

Place-on-the-Move: Space and Place for the Migrant

CLARENCE MONDALE

There are few systematic studies of the experience of the individual migrant. Most migration study is group-oriented and is derived from data that allow only glimpses at fragments of the individual experience.[1] To understand the full cultural implications of the individual experience, one must study it from the inside and as a whole.

Students of what can be called "inner geography" have been developing a framework for analysis that fully respects the totality of the individual experience. Research in this new mode is generating a growing scholarly literature. Its most lucid single expositor is Yi-Fu Tuan, and its most systematic exposition is Tuan's *Space and Place* (1977). "Inner geography" has to do with geography as it is experienced by the individual. Much of that experience is unselfconscious and is grounded in the world of everyday routine and habit. In his analysis of that experience, Tuan thinks in terms of polarities among values, rather than in simple contrasts. The great geographical rhythm in the individual life, for him, is between pause and movement, home and reach, space and place. Place, home, and pause supply orientation; space, reach, and movement thus derive their meaning.[2] This essay attempts to describe the experience of the first-generation migrant in terms of the general framework supplied by Tuan and his school of thought.

We speak of some experiences as "moving." We speak of others as "unsettling." Both terms connote an unmooring from the routines of everyday life, a profound shift in what can be taken for granted. Any considerable migration experience is at once "moving" and "unsettling." The migrant exchanges one home for another, and, in terms of inner geography, there are few cultural transactions that are quite so basic.

The drama of the transaction is likely to concentrate upon the events surrounding the migrant's departure from the old home and his arrival at the new. His old home, in its everydayness, supplied orientation. It was where he "belonged." When the migrant leaves home, he becomes disoriented (is "left at sea," as we say) and leaves part of himself behind too. As oral histories reveal, leaving home behind for good is an experience that is likely to be remembered for a very long time, in disproportionate detail, in much the way one recalls events surrounding the death of a loved one. In moving, a quintessentially familiar world of touch and smell is abandoned. It is as if the disproportionate details lodged in memory minister to the grief provoked by that emotional rupture.

Arrival at the destination in effect reverses the process. Lacking orientation, the migrant in the new place is "neither here nor there." Something of that traumatic experience of being "neither here nor there" is likely to linger on. First memories of the circumstances of arrival, like last memories of departure, are likely to be extraordinarily detailed. Over the longer term, the riddle in migrant accounts is how to work out the terms of exchange between incommensurates, between the culture of the old place and that of the new. For most migrants, the riddle is never fully resolved. Their lives take on a "hyphenated" quality between the culture of the old home and that of the new—and, for some, living with the riddle involves a lifelong unease, a not quite coming to rest.

The pull of the familiar in the inner life of the individual migrant is analogous to the pull of gravity in the physical world. Many of us ski or fly to outwit gravity and so pay tribute to a force we live by. Certain forms of migration (and certainly much recreational travel) indirectly evidence the generally prevailing pull of the familiar. Some migrants, and many tourists, make a point of moving great distances, to strange places, even to what they see as the end of the world. All migrants, probably, are in some degree excited and "moved" by the adventure of putting the familiar behind them, and some element of the utopian is likely to assert itself in their accounts. Most cultures provide for pilgrimages to places defined in large part by their unfamiliarity: for example, among Americans, to the natural wonders on the North American continent or to particular landmarks of ancient culture in Europe.[3] But such adventures are episodic and take on durable meaning only as they find their place in relation to the otherwise governing pull of the familiar.[4]

Students of migration often speak of how migrants "cluster" in leaving an old place, following a particular path to a new place, and settling down. Such clustering, such staying in touch with one's own, is central to the migration experience. It is place-on-the-move. A migrant clusters according to what is most basic to self-orientation, what is most immediately familiar, intimate, primordial.[5] Those migrants most threatened by the experience tend to cluster most tightly; those who are relatively unthreatened, especially those with means and education, tend to cluster most loosely; but clustering is what virtually all unsettled people do as a substitute for the home left behind.

My argument relies upon oral-historical evidence, drawing particularly upon two volumes by Robert Coles on American domestic migration from the South to the North during the 1960s; and upon *American Mosaic*, a volume of immigrant recollections assembled by Joan Morrison and Charlotte Fox Zabusky.[6] I am not arguing that those sources are in some way representative of migration literature, that there are not other equally useful sources here unexamined, or that oral history is a particularly privileged kind of evidence, given the objectives of this essay.[7] These three books are, simply, credible efforts to reconstruct the experiences of individual migrants.[8]

In his two volumes, Coles talks with mountaineers, sharecroppers, and migrant agricultural workers caught up in the migration experience. His subjects grope for meaning in the midst of prevailing perplexities. The immigrant accounts in *American Mosaic*, in contrast, are recollections of that experience, often after many years. Memory at a distance produces narratives with well-developed story lines tending to feature single themes, like success, adventure, exile, or endurance. The immediate and the retrospective views of the migration experience nicely complement one another, agreeing in many respects but also calling attention to what each kind of source leaves out or puts in.

The emphasis here is upon cultural persistence, rather than upon the striking out in new directions that is so important in migrant (and especially American migrant) lore. My purpose is to understand the taken-for-granted world that defines what is assumed to be adventure. I emphasize what different kinds of migration have in common, rather than their differences. Most of the oral histories to be examined here describe a more or less voluntary migration, and of course huge numbers of migrants have moved or been moved involuntarily. Without doubt, experiences vary between blacks, say, and whites, and between males and females, as well as between domestic and international migration. I am aware of those many and basic differences. The intent, here, however, is to discern general patterns in the inner geography of the individual migrant that hold across and among such differences.

My analysis of the oral histories is placed in the context of what has been discovered in recent years about small-group migration by historians like Jon Gjerde, geographers like Robert Ostergren, and sociologists like Charles Tilly. In stressing the small group, such scholars make the individual experience accessible in a new way. However, it is not just a matter of complementarity between small-group studies and this emphasis upon the individual. The approach taken here suggests its own array of researchable topics. Finally, this emphasis upon migration as experienced can make its own contribution to theory about the present-day cultural region. There is a regionalizing involved in our highly mobile culture, but it does not conform to classical regional theory. An applicable theory must take into account values in transit, what I am calling place-on-the-move.

In what follows I discuss the experience of the individual migrant in relation to the old home, clustering en route and upon arrival, and patterns of the "hyphenated" life for those who stay on in the new location.

THE OLD HOME

  Earlier forms of migration study emphasized the difference between the "rootedness" of the place being left behind (the farm in Europe or, for that matter, the farm in the United States) and the "uprootedness" of modern and urban life. Most recent scholarship emphasizes, instead, how unsettledness in the home culture prepared the migrant for the unsettledness of the move.[9] The logic of inner geography argues on behalf of the new interest in the connectedness between old place and new.

  Tuan and his school maintain that it is impossible to stay "home" or "in place," because those terms derive their meaning only in relation to movement and change. In terms of the journey to work, for example, home is what one leaves and what one returns to. Conversely, movement is movement from and to home. Such rhythms in the ordinary mobility of everyday life are continuous in kind with the less ordinary rhythms of temporary or seasonal migration, in which the individual moves fully intending to return to the home place, as well as with the extraordinary rhythms involved in what I am calling the "considerable" move.

  Charles Tilly distinguishes between "mobility" and "migration." "Mobility" denotes the ordinary movements of everyday life (e.g., to work and back). "Migration," in contrast, involves a move of extraordinary distance that is "definitive," involving some degree of displacement or social rupture.[10] In particular cases, however, definitiveness may have little to do with distance. A move from one house to another, under certain circumstances, or even a move from one room to another within the same house, can have all the traits of a long-distance move.[11] And movement across the Atlantic and back and forth across half of the United States can be seen in local, nondefinitive terms. A young Polish migrant to Chicago, needing a bride, looks up an acquaintance from the home village living in Chicago in order to get some recommendations. That acquaintance knows a girl from that village, then resident in Niagara Falls, who is single and of marriageable age. The youth travels from Chicago to Niagara Falls in order to propose to her formally.[12] Here actual distance is of little consequence; significant distance is calculated in provincial, Polish terms. Or, as a contrasting case with the same moral, an individual from suburban Chicago might be reassigned by her corporate employer to a new job landing her in suburban Seattle; the new place in that case may seem on many counts familiar, in spite of the great distance involved in the move.[13] One concludes that the degree of definitiveness or displacement is likely, but not certain, to be related to the distance of the move.

The more general point to be made, however, is, as Tilly argues, that local mobility, seasonal migration, and "definitive" migration are often indistinguishable. The great mass of immigrants to the United States came from regions in which seasonal migration had become commonplace as a dimension of everyday mobility. For many Italians, trips to and from the United States followed a seasonal rhythm. Polish migrants often took jobs in American steel mills for years at a time in order to earn the cash necessary to purchase land upon return home, which in effect constituted a prolonged seasonal cycle.[14] An extreme case of "seasonal" migration patterns (reported by David Lowenthal and Lambros Comitas in 1962) is that of Greek islanders who were depending upon remittances from emigrants abroad for economic survival, but who insisted (along with the emigrants, often long departed) that all such emigration was to be understood as temporary.[15]

Such patterns informed much domestic migration. Clyde V. Kiser has described how Sea Island blacks in the last years of the nineteenth century found themselves unable to make a living at home and so worked out patterns of movement that combined work at home with work in nearby Savannah and Charleston, the patterns varying according to gender and age. In time the great majority of Sea Island residents derived part or even all of their income from outside work.[16]

The oral histories we are examining reveal how the unsettledness of the old home prepares the individual for the unsettledness of the move. Coles studies domestic "betterment" migration, people leaving more or less voluntarily to improve their situations. He shows that, for such individuals, mobility and migration unsettle the very notion of home. In *Migrants, Share-croppers, Mountaineers* (hereafter *MSM*), he interviewed individuals who had not yet moved off the land. All of his interviewees know that there are great changes underway: the mountaineers are only half at home; the sharecroppers represent a kind of remnant culture; and the migrant workers are inured to lifelong homelessness.

The mountaineers have a fierce pride in place. They have grown up in mountain hollows where their ancestors have lived "forever" (*MSM*, 3–24, 578–617; on landscape, see especially 7–14). At the time of the interviews, few of the mountaineers could make a living staying at home. To find work, it was necessary to commute to a nearby town or move to a regional center or out of the region altogether (see, e.g., *MSM*, 221, 278). Money coming from the North became necessary to local survival (*MSM*, 304). Youngsters earning cash on the outside had become less attached to the home place: as a mountaineer observes, those youngsters "can like it up here in the hollow, but they're not tied to it so much" (*MSM*, 269). In the second volume, *The South Goes North* (hereafter *SGN*), interstate highways became a ligature between the home place and its northern colonies, especially on weekends (*SGN*, 571). Individual families became split between home and the colonies, with the young people moving to the colonies while the older and the less mobile stayed at home. For the individuals who stayed at home, the "outside" world became part of an increasingly "stretched" local geography that incorporated the home place and its colonies. All of these changes altered the old place: a returned native noticed that there was a new carelessness about local record-keeping and that, increasingly, people were no longer buried at home (*MSM*, 358).

For the sharecroppers interviewed by Coles, there was something fugitive about their very sense of place. For one thing, the land did not belong to them, as it did to the mountaineers. For another, most of their fellow sharecroppers had gone north; they had been left behind, stranded at home. Yet they had reasons to want to stay. As youngsters, they had developed an intimacy with the land that Coles found remarkable, a way of life governed by daily and seasonal rhythms rather than by the clock (*MSM*, 187–88; cf. 163–66). Their social life had depth by virtue of its cycle of holidays and, especially, its shared religion (*MSM*, 151–52, 604–14). But parents knew that they might have to move, and children grew up asking when the move would come (*MSM*, 132, 187–88). "Up North," especially Chicago, became part of the "stretched" local geography. That city had fearful meanings for the remnant culture, connoting rats, freezing weather, and lost souls (e.g., *MSM*, 157).

Coles says that the members of the third group, the migrant agricultural workers, could be said to live in exile (*MSM*, 105). They belong nowhere. The pull of the familiar, for them, has few charms. Among children of the migrant workers, Coles concludes, "care is lost; the child stops caring, hardens himself for the coming battle ..." (*MSM*, 84). Coles asks the children to draw landscapes. They draw roads without destinations and fields with guards and high fences (*MSM*, 93–115). Young adults drift into the endlessly migrant life of their parents (*MSM*, 546, 547). In terms of inner geography, such individuals represent the extreme case, in which any sense of home is at best elusive and fragile, all but lost in the continuous movement.[17]

The immigrants in *American Mosaic* (hereafter *AM*) move from one national culture to another. Nevertheless, many of them are, like Coles's subjects, "betterment" migrants, whose accounts tell of a more or less voluntary youthful migration as an escape from hopelessness at home, in implicit contrast to conditions in the United States. "Work, work, all the time. No end. No compensation. Only an existence," says a Swede (*AM*, 5). "In the crowded valleys of Wales," one migrant remarks, ". . . they was almost waiting for dead man's shoes, you know" (*AM*, 109). After describing the round of chores characterizing her Irish childhood, a woman remarks, "There was nothing in Ireland" (*AM*, 41). A woman from Hungary says that she moved to America out of desperation: "There was no work over there. . . . We wanted to make some money and come back better. But we found it was different here. . . . It was better than over there" (*AM*, 58).

In contrast to Coles's subjects, many of the individuals in *American Mosaic* are involuntary migrants who were required to flee their homelands to escape hostile police and armies.[18] For some among them, America is exile, and, like members of a colony of Yugoslav royalists in New York City, they dream of the day when the homeland will be back in their hands (*AM*, 270; cf. 327). For most of them, there is no possibility of return. For example, a Pole returns to search for his home neighborhood in Warsaw, but finds it in ruins (*AM*, 169–70). As an extreme instance: a Polish Jew returns to what had been her hometown before World War II to discover that all her family and kin are dead and that all of their property has been confiscated by gentiles (*AM*, 159).

Whereas Coles's subjects are uniformly poor, some of the immigrants in *American Mosaic* are relatively well off. The narratives of such individuals suggest that money and education make a qualitative difference in how migration is perceived and how its story is told. A Yugoslav refugee concludes by saying, ". . . you are not as culturally narrow when you have the wherewithal to travel, to collect, to go to school" (*AM*, 272; cf. 174–81, 286–94). That is to say, for the fortunate the sense of home is likely to be more spacious, even among refugees. An Egyptian doctor and his wife can be said to live comfortably in both worlds. The husband enjoys the professional challenges involved in working in the United States, his wife is able to make frequent trips to Egypt, and the two are in regular touch with family and friends there (*AM*, 379–84). Denise Levertov, in *American Mosaic*, has the wherewithal to take off with a friend on a hitchhiking jaunt around postwar Europe, during which she meets and marries a book-loving GI and savors the adventure of being half-American while still in Europe (*AM*, 239). Alistair Cooke comes from England to America as a young man intending to have a very good time. He uses an academic fellowship in the United States as an excuse for a prolonged vacation at school and an extended ramble through the American West (*AM*, 126–30). Cooke talks as if his choosing to stay on in the United States simply prolonged the vacation.

Even those in fortunate circumstances, however, may be devastated by the move. Ilona Bertok describes a life of endless moving, from Hungary, to New York, to Tennessee, from one impossible situation to the next. She concludes that she belongs nowhere: "Everywhere I was a changeling" (*AM*, 282). A Russian exile is well off, but her life in America is empty of meaning, because she belongs to the dead world of Czarist Russia (*AM*, 88–93).

The Coles volumes show how the old home, when seen close up in migrant accounts, is an unsettled place. In *American Mosaic*, the betterment migrants are likely to represent their own movement as part of a more general restlessness back home; the involuntary migrants leave behind upheaval rather than restlessness; and the more fortunate migrants overall seem to be less threatened by unsettledness than are those of lesser means. But, generally, unsettledness at home prepares the migrant for the unsettledness of the "considerable" move.

THE MOVE

In terms of inner geography, clustering of the "near and dear" is the means by which a migrant keeps a sense of place while on the move and upon arrival. Like place itself, such clustering has to do with the immediately familiar. It relates to the special value the migrant puts upon what remains of place once the old home is left behind. Clustering serves to sustain what is intimate and familiar in the midst of otherwise strange circumstances. It is elemental to cultural survival.

A person makes a considerable move only under unusual circumstances. Much of the migration to and within the United States has been what I earlier described as betterment migration. G. J. Lewis, in his review of migration literature, concludes that most long-distance migration is economically motivated.[19] The central motivation for such migration is easily demonstrated, as by Jon Gjerde, who shows that the ups and downs of immigration from Norway followed the ups and downs of wheat prices in the United States. But, of course, much else enters in. Gjerde is describing migration from Balestrand, a small rural community in western Norway. The Balestrand migrant knew the level of American wheat prices, but also needed to know where and how to buy American farm land, how to make the trip from Old World to New, and how to close out affairs in Norway. When the migrant risked so much, this information had to be absolutely reliable. Generally that meant that the information had to come from kinfolk and townfolk or their surrogates.[20] Thus the importance of "America letters," from kin and townfolk in the New World to kin and townfolk back home, describing what lay in store for migrants.[21] Bernard Bailyn, in his study of eighteenth-century English migration, comments that successful recruiters of migrants had to know and have the trust of the local communities they visited; "outsiders" were unsuccessful.[22] For such betterment migrants, the more local the knowledge, the more trustworthy it was.

Under the circumstances, it is not surprising that such migrants exercised a local logic in following a precisely defined path from old home to new. The Balestranders, for example, moved west from Norway to Long Prairie, Illinois, to Koshkonong, Wisconsin, to Norway Grove, Wisconsin, to particular farm communities in Iowa and Minnesota. Generally, the latest western settlement became the base for migration yet further west. A young man would set up a farm in a western outpost during the summer, return "east" for the winter and, often, for a bride, and then complete his move. The whole process was locally enclosed, a movement from one Balestrand colony to the next.[23] Bailyn documents a very similar pattern in the 1773–1776 period for Yorkshiremen moving to Nova Scotia and for Scottish highlanders moving to North Carolina.[24] Kiser describes in detail the evolution of migration north on the part of residents of the Sea Islands, with local knowledge of Philadelphia and Boston leading to local knowledge of New

York City and, eventually, to the formation of a Sea Island colony in that metropolis.[25]

A close study of early migration to and from Syracuse, New York, details movement from particular towns in Connecticut to settlements in the Syracuse area and, later on, movement from rural communities in the Syracuse area to Michigan and points west according to where kinfolk or townfolk had gone before.[26] Syracuse and Balestrand migration both followed a local logic, but with a difference. The Balestranders clustered tightly, if over an extended geography. The tightness of the clustering seems to be a function of the social distance felt between the migrants and host culture at the point of arrival. Characteristically, the Balestranders settled side by side; Balestranders as a group settled next to emigrants from nearby areas in Norway; and Norwegians in general clustered together in relation to both immigrants from elsewhere and native-born Americans.[27] The Syracuse migrants seemed to move in a more scattershot pattern. They followed kin and townfolk west, but perhaps to Michigan, perhaps to Illinois. Wherever they settled, they found themselves among great numbers of fellow New Englanders, among their own kind.[28] The pattern of these new settlements represents a relatively looser form of clustering than with the Balestranders, but for both groups, however tight or loose the clustering, there was a local logic to patterns of movement.

Patterns of migration from the Midwest to southern California during the 1880–1940 period seem to be continuous in kind with those I have been describing. The evidence is fragmentary, but, I believe, convincing. Midwesterners moving to the Los Angeles area came in clusters, but the clusters were still more stretched and scattershot than those in the Upper Midwest. Also affecting movement and settlement among these latter-day migrants was the fact that they seem to have been generally better-off than the Balestranders or New Englanders.

Carey McWilliams, in *Southern California* (1946), lovingly chronicles the misadventures of midwestern migrants in the Los Angeles area during the 1880–1920 period. He represents midwesterners in California as pursuing the amenities in disregard of "normal" concerns about work, place, and kin.[29] By his account, they are entirely unprepared for the realities of California life, driven by a fervent wish to escape long, hard midwestern winters, thinking that some cash on hand may buy them the never-never land described by public relations experts and real estate sharks. McWilliams represents the migrants as an extreme type of the culturally displaced. In fact, there may well have been a factitious quality to social life among those newcomers in their very strange environment. That is all the more likely because so many of those initiates to California came as retirees. If one looks to other sources, however, one gets a different story.

Gregory H. Singleton, in *Religion in the City of the Angels*, describes familiar patterns of clustering in the translation of a church-centered and localistic social order from the Midwest to the Los Angeles area during the early years of midwestern settlement.[30] Robert M. Fogelson, in his history of Los Angeles, carries the story forward and takes specific exception to McWilliams, emphasizing the importance of family to the emigrants and detecting among them a "betterment" emphasis upon material acquisitions.[31] McWilliams can be brought to bear against his own argument: he describes the ways in which county fairs, vacation travel, and local newspapers kept Californians and midwesterners in touch; and he is clearly conscious of the existence of midwestern colonies, as at Long Beach, even if he does not pause to examine the colonization process. Jon Gjerde has studied migration between Iowa and Pasadena and discovered that his subset of Iowans came from a particular but relatively large area in northeast Iowa, to settle in a relatively spread-out way in a particular part of Pasadena.[32] No doubt other northeastern Iowans were loosely clustered elsewhere in the state. Our fragmented evidence argues that among midwestern migrants to southern California what is local takes in a larger territory, but locale (as the locus of the familiar) still counts.

I have been describing clustering in general terms. Oral histories show how the process of clustering worked for particular individuals. The decision to migrate, these histories suggest, is likely to have a family logic. Decisive moments, at given life-stages, provoke or permit the move. A woman described by Coles would not think of leaving Alabama while her mother needed her care, but left with a clear conscience upon her death (*SGN*, 544). A mountaineer, long restless, left the moment his father died (*SGN*, 368–70). Kiser supplies numbers: one-fourth of his subjects left their Sea Island homes upon a death in the family.[33]

Many of the narratives in *American Mosaic* have to do with young people coming of age in an area in which long-distance migration has gained local currency. A young Swede describes the circumstances of his move. He was out of school and knew of the New World through family friends and books. His father finally said he could migrate or stay home, as he wished. He recalls his reaction: "Sure I'd go. I was seventeen years old. Strong. Weighed a hundred and fifty pounds. A bargain in the labor market of the New World. Besides, I had an uncle in Minnesota. He'd fix it for me. Everything would be as easy as pie" (*AM*, 6; cf. 53–54). A female Irish migrant left home at age eighteen, like many others from her home area. "You know what they needed then, mostly? I'll tell you. Strong and healthy. . . ." She knew what to do upon landing. She immediately contracted with an employment agency for work as a domestic (*AM*, 42).

A whole category of migration is marriage-related. Many of the immigrants in *American Mosaic* have arranged marriages, often with mates from "the other side," from "two, three miles away from my village" (*AM*, 59). The fact that the man from the "other side" happened to live in the United States does not much affect the pattern. A kind of swarming is involved, with an Old World local logic determining suitability of mates on either side of the ocean. An Italian-American comments: "In fact, my mother . . . wouldn't *allow* me to marry anybody else from a different town. It's got to be from the same town" (*AM*, 65).[34] In such cases, the linkages among culture, family, migration, and marriage are institutionally channeled.

The complexities of those linkages become manifest when the choice of mate becomes problematical, as, for example, in the case of a young Italian who has his parents on one side of the ocean and other kin and his girl friend on the other and must choose one group against the other (*AM*, 365–66); or, under different circumstances but involving the same dilemma, the case of a Dayton, Ohio, young man who nearly proposes to a Kentucky girl and so nearly commits himself to the old mountaineer way of life (*SGN*, 359–61). One mother explains that if her daughter marries a German instead of a German-American "it's a completely different relationship when they are together. Because they got more in common. They can talk about more. They can even sing a song together" (*AM*, 214; cf. Polish version, *AM*, 168).

It is fascinating, in *American Mosaic*, to see who among the immigrants ends up marrying an American. For example, the German mother just described, with her distinctions between German and German-American mates, rejoices in living in a neighborhood in which she can get by without any English at all (*AM*, 213). In contrast, a Welsh immigrant looks back upon a fulfilling American life by concluding about it and his American-born wife: "Of course it's all Louise's and my relationship. . . . And it's difficult to separate the United States from Louise. It's Louise to me" (*AM*, 223).

Human migration usually involves movement of kin.[35] A familiar pattern among what are called "chain" immigrants is one in which a male migrant prepares the way for a succession of relatives, from his wife and children, to his siblings, to his parents, to his more distant kin. Over time the entire family, or even something like an entire village, is transported overseas, so that it eventually regains something like the old family and sometimes even the old village unity. An extreme example of the pattern is a Scotch Plains, New York, Italian-American colony in which settlers virtually duplicated the life they had known overseas. For example, the women gathered wood in the forests and carried it on their heads back to the house, for use in outdoor ovens (*AM*, 29–30). More characteristically, the story line is like that followed by an Italian immigrant, describing her particular urban neighborhood: "We were a group all from our town that we came together. This uncle of mine, my mother's brother, he brought his whole family over here, too. We lived close, about four blocks away . . ." (*AM*, 65). Domestic migrants in Coles follow similar patterns: a sharecropper, once established in New York, sends for his wife and children, "and after a while we sent for my cousins, too" (*SGN*, 20–21); a mountaineer father tells how he followed his daughters north (*SGN*, 337–49).

Of course, movement of kin between old place and new leads to straddled family and regional loyalties, as in the cases of the young men from Italy and from Dayton, Ohio, mentioned above. For many migrants, family unity, however desirable, is hard to come by. For example, a family lives in Boston, along with two of the mother's sisters. The child's grandparents live in North Carolina, which the child calls "back home." He visits them regularly. The grandparents make visits to Boston and to two other cities along the way, where the child's uncles live, but the grandparents have no wish to move north (*SGN*, 83). A migrant family may be reconstituted on a new basis, as when a sharecropper father leaves home upon the birth of his child, whereupon the mother, grandmother, and child catch a bus north to join the child's maternal uncle (*SGN*, 114).

I earlier examined the "stretched" geography linking the old home to its colonies, emphasizing the first of the two Coles volumes. The subjects of Coles's second volume describe that geography from the point of view of the colonists. For example, a mountaineer family, whose loyalties are split between Cleveland and Kentucky, divides its members accordingly: a husband and a wife in Cleveland provide room and board for the wife's sister's husband, while the wife's sister stays down in Kentucky to care for her mother and a retarded younger sister. The wife's father tried Cleveland but returned home (*SGN*, 315–16). Mountaineer mothers, resident in the North, make a custom of returning home to give birth to their babies (*SGN*, 325, 418, 559). The automobile that links geographically removed parts of the family takes on a special meaning for a mountaineer child, who becomes remarkably familiar with the exact route followed in weekend drives to the old home and back—which interstates, which turnoffs (*SGN*, 571). When migrants reach a certain age, debates about where to be buried are likely to be intermixed with debates about where to call home. One mountaineer who did not migrate comments about how the old-timers come back to Kentucky to "have a happy last few years," to be "back for good," to "die in peace" (*SGN*, 318).

Again, the pattern for the "fortunate" differs from that for the ordinary migrant. A number of accounts in *American Mosaic* are by professionals (e.g., writers, physicists, actors) with international connections. In such cases, kinfolk usually play a smaller role in the migration story, and professional colleagues figure more prominently (see, e.g., *AM*, 192–95). But, I suspect, kin or their surrogates always count.

For example, take the case of Carey McWilliams, a young man with interregional connections. In a 1973 preface to his 1946 book, McWilliams recalls his own migration experience, in which kinship and local loyalties played their part, along with fortunate circumstances. He grew up in Colorado. In general, he remarks, Coloradans leaving the state migrated to southern California. Upon the death of his father, his mother moved to Los Angeles. There she joined her brother, his uncle. He notes that his mother's best friends in her new location were always other ex-Coloradans. McWilliams himself moved to Los Angeles after he had been expelled from a university. He was met at the Los Angeles train station by his uncle, who then helped him look for a job. In short order, he was followed to California by a brother who had remained in Colorado.[36] McWilliams went on to make a name for himself as a journalist and writer. In his account (as in that of Alistair Cooke, described earlier), the new home is represented as wonderfully spacious. McWilliams recalls his many Los Angeles years as an extended good time, "a ringside seat at the circus." But, especially upon initial arrival, kinship and local loyalties were crucial.[37]

An alternative to clustering, for the migrant, is to go it alone, to be what can be called a "pioneer" migrant, the first of a particular group to settle in a strange place. In the oral histories under review, such pioneer migrants are few and far between. There is, in *American Mosaic*, the case of a young Nigerian who through ham radio and church connections ends up in Bristol, Rhode Island, as the only one of his kind. He later introduces some of his compatriots to the advantages of the area, who until then had not thought of settlement outside of the big coastal cities (*AM*, 405, 407). A black lawyer in *The South Goes North* recalls the pioneering journey of his father, who had left Memphis when only nine at the urging of his parents and a teacher. The teacher paid for the trip north and secured housing for him there with her brother (*SGN*, 178–79).[38] There is, in *American Mosaic*, the instance of a Hungarian refugee who grew up resenting the Communist regime back home and jumped at the chance to come to the United States, in spite of the fact that he came as a stranger (*AM*, 302).

When a pioneer looks back after a successful move, it makes a great story—one thinks of the young Benjamin Franklin's move to Philadelphia as a classic of the type. It makes a great story because it represents a dramatic break with normal behavior. Pioneers might well be enshrined in public memory, as part of an important fiction about collective identity. The Sea Island colonists in New York City, for example, continue to celebrate the memory of the handful of schoolchildren who had been brought north from the old home by northern philanthropists just after the Civil War, and who thereby set the stage for the mass migration of the 1920s.[39] But pioneer migrants are the exceptions that prove the rule.

Overwhelmingly, migrants, fortunate and otherwise, choose a particular destination because family members or their surrogates live there. Coles describes the new migrant to the northern city as coming armed with addresses of kin, not necessarily close kin, "but above all, kin" (*SGN*, 18). "We had kin here and we just went to them," says a mountaineer. An unsympathetic landlord says that blacks move north "because there's a relative or a friend here . . . and they move in . . ." (*SGN*, 613). The pattern, I suspect, is all but universal. When we move, we might well idealize the pioneer, the adventurer, but we are almost certain to keep handy and put to quick use the address of someone "near and dear," some home connection in the strange place. As remarked earlier, clustering is what virtually all unsettled people turn to as a substitute for the home left behind.

THE NEW HOME

The newly arrived migrants must make something of a home of the new place. The effort is likely to consist in a patchwork of expediencies. They live with their own, their near and dear. Their own, as a group, move near their kind. What is understood to be their kind is continuously redefined by the changing circumstances of the new place.[40] Over the years subsequent to arrival, the migrant must puzzle out the meaning of the migration experience. Central to that effort are recollections of events surrounding departure from the old place and arrival at the new, and the light they throw on what becomes a more or less hyphenated life between "here" and "there."

Strong biases affect conventional representations of the move itself. We need to understand better the view the home culture takes of the act of moving away. Most people stay at home, and many people who stay at home are better off for doing so.[41] Movement away from the group and homeland has at best an ambiguous moral quality. For many immigrant groups and for the mountaineers described by Coles, to move is in some measure distasteful, even disgraceful. Groups such as Italians and Poles, with a high incidence of remigration, are likely to see return to the homeland as the object of migration and become Americans almost in spite of themselves. Many migrants return, yet we know very little about the remigrant experience.[42] Finally, there needs to be much more attention to the whole phenomenon of continuous intermigration linking one home to another and to the "stretched" geography, incorporating both, that comes to be taken for granted by the home culture and its colonies.[43] Leaving the old home behind in the years subsequent to the move is a culturally complicated affair.

Caroline Golab describes the twelve Polish settlements in Philadelphia at the turn of the twentieth century as an amalgam of migrants from various villages and provinces. The immigrants are grouped roughly by subgroup (e.g., Galician, Prussian), in some conjunction with like subgroups (e.g., Prussian Pole with German), all in an urban setting that may well be shared among several distinct ethnic groups. Out of some such geographical pattern emerge ethnic communities and the institutions that are developed to serve them.[44] John Bodnar traces such patterns over time among Polish and Italian immigrants in Pittsburgh. On arrival, the migrants had to live near the job, and clustering was inhibited by that necessity. With more money and affordable transportation, the clustering within the Polish and Italian neighborhoods became more exclusive; given the means, these ethnic groups concentrated with a new intensity. Later, when young Polish couples moved to the suburbs, they chose places convenient to their old urban neighborhoods and to one another. The whole process amounts to a kind of continuous reclustering.[45]

Group identity is necessarily redefined in the new place. Over time mountaineer migrants to Chicago begin to see themselves in city terms, as from "Appalachia," as well as being natives of a particular Kentucky county or hollow; and sharecroppers from particular areas in rural Mississippi come to see themselves as from the "South." In like manner, San Francisco Italians in time see themselves as northern or southern Italians, rather than as coming from particular villages, and later simply as Italians.[46]

Recollections of the experiences immediately surrounding the move resonate for a lifetime. William Thomas and Florian Znaniecki's classic study of Polish migration includes a remarkably full account of one individual's experience at the time of departure. The individual, who goes by the name of Wladek Wiszniewski, decides to move to America only after he concludes that he is a failure at home. To mark his farewell from the homeland, he goes through an elaborate ritual—a formal speech to his parents; a final dinner with his two brothers, asking each to write down advice to guide him on his journey; a farewell to his ex-betrothed; and, finally, a farewell to the family as a whole, together in evening prayer at the church, and then, the next morning, one by one at the family home.[47] A Swede, remembering his move as the best thing in his long life, calls up a wealth of remembered detail about the last few days at home, climaxed by a meal of home-baked beans and salt pork prepared by his mother. He recalls her as unusually quiet at the moment of farewell (*AM*, 6). Sometimes inarticulateness is eloquent. A Polish emigrant in *American Mosaic* remarks: "Of course I was very anxious to go, to see the world. My husband's taking me to see America and to see the whole world. Everybody was crying. I can't understand why they're crying. When the train started moving, then I was crying, too. My mother, my father, my sisters and brothers, all crying." At that point in the telling of her story, the woman, some fifty years after the event, burst into tears (*AM*, 68).

Denise Levertov, in *American Mosaic*, was surprised by her own behavior as she was preparing to leave her English home. Her parents had kept her childhood room intact. She went through belongings and memorabilia there, "systematically throwing out all sorts of things—in a sort of ritualistic way, because it was really quite unnecessary. It was a kind of ritual, like closing up a house" (*AM*, 239). Pets sometimes act as surrogates among migrant children for the world of touch and smell being left behind. Ilona Bertok, remembering herself as a child in flight from Hungary, recounts the details of her departure. The family had selected a few precious and portable items to take with them. Friends stood outside the train window waving farewell. She concludes: "Someone was holding my pet cat, and I think that cat was the creature I cried about most" (*AM*, 275). Coles describes how a mountaineer child, long after his move, draws pictures of the dog he had been forced to leave behind (*SGN*, 85; cf. *SGN*, 24).

Surely the journey overland or overseas, from old home to new, filled the thoughts of earlier emigrants, but it receives slight attention in the sources. The arrival at the new place is another matter. The wonderfully articulate Levertov recalls a utopian moment as the New World came into her view. She saw the New York skyline from the boat, "with those skyscrapers sticking up out of a rose-tinted mist. It was sort of Venetian looking, because they were kinds of palaces coming up out of the water. It was incredible! I never saw it like that again" (*AM*, 239). In the same spirit, a French chef reacts to the same skyline: "You see this, you forget you seasick, you forget everything. This is my dream coming true, my dream coming true" (*AM*, 338). Although the experience comes after he has been in the country and away from England for a year, Alistair Cooke's romp through the American West has something of the same utopian flavor. The firsthand experience of the grand spaces of the West is, for Cooke, cause for lifelong wonder, and even nondescript experiences along the way are given drama by the extravagant youthful fantasies he had about the region—for example, the "badger game" and the "buffalo moth," and, of course, Hollywood (*AM*, 129–30).

Levertov's utopian excitement about the New York skyline as first encountered collapsed during the trip to her husband's brother's home upon debarking in New York. Being pregnant colored her mood, she recalls. She suddenly felt tired and queasy. She had thought of New York as clean, "like Switzerland."

> Well, the first thing I know, we're driving through the Bowery, and there are bodies just lying on the streets. It's not what I'm expecting at all. It looked sort of dreamlike to me—just weird, totally weird. I'd never seen a neighborhood like that—wastepaper and bottles and bums flat out on the sidewalk. Then I saw a big electric sign that said *Kinsey*, over on the Brooklyn shore, and I thought it was an ad for the *Kinsey Report*, which had just come out. "Wow, they advertise books with big neon signs in America," I thought.
>
> (*AM*, 240)

Levertov's sense of "weirdness" and the earlier dreamlike vision are both remarkable to her precisely because they are so much at odds with what she had always taken for granted.

One of the finest sections in the Coles volumes is entitled "The Streets." It describes the shock felt by country folk when they first take in the rush and noise of city life, and the strangeness of its built environment (*SGN*, 3–27). A New York cabbie up from Georgia says that he will always live with "a little bit of that first day in me." Nothing was familiar; nothing could be taken for granted. "I'd have my eyes watching all over, and my ears as open as they could be—and the result was that I didn't know what to do" (*SGN*, 20–22). A Kentuckian, remembering the moment the city became visible from the highway, says, "I saw the city from a distance, you know, and I thought I was having myself a dream. . . . Well, we got closer and closer, and all I could think was that we were going to die, once we got in the middle of the city . . ." (*SGN*, 18). One recently arrived Colombian woman in *American Mosaic* wandered about a strange section of Miami for an entire night because she was afraid to ask how to take the bus or taxi, unable to find a telephone, and too unsure of her English to stop at a restaurant to ask for help (*AM*, 359).

An extreme case of felt disorientation and "weirdness" is that of a Polish refugee family whose members can be described as involuntary pioneers. Just after the last world war the family decided to move to rural Minnesota, in response to a newspaper advertisement soliciting applications for farm work. They knew nothing about the place and came as isolates, as, corporately, a cluster fragment. The son recalls the moment of arrival, in exquisite detail:

> We arrived in the afternoon in St. Cloud, Minnesota, and this was the funniest—I wish I would have had a camera at the time. You can imagine: a family of four immigrants, everybody dressed to kill, because we wanted to make an impression. We had only one suit per person, made by a German tailor by paying American cigarettes. And my mother had a dress made out of a curtain from a window. And we got off in the middle of nowhere! There's nothing. The train stopped, they put this little step, and they said, "Get out." The train left and we're standing there and—nobody! We said, "Where are we? No it can't be here."
>
> (*AM*, 167)

As soon as possible thereafter the family rejoined their kind in Ossining, New York, "a big Polish community" (*AM*, 168).

In spite of clustering, the most intimate relations change in the new location. A young Chinese immigrant in New York City is unconsoled by the local "family associations," groups of people from particular home villages. Such people are "like acquaintances. Nobody's intimate. The biggest adjustment is when . . . you have sickness and you are alone" (*AM*, 77).[48] Wladek Wiszniewski's sister tells the newly arrived immigrant that he will get free room and board for one week, but then will have to pay his way, explaining, "in America everyone lives for himself."[49] In Coles, a devoutly religious mountaineer woman says that her sense of God's presence has changed in her new surroundings: "He wants us to be more on our own. . . . everywhere you turn it's new and strange and we're being tested" (*SGN*, 315). Coles comments that sharecroppers in the northern cities, in spite of the harshness of life in the South, "cradle themselves" with recollections of southern place and kin. A woman's eyes fill with tears, to her own frustration. She says, "I'm glad we're here, and I wish I was back there; that's what I tell my children" (*SGN*, 315–16). Years after the event, an elderly woman keeps the stub of her bus ticket from Mobile to Boston in a bedroom drawer as a keepsake (*SGN*, 71).[50]

Coles comments, as Tuan might, that with time the past is recalled "with decreasing frequency and increasing self-consciousness" (*SGN*, 23). The feeling of being in limbo gives way to resignation to being "up here, even if it is for just a while," to staying on without realizing it (see *SGN*, 318,

323, 399). Students of migration seem to agree with what the logic of inner geography would argue: that the longer the migrant stays in a new place, the more likely she is to continue to stay.[51] The first thought upon arrival may well be to turn around and go home (*SGN*, 21–22; cf. *AM*, 304–5). Over time, the pull of the old home asserts itself less frequently, if at predictable times. For example, a German immigrant remarks, "Well, I don't feel unhappy all the time, but . . . on holidays, you get homesick" (*AM*, 214).

Familiarity with the new place and the decision to settle there are of course related to one another, but they are nevertheless distinct. An Israeli couple persisted over nearly a decade in putting off the decision to stay in the United States. In their minds, "This was still temporary. We were living out of suitcases for a long time. I was visiting, just visiting all the time" (*AM*, 388). Their dilemma meant nothing to their American-reared children, who finally forced the parents to realize that they had in fact become Israeli-Americans. Coles tells of a mountaineer father who has made all the arrangements to return home, but, in the midst of packing up, says, "I believe we'll stay." He thereafter goes at adjustment to life in the city with new purpose (*SGN*, 402–3).[52]

After any considerable migration, the question over the long term becomes what to make of a more or less hyphenated life. Coles, the psychiatrist, is well aware of the fact that what a migrant thinks of his past is an important indication of how he feels about present prospects. Thus, a well-adjusted black father remembers his Virginia home with affection but with no thought of return (*SGN*, 202–3). The Washington cab driver who too strenuously insists that "the past is past" is also too strenuous in the care of his suburban lawn and in his hopes for his achievement-oriented only child (*SGN*, 361–72).

All of the recollections in *American Mosaic* dwell upon the nature of the hyphenated life. All agree that one should not give up one culture for another, but must instead retain the best of both. But how do you decide what is the best of both?

A few of the accounts suggest that such concerns do not constitute a problem. At one extreme is Lynn Redgrave, who after a relatively brief stay in this country feels that she is accepted as a New Yorker and is yet free to be English: "I cry when Princess Anne has a baby, and I love all that." "Unlike any country in the world," she remarks, "you actually can be accepted here" (*AM*, 417). For her the hyphen seems to function as an amusement. The Yugoslavian (mentioned above) who contrasted the fortunate to the unfortunate migrant says with some complacency: "I'm an American who happened to have spent a lot of time in his childhood in other countries" (*AM*, 273). For him, the hyphen is there, but it is not obtrusive. At the other extreme are the exiles, who refuse to think of any exchange at all, such as the Yugoslav royalists in New York City plotting their return to power, the Pole whose home was obliterated during the war, and the Russian exile whose American life is empty because her heart belongs to a Czarist Russia that no longer exists, or, as a type of them all, the Hungarian emigrant who is never able to get her American bearings (*AM*, 270, 159, 88–93, 282).

Much more characteristic than such extreme cases is life as described by a thoughtful Pole looking back after many years in this country. He has no regrets about moving to America, in spite of the time lost in mastering a strange language. As a Jew married to a gentile, he is much less self-conscious about his mixed marriage in the United States than he would have been in Poland or in Israel, where he also lived. He decides, with some misgivings, deliberately to ignore Polish culture and history as ingredients in his children's education. "I think if my children live in this country, they have to be American. Why mix?" For all that, he comments, "No matter how well you speak English, there is slightly a different mentality. . . . Let's face it, no matter how much I feel myself right now American, still, when it comes to friendship, I look more or less for what has the same background I have" (*AM*, 249).[53]

Remnants of the early homesickness can be amazingly persistent. Levertov, after a quarter-century in the United States, decides "she *must* go back" to England. On the day of return to her former homeland, she is overcome with a rush of familiar but forgotten feelings: "I went for a walk that evening. It wasn't a neighborhood I was familiar with . . . but [the streets] had those features which were of the most astonishing familiarity, and that familiarity was astonishingly moving to me." "I understand why people kneeled down and kissed the soil. I felt just like that" (*AM*, 242). A Scottish immigrant takes delight in a family reunion between New World and Old World branches which had been long separated. The host was elderly Uncle Angus, who had been at odds with the family over the years. The immigrant concludes, "Uncle Angus died about six months after the reunion. I'm glad we were able to do that, to get everyone together for the last time" (*AM*, 148). The reunion is of course personal as well as familial: the immigrant thereby effects a "last" reunion across the deep divide in her own life.

For mountaineers, the old place is continuously accessible, reunions are recurrent, and the thought of remigration persistent, including the thought of return as old age approaches and of burial back home. Elderly Poles decide to be buried in a cemetery site removed from their American residence but dedicated to Our Lady of Czestochowa. Their son remarks, "They say they want to lie among their own people" (*AM*, 171). A German lady who has never been reconciled to life in America declares, "That's what I keep telling [my husband]. I say, 'Send me over.' If I know I'm dying, I would go over" (*AM*, 214).

Any real trip "back" returns the migrant to a changed place. One German immigrant has the luxury of living in the United States while keeping an apartment back home. She thought of moving back to Germany, "but as you get older and older, you don't want to go back. You know, if you live that long so far away, your friends drift, too." She now knows a lot of people from her old home, she says, but "no close friends anymore," especially since her mother died. Yet she keeps the apartment just in case anything happens to her husband (*AM*, 227; cf. 206).

One can, however, travel back in one's imagination to effect some kind of reunion with one's lost self, as in the case of the Swede (with the quiet mother) who, just before being interviewed, had attended a lecture about the mysteries of antimatter. It was antimatter, he was told, that had caused a flash of light throughout northern Europe back in 1908. "Just think," he says. "I had seen that flash from my farmyard in Sweden when I was a boy, and I had to wait till I was eighty-three years old to learn what it was. Isn't that strange!" (*AM*, 8). Thus, the far ends of life are mysteriously rejoined. Ancient memories of a place long left behind can take on a formulaic quality, effecting the same end. One Sea Islander in Kiser, long resident in New York, claims to still hope to return back home "before life's journey is over"—the very phrasing invokes hope without commitment. Another speaks in a similar vein of how, despite the thousand miles separating him from his old home, "I still see St. Helena." Kiser includes autobiographies of Sea Islanders, which conclude with what one feels is a ritualistic invocation of their place of origin.[54]

In such accounts we begin to ascend into the timeless stuff of fiction and myth. It seems right that *The Cotter's Son* should have been the most popular novel of emigrant years among Norwegian-Americans. Its hero is able to obliterate all hyphens and return in triumph to his cultural nest. The story involves a young man, denied his true love because of his low station in Norwegian society, who moves to the New World and makes a fortune. He then returns to Norway, toting two six-shooters, buys out the sweetheart's father (who has become a drunk), marries his sweetheart, and lives happily ever after.[55] Except for his changed status, his money, and his guns, it is as if he had never left home—and as if home never changed.

The riddle in the migrant accounts is that of how to work out the terms of the exchange between the culture of the old place and that of the new. On one level, it involves the continuous reclustering of people only half at home in the new place. At another level, it involves the emotional turmoil of being "neither here nor there," revealed in the extraordinarily detailed recollections of the circumstances at the time of the move and in what is often a lifelong—if intermittent—homesickness.

CONCLUSION

This essay is exploratory in nature. It is based upon a very few sources among the multitude of materials that might have been consulted. It depends upon oral history, which has its own problems as evidence and, in any event, is just one kind of resource relevant to this inquiry. It slights the involuntary aspects of the migration experience and the manifest differences in migration experience based upon race, gender, and movement within as against movement across national boundaries. In any extended study of the subject, there would have to be more attention to the many distinctions between recent memory and memory at a distance, as well as to the nature of narrative as a means of imposing order on seemingly miscellaneous events. Such differences are immensely important and are the proper concerns of any work following up on this first attempt to apply the postulates of inner geography to the experience of the first-generation migrant.

Two ongoing major efforts at historical-geographical synthesis emphasize small-group migration patterns and urge that scholars give more attention to the experience of the individual migrant. The basic units in Bernard

Bailyn's Peopling of British North America project are "local, small-scale exoduses and colonizations." His study "concentrates on individuals and their fortunes." "Peopling" is to be understood in relation to "*domestic*" mobility patterns in the sending country, in their countless varieties, and to the countless variations in the local circumstances of arrival in the New World. Bailyn's *Voyagers to the West*, a first substantial volume in the Peopling series, has been useful for this paper because of its effort to come as close as possible to the experiences of migrant individuals.[56]

D. W. Meinig, in a project as ambitious as Bailyn's, is in the process of describing "the shaping of America." Meinig makes a real effort to particularize the circumstances of small-group migrations during the colonial period. He tabulates 130 "regional-ethnoreligious" subgroups in the mosaic of settlement patterns in British North America in 1750, but then admits that for a full definition of the migration process "it would be useful to know more than birthplaces and ports of departure; one would like to know something of the sociographic experience of every individual."[57] For some time, a number of geographers and historians have been carrying out the agenda recommended by Bailyn and Meinig. In describing individual migrants in this paper, I have cited the work of Jon Gjerde, Dino Cinel, David Cressy, John Bodnar, Roberta Balstad Miller, Virginia Yans-McLaughlin, John C. Hudson, Robert Ostergren, and Charles Tilly, because their attention to small-group migration patterns was so helpful to me in understanding the individual experience.[58]

My emphasis upon inner geography is fully consistent with the emphasis in the studies just mentioned upon the continuum between "considerable" migration on the one hand and ordinary or everyday patterns of mobility on the other, with intermediate activities such as seasonal migration having the qualities of both. My emphasis upon clustering as seen from the inside parallels their emphasis upon clustering as revealed in statistical analysis and in settlement patterns. However, it is not just a matter of congruity between their approach and the one taken here.

An interest in inner geography suggests its own set of researchable topics: in view of the large numbers involved, the experience of remigration has received surprisingly little scholarly attention.[59] Pioneer migration, often the subject of individual narratives, has not been investigated as a cultural category along the lines suggested above. The qualitative differences between "fortunate" and other migrants, as seen from the inside, deserves study, as does the "stretched" geography attending continuing back-and-forth movement between two or more homes.

I have said that the exchange of one home for another is a basic cultural transaction. It would be more precise to describe it as a cultural-geographical transaction, requiring attention to geography as well as to history. Geographers, Meinig included, have described American cultural regions as geographically contained wholes formed by diffusion from particular hearth areas, largely as a result of migration.[60] Bailyn, although lacking Meinig's geographical sophistication, describes colonial regions in much the same way.[61] That traditional interpretation of the cultural region becomes increasingly inapplicable as one approaches the present and settlement west of the Mississippi, although it is important, I think, to look for geographical and historical continuities in relation to present circumstances, rather than to hypothesize that there are radical historical breaks in pattern.[62] Present-day regional studies must proceed in such a way as to allow for noncontiguous settlement, for repeated migration and for remigration, and for the dramatic changes in the technologies of transportation and communication of the more recent past.[63] Attention to the individual case is one way of understanding what region means under recent circumstances. Most scholars agree that migration, more and more, is becoming an individual matter.[64] Attention to cultural persistence or inertia in the individual migration experience discloses cultural-geographical connections among continuously mobile people, of the kind I have been describing. Any currently relevant theory about the nature of the cultural region must help in the explication of the meaning of those connections.[65] This paper is intended as a contribution to that end.

NOTES

I want to express my deep thanks to Sarah Mondale, Jane Loeffler, and Jon Gjerde for their careful critiques of earlier versions of this paper.

1. See G. J. Lewis, *Human Migration* (New York: St. Martin's Press, 1982), for a competent general survey of migration literature from a geographical perspective. The book makes a good-faith effort to pay attention to social and cultural dimensions of migration as well as to economics, although the general approach is behavioral rather than humanistic. Lewis comments (126) that generalizations about

group migration behavior have not been very helpful in understanding the "micro scale" of particular migration events.

2. Yi-Fu Tuan, *Space and Place: The Perspective of Experience* (Minneapolis: University of Minnesota Press, 1977). Anne Buttimer is another principal spokesperson for "inner geography." See, for example, her "Home, Reach, and the Sense of Place," in *The Human Experience of Space and Place*, ed. Buttimer and David Seamon (New York: St. Martin's Press, 1980), 166–87. The distinction between inside and outside perspectives on geography is important in E. C. Relph, *Place and Placelessness* (London: Pion Limited, 1976). Perla Korosec-Serfaty, "Experience and the Use of Dwelling," in *Home Environments*, ed. Irwin Altman and Carol M. Werner (New York: Plenum Press, 1985), 65–86, traces out the philosophical roots of the idea of geography from the inside to Edmund Husserl, Martin Heidegger, and Jean-Paul Sartre. Her article, in large part, is a critique of Gaston Bachelard, *The Poetics of Space* (Boston: Beacon Press, 1970), another principal source. David Seamon, *The Geography of Lifeworld: Movement, Rest and Encounter* (New York: St. Martin's Press, 1979), emphasizes Maurice Merleau-Ponty.

3. See, for example, John F. Sears, *Sacred Places: American Tourist Attractions in the Nineteenth Century* (New York: Oxford University Press, 1989).

4. The pull of the familiar is implicit in generalizations made in quantitatively oriented studies of migration patterns, as summarized in Lewis. Such studies agree that among age groups, it is young adults that are most likely to migrate. At other ages, people stay home. The implication is that except at the physical prime of life we prefer, overall, to stay where we are. Such studies agree that there is an inverse relationship between distance and movement. The long move is the exception. If we can, we stay close to what we know. In moving longer distances, we often move by "stage" or "step," from a small place to a nearby larger place, so as to stay in touch with what we have left behind. If we move on from there, it is not until we have become familiar with that first step, and, for that matter, with the process of moving. "Chain" migration, a pattern common to much of the immigration to the United States, systematically reduces the sense of displacement for the migrants by locating family and townspeople along the way.

To compare the pull of the familiar to gravity is, of course, to indulge in metaphor. Even as metaphor it fails in at least one respect: if notions of individual identity shift dramatically, as at moments of religious conversion or mystical insight, the whole meaning of the everyday world can be transformed. On the general topic, see Tuan, *Space and Place*: "A brief but intense experience is capable of nullifying the past so that we are ready to abandon home for the promised land" (184).

5. Josef J. Barton remarks that "people ordinarily long, not for an abstract heritage, but for immediately experienced personal relationships, evolved in specific

cultural and social settings, that any deracination such as migration may destroy." See his "Land, Labor and Community in Nueces: Czech Farmers and Mexican Laborers in South Texas, 1880–1920," in *Ethnicity on the Great Plains*, ed. Frederick Luebke (Lincoln: University of Nebraska Press, 1980), 198.

6. Robert Coles, *Migrants, Sharecroppers, Mountaineers* (Boston: Little, Brown, 1971), and *The South Goes North* (Boston: Little, Brown, 1971); Joan Morrison and Charlotte Fox Zabusky, *American Mosaic: The Immigrant Experience in the Words of Those Who Lived It* (New York: New American Library, 1980).

7. Countless autobiographical and fictional accounts of the migration experience could and should be examined in any extensive treatment of this essay's theme. Materials emphasizing commentary about migration by the migrants themselves, not here examined, include Tamara K. Hareven, *Amoskeag: Life and Work in an American Factory-City* (New York: Pantheon Books, 1978); Charlotte Erickson, *Invisible Immigrants: The Adaptation of English and Scottish Immigrants in Nineteenth-Century America* (Coral Gables: University of Florida Press, 1972); and Thomas Kessner and Betty Boyd Caroli, *Today's Immigrants: Their Stories* (Oxford: Oxford University Press, 1982). Virginia Yans-McLaughlin, "Metaphors of Self in History: Subjectivity, Oral Narrative, and Immigration Studies," in *Immigration Reconsidered: History, Sociology, and Politics*, ed. Yans-McLaughlin (New York: Oxford University Press, 1990), 254–90, makes an eloquent plea for the use of "subjective documents" in the study of immigration.

8. Coles, in the two volumes of his under examination here, is interested in the effect of poverty on children during the 1960s. The migration studied is that from farm to city. His materials are biased by those central interests (generous biases, but biases nevertheless). The editors of *American Mosaic* discuss their methodology (xviii–xix). They attempted to interview "representatives of all countries from which immigrants came in significant numbers and from all periods for which there were still living members." Their interviewees were to come from all social and economic classes and were to include individuals coming to the United States for all kinds of reasons. Representativeness in such matters counts, no doubt; but also, obviously, they looked for the good stories. Coles apparently did not use a tape recorder. He is good at suggesting differences among individuals interviewed, but their language as recollected always includes certain expressions characteristic of Coles. Morrison and Zabusky were careful to tape-record their interviews and to stay as close as possible to the language, meaning, and intent of the speaker.

9. The classic example of the old emphasis upon the discontinuities between Old World and New is Oscar Handlin, *The Uprooted: The Epic Story of the Great Migrations That Made the American People* (Boston: Little, Brown, 1951). An early example of the new approach, taking specific exception to Handlin, is Virginia

Yans-McLaughlin, *Family and Community: Italian Immigrants in Buffalo, 1880–1930* (Ithaca: N.Y.: Cornell University Press, 1971), especially 17–24 (introduction). Similar contrasts hold in the study of domestic migration. An older kind of analysis of rural-urban migration emphasized discontinuities in the experience (as in the work of Robert Park); Robert McMath, in "Community, Region and Hegemony in the Nineteenth-Century South," in *Toward a New South?: Studies in Post–Civil War Southern Communities*, ed. Orville Burton and McMath (Westport, Conn.: Greenwood Press, 1982), 281–300, emphasizes "unsettledness" in the rural communities in which increasing numbers were preparing to move to the city.

10. Charles Tilly, "Migration in Modern European History," in *Human Migration: Patterns and Policies*, ed. William H. McNeill and Ruth S. Adams (Bloomington: Indiana University Press, 1978), 48–72, especially 51–57. For a recent reformulation in some respects of that earlier essay, see Tilly's "Transplanted Networks," in *Immigration Reconsidered*, ed. Yans-McLaughlin, 79–95, in which he talks of reconstituted social networks rather than "definitiveness," although he still sees distance as a critical variable.

11. J. A. Jackson, "Editorial Introduction," in *Migration*, ed. Jackson (Cambridge: Cambridge University Press, 1969), 1–2, argues that moves within the household are instances of migration. Robert M. Butler, *Why Survive? Being Old in America* (New York: Harper and Row, 1975), 104, vividly describes how, for a particular poor elderly woman, eviction from her home was all but life-threatening.

12. William I. Thomas and Florian Znaniecki, *The Polish Peasant in America* (New York: Alfred A. Knopf, 1927), 2:2218–19.

13. Lewis, *Human Migration*, 65–66, discusses "same place" migration—migration between places sharing many of the same characteristics. One analysis of residence histories reported on there concluded that as many as half of the migrants studied were "same place" migrants. Charles F. Longino, Jr., "American Retirement Communities and Residential Relocation," in *Geographical Perspectives on the Elderly*, ed. Anthony M. Warnes (Chichester, Eng.: John Wiley and Sons, 1982), 239–62, describes "same place" migration among the elderly (e.g., the choice of a retirement home for ex-suburbanites is likely to be suburban in plan).

14. John Bodnar, *Lives of Their Own: Blacks, Italians, and Poles in Pittsburgh, 1900–1960* (Urbana: University of Illinois Press, 1981), 122–23, discusses the "birds-of-passage" phenomenon among Italians and Poles who worked in the United States in order to take money back home. Thomas and Znaniecki, *The Polish Peasant*, 2:1495–1500, discuss the continuities between seasonal migration and migration to the United States. Their Wladek Wiszniewski (the individual who searched out a bride in Niagara Falls) spent time in seasonal agricultural labor in Germany and as an itinerant baker in Poland before deciding to emigrate to the United States.

Place-on-the-Move 83

15. David Lowenthal and Lambros Comitas, "Emigration and Depopulation: Some Neglected Aspects of Population Geography," *Geographical Review* 52 (1962): 195–210. Theodore Saloutos, *They Remember America: The Story of the Repatriated Greek-Americans* (Berkeley: University of California Press, 1956), describes Greek-American migration and remigration in the context of the particularly Greek notion of undying loyalty to the homeland.

16. Clyde V. Kiser, *Sea Island to City: A Study of St. Helena Islanders in Harlem and Other Urban Centers* (1932; rpt. New York: AMS Press, 1969), 150–51.

17. In *SGN*, 131–41, Coles describes a wandering couple who are never able to keep jobs or stay in one place. What is amazing about the account is the degree to which their movements are guided by what is described as "an informal network of friends and relatives and comrades-in-distress" that they have been able to find all over New England.

18. My effort throughout the paper is to make out similarities in the migration experience among very different kinds of people and situations, but surely at some point, among the Jews, especially, the extremities of the experience of dispossession and torture for the survivors places their migration experience outside any projected continuum between voluntary and involuntary migration.

19. Lewis, *Human Migration*, chap. 7.

20. Jon Gjerde, *From Peasants to Farmers: The Migration from Balestrand, Norway, to the Upper Middle West* (Cambridge: Cambridge University Press, 1985), chaps. 6, 7.

21. For a fine collection of such letters, see Theodore Blegen, ed., *Land of Their Choice: The Immigrants Write Home* (Minneapolis: University of Minnesota Press, 1955). A vivid fictional account of the effect of "America letters" on one Russian-Jewish youngster appears in Abraham Cahan, *The Rise of David Levinsky* (1917; rpt. New York: Harper Torchbooks, 1960), 61.

22. See, for example, Bailyn's description of successful recruitment in Yorkshire, in *Voyagers West: A Passage in the Peopling of America on the Eve of the Revolution* (New York: Alfred A. Knopf, 1986), 374–79.

23. Gjerde, *From Peasants to Farmers*, 143–64.

24. Bailyn, *Voyagers West*, 406–29, 503–6.

25. Kiser, *Sea Island to City*, 92–93, 144–46. The Coles volumes describe migration paths, if not in the detail one would wish. Mountaineers are described as moving in step fashion, in succession from the farm to a local community, mill towns, regional urban centers, and then to Cincinnati, Dayton, Chicago, Cleveland, or Detroit, as required by the search for work (*MSM*, 494–95). One of his mountaineers describes with pride the success of one son in Dayton, another in Knoxville, and a daughter in Knoxville (*MSM*, 339). Coles describes Mississippi blacks

as moving to Greenwood, Greenville, Memphis, and Chicago (*MSM*, 364) and Alabamans from Monroe County as moving to Montgomery, Birmingham, Mobile, or up north (*MSM*, 406).

26. Roberta Balstad Miller, *City and Hinterland: A Case-Study of Urban Growth and Regional Development* (Westport, Conn.: Greenwood Press, 1979), 20–21 (on patterns of migration from New England to the Syracuse area). For general figures on migration west from Syracuse and description of the interconnections among kin in New York and Michigan, see chap. 6, especially 144–47.

27. See maps depicting the pattern of farm ownership in areas settled by Balestranders in Gjerde, *From Peasants to Farmers*, 146, 156, 159. Cf. the patterns described for Swedes settling in South Dakota in Robert C. Ostergren, "Prairie Bound: Migration Patterns to a Swedish Settlement on the Dakota Frontier," in *Ethnicity on the Great Plains*, ed. Frederick C. Luebke (Lincoln: University of Nebraska Press, 1980), 73–108, especially fig. 7 (87). For students of the cultural implications of migration, a wonderful complement to the above sources is Einar Haugen's classic description of language usage within and among Norwegian farm clusters in "Language and Immigration" (1938), reprinted in *The Ecology of Language: Essays by Einar Haugen*, ed. Anwar S. Dill (Stanford: Stanford University Press, 1972), 1–36.

28. The general likelihood of moving with and among fellow New Englanders is suggested in John C. Hudson, "North American Origins of Midwestern Frontier Populations," *Annals of the Association of American Geographers* 78 (1988): 395–413.

29. Carey McWilliams, *Southern California: An Island on the Land* (1946; rpt. Salt Lake City, Utah: Peregrine Smith, 1973). The subject of amenities migration has its own literature. On California and amenities, see James E. Vance, Jr., "California and the Search for the Ideal," *Annals of the Association of American Geographers* 62 (1972): 192–210. An old but still useful essay on the same topic is Edward L. Ullman, "Amenities as a Factor in Regional Growth," *Geographical Review* 44 (1954): 119–32. For a sweeping general review of literature on amenities migration, see Jerry M. Svart, "Environmental Preference Migration: A Review," *Geographical Review* 66 (1976): 314–30. A brief analysis of amenities migrants in what is becoming exurban Wales appears in Lewis, *Human Migration*, 177–78. Lewis categorizes such migrants as second home owners, retirees, individuals who can fully divorce place of work from place of residence, and urban dropouts moving "back to nature."

30. Gregory H. Singleton, *Religion in the City of the Angels: American Protestant Culture and Urbanization* (n.p.: UMI Research Press, 1979).

31. Robert M. Fogelson, *The Fragmented Metropolis: Los Angeles, 1850–1930*

(Cambridge, Mass.: Harvard University Press, 1967), 197–98. Fogelson also comments upon an emphasis among southern Californians of the period upon "personalism" or what today would be called privatism.

32. Jon Gjerde, "The Seacoast of Iowa: Chain Migration from the Middle West to California, 1880–1930," unpublished manuscript, no date.

33. Kiser, *Sea Island to City*, 134–35.

34. The acceptance of intramarriage on such terms is amazing to a modern reader. It is apparently a pattern of long standing: cf. Bailyn, *Voyagers West*, 427–28, on intramarriage among eighteenth-century immigrants from Yorkshire in Nova Scotia.

35. As evidence of that point, see Bodnar, *Lives of Their Own*, 47–48, 208; and Gjerde, *From Peasants to Farmers*, 131.

36. McWilliams, *Southern California*, vii–ix.

37. The phrase is from McWilliams, *Southern California*, 376. David Cressy, studying seventeenth-century migration patterns, suggests that the role of kin was more important for the better-off than for the ordinary folk. See *Coming Over: Migration and Communication between England and New England in the Seventeenth Century* (Cambridge, Eng.: Cambridge University Press, 1987), 274–75.

38. Lawrence Levine, *Black Culture and Black Consciousness* (New York: Oxford University Press, 1977), 261–64, argues persuasively that with the end of the Civil War black movement north took on a mythical quality, as an escape from bondage into freedom. The South as land of oppression for the now liberated black shows up in the story a black man tells Coles about his father's leaving the South because he had been arrested for telling a white man to go to hell (*SGN*, 168) and in a mother's pride in having told her son to leave the South and never come back (*SGN*, 131). James Baldwin, in *Go Tell It on the Mountain* (1953; rpt. New York: Dell Publishing, 1971), fictionally recreates the circumstances of black migration north in the 1920–1940 period as escape from bondage, if into something less than freedom.

39. Penn School sponsored early migration north. When Kiser wrote his book in 1932, there was a Penn School club among Sea Island residents in New York City, whose forty members met once a month (Kiser, *Sea Island to City*, 96–97, 211–12).

40. Charles Tilly lucidly describes "Transplanted Networks" in *Immigration Reconsidered*, ed. Yans-McLaughlin, 79–95.

41. Lewis, *Human Migration*, chap. 3, estimates that one in five Americans move every year, which means that four out of five stay home. Also, the movers may be people who have moved before and will move again, so that in effect more than four out of five are stayers. He also estimates that some 3/1,000 of the European population emigrated during the 1846–1935 period, which was a higher rate than

elsewhere in the world and a higher rate than had characterized Europe in previous years. Emigration is much rarer than internal migration, of course. Such statistics seem to imply that one is generally better off staying at home. Robert H. Brown, "The Upsala, Minnesota, Community: A Case Study in Rural Dynamics," *Annals of the Association of American Geographers* 57 (1967): 267–300, does compare stayers to movers and finds stayers better off.

42. The two best accounts of that experience that I know of can be found in Dino Cinel, *From Italy to San Francisco: The Immigrant Experience* (Stanford: Stanford University Press, 1982); and Saloutos, *They Remember America*. Both comment on the paucity of scholarship on the subject.

43. The Coles volumes, in combination, amount to a description of the stretched geography of particular streams of farm-to-city migration from the South to the North during the 1960s. I do not know of work that similarly describes the stretched geographies incident to immigration.

44. See Caroline Golab, *Immigrant Destinations* (Philadelphia: Temple University Press, 1977), 112–13, 139, 147, 153–55. Robert Slayton, *Back of the Yards* (Chicago: University of Chicago Press, 1986), describes in detail the history of one famous interethnic neighborhood in Chicago. One cannot help but be struck by the similarity of pattern among these urban immigrants and that among the rural migrants described by Gjerde and Ostergren (see above, note 27).

45. See especially Bodnar's discussion of seven Pittsburgh neighborhoods, *Lives of Their Own*, 207–36. The northern urban neighborhoods of mountaineers and sharecroppers to which the migrants interviewed by Coles move are in the very early stages of articulation. Obviously, different patterns would characterize black urban settlement because of systematic discrimination against blacks of the kind described in Arnold Hirsch, *The Making of the Second Ghetto* (Cambridge: Cambridge University Press, 1983).

46. Cinel, *From Italy to San Francisco*, chaps. 8, 9.

47. Thomas and Znaniecki, *The Polish Peasant*, 2:2203–9.

48. "Unique to human beings among primates," says Tuan in *Space and Place*, "is the sense of the home as a place where the sick and the injured can recover under solicitous care" (137).

49. Thomas and Znaniecki, *The Polish Peasant*, 2:2211.

50. The rhythms of adjustment no doubt vary according to gender. In *American Mosaic* there is what must be an extreme case, that of a Russian immigrant couple, long since divorced, who recall the same experiences in drastically different ways, the differences having to do with gender (*AM*, 93–105). Yans-McLaughlin, in "Metaphors of Self in History," 278–82, sees oral-historical materials as important for getting at gender differences in the individual migration experience.

51. See Lewis, *Human Migration*, 70; cf. Bodnar, *Lives of Their Own*, 119.

52. Joan Didion, in *Slouching towards Bethlehem* (New York: Simon and Schuster, 1968), 225–38, describes her dwindling resolve to stay in New York City as a young woman newly arrived from California. She becomes disconcerted by her own behavior, unable to finish arranging her room or to fully unpack her belongings (a map of her home state is a kind of fugitive ornament). She finds her social life increasingly limited to southerners and other non–New Yorkers. Her return to California solves that set of problems.

53. *American Mosaic* abounds in interesting reflections on the importance of language in adjustment to the new scene. A first assignment upon arrival, for the non-English speaker, is to master the new language. An Italian immigrant and his brother made a point of watching the same movie as many as five times to master the English involved: "It was the only way" (*AM*, 178). And, of course, any English mastered is still a second language: a Hungarian, after many years in this country, reflects upon the lasting pull for him of poetry in the mother tongue (*AM*, 303).

54. Kiser, *Sea Island to City*, 264, 247.

55. Gjerde, *From Peasants to Farmers*, 232.

56. The Peopling project is outlined in Bernard Bailyn, *The Peopling of British North America: An Introduction* (New York: Vintage Books, 1986), 4, 8, 20, 49–60 (the italicizing of "*domestic*" is Bailyn's).

57. D. W. Meinig, *The Shaping of America: A Geographical Perspective on 500 Years of History*, vol. 1, *Atlantic America, 1492–1800* (New Haven: Yale University Press, 1986), 215–18.

58. Gjerde says that his individual Norwegians thought in group terms. That is surely also true for the Poles and Italians described by Bodnar. In emphasizing individual experience I am not denying such group loyalties, as should be clear from my discussion of marriage patterns among chain migrants. My perspective is simply different. The same can be said for differences between the approach here and the small-group-oriented approach taken by Charles Tilly, particularly in his most recent essay, "Transplanted Networks."

59. Jane Loeffler has called my attention to the fact that there was a Finnish-American society in Finland, made up of Finns who had returned home after stays in America. That society was crucial to the upbringing of an influential Finnish architect and philosopher. See Malcolm Qauntrill, *Reima Pietilä: Architecture, Context, and Modernism* (Helsinki, Finland: Otava, 1985), 26–27. There must have been and must still exist many other such organizations in other places with such cultural consequences.

60. Meinig describes his method in "The Continuous Shaping of America: A Prospectus for Geographers and Historians," *American Historical Review* 83 (De-

cember 1978): 1186–1205. Two of his well-known essays exemplify how that kind of regionalism works: "The Mormon Culture Region: Strategies and Patterns in the Geography of the American West," *Annals of the Association of American Geographers* 55 (1965): 191–220, and "American Wests: Preface to a Geographical History," *Annals of the Association of American Geographers* 62 (1972): 159–84. In this last essay, Meinig predicts that any lingering western regional identity will be swallowed up in what will surely become a uniform national culture.

61. Bailyn, *The Peopling of British North America*, 89–112.

62. John C. Hudson, studying migration to North Dakota in the late nineteenth century, concludes that the traditional culture-area approach is of limited use in that case. See "Migration to an American Frontier," *Annals of the Association of American Geographers* 66 (1976): 264–65.

Henry Glassie, in *Patterns in the Material Folk Culture of the Eastern United States* (Philadelphia: University of Pennsylvania Press, 1968), flatly opposes traditional regions to a regionless modernity. (That is less the case in his more recent work.) Eric Wolf, *Europe and the People without History* (Berkeley: University of California Press, 1982), supplies a panoramic view of how modernity and tradition have interacted since at least the fifteenth century. The thing to be understood, it seems to me, is that interaction or interplay between change *and* persistence.

63. A provocative essay on the regional implications of current changes in communications is Ronald F. Abler, "Monoculture or Miniculture: The Impact of Communications Media on Culture in Space," in *An Invitation to Geography*, ed. David A. Lanegran and Risa Palm (New York: McGraw-Hill, 1973), 186–95.

64. This is reflected in Wilbur Zelinsky's speculations about "voluntary regions" and personal preference patterns. See Zelinsky, "Personality and Self-Discovery: The Future Social Geography of the United States," in *Human Geography in a Shrinking Planet*, ed. Ronald Abler (North Scituate, Mass.: Duxbury Press, 1975), 108–21, and "Selfward Bound: Personal Preference Patterns and the Changing Map of American Society," *Economic Geography* 50 (1974): 145–79. See also R. C. Harris, "The Historical Geography of North American Regions," *American Behavioral Scientist* 22 (1978): 115–30.

65. As earlier attempts to sketch out the new kind of region, see the "Introduction" to Michael Steiner and Clarence Mondale, eds., *Region and Regionalism in the United States: A Source Book for the Humanities and Social Sciences* (New York: Garland Publishing, 1988), xi–xiii; and my "Babies and Baths: Cultural Region and Place," *Architecture California* 13 (1991): 8–14.

"To Lose the Unspeakable": Folklore and Landscape in O. E. Rolvaag's Giants in the Earth

APRIL SCHULTZ

The ambiguity and irony in O. E. Rolvaag's *Giants in the Earth*, a tale of Norwegian immigrant pioneers on the Dakota plains, are present in the very title of the work. The epigraph from which the title is taken is from Genesis 6:4. "There were giants in the earth in those days; and also after that, when the sons of God came in unto the daughters of men, and they bare children to them, the same became mighty men which were of old, men of renown."[1] For the American reader imbued with the cultural myth of the mighty pioneer paving the way for American progress, the "giants" very likely refer to the stalwart Norwegian settlers. Indeed, at least one scholar has claimed that Rolvaag's narrative is a striking illustration of Frederick Jackson Turner's frontier claim: that the frontier stripped the settlers of Old World constrictions and transformed them into "new" Americans who went about the crucial, democratic task of settling the continent.[2] For these readers, Per Hansa's tragic death is no doubt an anomaly. Instead of resonating with irony, the last sentence—"his eyes were set toward the West"—confirms the optimistic promise of the frontier experience.[3]

Read this way, Rolvaag's novel loses much of its irony and its richness. In one sense, the "giants" may very well be Rolvaag's protagonists—Per Hansa, Beret, and the other settlers. But there are other, perhaps more significant, allusions in the title that may undermine this interpretation. The subtitle of Genesis 6 is "The Wickedness of Man," and the verse following the one above states that "God saw that the wickedness of man *was* great in the earth, and *that* every imagination of the thoughts of his heart *was* only evil continually." In their biblical context, the "giants" are superhuman creatures or monsters who are the children of the sons of God and the daughters of men. They appear as a sign of increasing wickedness and imminent destruction on earth. Along with humankind and civilization, they will be destroyed by God in the great flood.

Similarly, in Norwegian folklore, giants or trolls are living spirits in nature who embody evil and foretell disaster. In the novel, Per Hansa conceives of the prairie as a brooding troll who has the power to unleash the hostile forces of storm, drought, pestilence, hunger, and loneliness. He and the other settlers must wage a battle against these "giants" in order to realize their dream on the prairie. Read in this context, the story becomes not a tale of manifest destiny but, at least for Per Hansa, a fatal battle against evil. Furthermore, as one biblical scholar asserts, the "giants" can be seen as symbols of the "demonic" quality of the "great" in every age. In later chapters, the arrogance of these superhuman creatures illustrates how the "gifts from God become instruments of domination."[4] If we can extend this arrogance to Per Hansa's pride, which indeed informs much of the tragedy of the novel, the evil against which he must fight is not only external but also internal.

This is only one instance, albeit a crucial one, of how an understanding of Rolvaag's allusions to Norwegian folklore—both pagan and Christian—can illuminate the complexities of *Giants in the Earth*. Published in 1927, the novel can be and has been interpreted in many ways. It has been viewed as a story of the rational Western individual battling against nature; as a paean to the heroic settlers of the frontier who risked both physical and mental well-being in the struggle; or as a tragic account of Americanization and the loss of traditional culture.[5] Part of the power of Rolvaag's novel is the possibility of these multiple readings. An actor in the immigration narrative itself, Rolvaag eloquently presents the complexities of each of these possibilities. We, like Rolvaag, feel for both Per Hansa and Beret. But if we place the novel in its cultural/historical context and examine its codes carefully, we can uncover a more specific message that situates it and its author at the center of an important moment in the history of the Norwegian-American community.

Rolvaag wrote *Giants in the Earth* in the context of an intense national drive to Americanize the immigrants. This drive by civic and cultural leaders deeply touched a long-standing debate in the Norwegian-American community over assimilation and Americanization.[6] The novel holds a significant place in this dialogue, for through his literary codes Rolvaag the teacher and proselytizer specifically addressed the Norwegian-American community about the tragedy of both immigration and the dangerous hubris of the dominant American narrative of individualism and inevitable expansion. From the connotative structure to specific episodes, Rolvaag imbued his novel with folkloric references that most critics have either ignored or dismissed as "local color." Though Rolvaag's characters confront a new and alien landscape in very different ways, their perspectives are grounded in folk ideas about space, place, and the human being's position in both. The contrast between Per Hansa and Beret—between Per's prideful optimism in the vast, open landscape and Beret's profound loss of place—forms the core tension in the novel and unmasks the very real tensions in the Norwegian-American community in the 1920s.

Through his characters, who populated a new landscape with Old World trolls and legends in order to make sense of their new experience, Rolvaag admonished his readers for—in his view—willingly giving up their Norwegian culture. *Giants in the Earth* and the subsequent novels in the trilogy, *Peder Victorious* and *Their Father's God*, spoke directly to the Norwegian-American community. Though *Giants in the Earth* was first published in Norway, the author's primary audience in his own view were immigrants and their children, including—and perhaps especially—his own academic folk-group at St. Olaf College in Northfield, Minnesota. The Norwegian-American community was one that, according to Rolvaag, had "'become something apart, something torn loose, without any organic connections either here in America or over in Norway.'"[7] In an earlier novel, *Amerika-Breve*, written in 1912, Rolvaag has an anonymous Norwegian address this group at a Fourth of July celebration. After recounting certain gains the Norwegians made by coming to America—a pragmatism born of hard work, new thoughts and ideas, political and religious freedom, and the possibility of upward mobility and material prosperity—the speaker then recounts the losses, the greatest of which is the loss of land and family, which he defines as

> the intimate spiritual association with our own people and our own nation. . . . [We are not just] strangers among strangers, *but we came away from our own nation and became strangers to our own people.* . . . We have thus ceased to be a harmonizing part of a great whole; we have become something by ourselves, something torn off, without any organic connection here or there. . . . In short we have become rootless. . . . We lost that which does not permit itself to be expressed in words, *we lost the unspeakable.* The saddest of all is that we do not comprehend these things until it is too late. Could, in truth, the people in the old country see it as you and I see it, it would not be long until the stream of emigration would be nearly dried up.[8]

Rolvaag's main character, Per Smevik, sends a copy of this speech home to Norway to his father, warning him against emigration. The immigrant's pain is most profound and obvious here. To "lose the unspeakable" is to lose one's culture, the unspoken and assumed stories about oneself that bind one to others, the "life-vision" that gives meaning and depth to one's everyday existence.[9] But while this early spokesman believed that such cultural ties were irrevocably lost in the process of emigration and assimilation, the later Rolvaag was at least outwardly more hopeful. In an opening lecture for a course on Norwegian immigration history at St. Olaf in the early 1920s, for example, Rolvaag admonished his Norwegian-American students for forgetting their past: "I am giving this course in the hope that those who take it may become better Americans." Patriotism, according to Rolvaag, was only possible if one loved one's home and one's past. He encouraged his students to "press onward into the future with all possible energy," but not to the exclusion of "faithfulness to your race, to the cultural and spiritual heritage which you have received and which you may receive in still larger measure, if you care. You must *not* erase your racial characteristics in order to become better Americans. You must deepen them, if possible. . . ."[10] By cultivating and keeping alive Norwegian culture, then, Norwegian-Americans could best contribute to American culture. Rolvaag was attempting to do this in his own life by keeping alive a particularly Norwegian literary tradition at the same time that he sought to contribute to the ranks of the American literary canon. While it is a hopeful and seemingly simple task on one level, on a deeper level a thread of pain runs through Rolvaag's lectures and admonitions, a pain that comes to full fictive life in *Giants in the Earth.*

In this novel, the American historical themes of westward movement and immigration are only one part of the story, the other being, in Rolvaag's words, "the human cost of this thing that we call Empire-building. In order to bring this idea out, I married a natural-born pioneer to a fine, sensitive woman; then I turned them loose on the prairies and watched what would happen."[11] What "happens" is a painful reminder of the cost of immigration and an admonition to not strip oneself bare on one's "life-vision."

The novel centers around Per Hansa and his wife, Beret, as they attempt to settle on the Dakota prairie. Beret's growing madness and fanatical attachment to the Old World are juxtaposed to Per's New World optimism and hope for the future. While Rolvaag admires Per's inventiveness and perseverance, his sympathies lie with Beret, for her madness is a consequence of her separation from her land and her culture. As Rolvaag's speechmaker observes in *Amerika-Breve*, Norwegian immigrants are "strangers among strangers. . . . How many brave Norsemen have not landed in insane asylums just on that account? All the coldness and strangeness, and then the homesickness—that sick, sore gnawing yearning drove them finally into insanity."[12] But an obsessive clinging to the past can also destroy. Beret becomes unyielding and unforgiving, refusing to make changes that are necessary for survival in the new land. Per's death is a tragic consequence of Beret's fanaticism and of his excessive pride and optimism about his own abilities.

At the core of the novel is the tension between Beret's Old World and Per's New World. How is this tension to be resolved? Do we toss away our culture and blindly follow the new? Or do we hang onto those values that give meaning and richness to our lives while also contributing to our new culture? Do we have a choice if one extreme leads to madness and the other to death? To gain a fuller understanding of Rolvaag's own answers to these questions, one must understand his use of folklore and landscape imagery in creating a specific message for his Norwegian-American audience. In light of this, it is significant that the Norwegian version of the novel contained explanatory footnotes for the American cultural references, and the American version did the same for the Norwegian references. A full appreciation of *Giants in the Earth*, therefore, depends on the readers' acquaintance with both the Norwegian and the American cultural elements.

The connotative structure of the novel would be very familiar to Rolvaag's Norwegian-American audience. The subtitle of the English version is "A Saga of the Prairie." There is no such title in the original Norwegian version, suggesting that Rolvaag's use of the term "saga" held particular meaning for his Norwegian-American audience. The dedication of the book reads as follows: "To those of my people who took part in the great settling, to them and their generations I dedicate this narrative."[13] The English phrase "the great settling" is translated from the Norwegian *det store landnam*. To the Norwegian reader, *landnam*, literally meaning "landtaking," refers to the settlement of Iceland by Norwegians between A.D. 870 and 930.[14] This migration was described in the heroic and epic Icelandic family sagas, particularly *Landnamabok* (The Book of the Landtaking). Thus, Rolvaag makes a pointed connection between two Norwegian migrations. While many studies of the novel acknowledge this reference, very little is done with the allusion in terms of interpretation. In fact, the structure and thematic content of the sagas help to inform the very structure and content of Rolvaag's novel.

The written sagas are based on an oral tradition of saga-telling dating from the tenth and eleventh centuries. At the time *Giants in the Earth* was published in 1927, thirty to fifty Icelandic sagas were still popular reading in Norway.[15] Though sagas differ in their form and in their aims, every

Icelandic saga has certain elements in common: sagas are episodic, with very little attention paid to plot development; they continually prepare the listener or reader for the fatal ending; they give no direct rationalization for behavior, but depend on the action to provide characterization; they have a dominating psychological interest, intent on building complex portraits of their characters; and they evince an overriding fatalism as perhaps their most essential element.[16]

Rolvaag's work has often been criticized because of its inattention to plot development. Indeed, the story of the Norwegian settlement of the Dakota prairie in the 1870s is a collection of seemingly unconnected episodes. One scholar asserts that Rolvaag presented his narrative in this way because it more nearly approximates the episodic nature of real life.[17] Perhaps, but the similarity to the saga is striking. The formula for the saga, again, requires a series of events or episodes that are linked together by character development rather than by plot development. The art of the saga, according to one scholar, "is dominated by a destiny that leads events and characters to their fatal consequences."[18] It is this preparation through character development that provides much of the unity between the episodes in Rolvaag's novel.

Indeed, every episode in *Giants in the Earth* develops such fatal characterization. In the episodes depicting Per Hansa building his sod house connected to a barn for warmth, whitewashing the inside walls of his home, weaving a fish net to capture ducks for food, carrying on fur trade with the Indians, and so on, we develop a view of the man as inventive and ambitious, intent on beating his neighbors in founding his dream "kingdom" in America. Through these disparate episodes we also see gradually that Per Hansa's tragic flaw is his pride and his need to "outdo" others in his community. Furthermore, the episodes build a contrast between Per and the other characters, particularly his wife. In Beret's reactions to her husband and in her own peculiar behavior—covering the windows at night to ward off evil, packing and unpacking her father's chest and finally crawling inside it to die, not taking part in the gaiety when the families decide to change their names, and so on, we see a character antithetical to Per Hansa. Beret is lonely and inward-looking, very tied to the Norwegian community that she left behind, while Per looks only to the future and his own personal gain.

In the saga, character is slowly revealed through such situations as well as through conversation in which "terse utterances and rejoinders can fall with fateful weight and sharpness."[19] As the reader comes to comprehend Beret and Per Hansa, the dialogue becomes emotionally charged. For example, halfway through their first difficult winter, Per makes a beautiful pair of warm clogs for Beret. When he gives them to her "it was plain to be seen that she was touched by the gift; but then she said something that he wished she had left unspoken: 'You might have thought of this before, it seems to me. Here I have gone with cold feet all winter.' The words were uttered quietly; she meant no reproach by them, but merely said what came into her mind. . . . Per Hansa felt that now he needed to cry. . . ."[20] This is merely one more example of the great distance that has grown between the couple on the prairie, and this chasm between characters is crucial in sagas, for "by comprehending the psychology of the actors you grasp the real meaning of the events."[21] It is this clash between Beret and Per Hansa, simplistically put, between the Old World and the New, that provides much of the dramatic unity between the episodes.

Perhaps the most important element in the saga, and in understanding *Giants in the Earth*, is fatalism, a conception of "existence as ruled by inescapable and immutable necessity." In the saga, the moral standard of a character is set by his attitude toward fate. "He can succumb to his fate, broken and resigned, or he can meet it unbroken and with heroic affirmation. . . . For it is primarily not fate, immutable and dark, which holds the attention of the reader, but rather the heroic attitude of the character toward his fate—not defeat, but victory."[22] The presence of fate in *Giants in the Earth* is made clear in the title with its allusion to biblical and folkloric evil and impending disaster. Per Hansa, as the hero, battles fate with heroic resolve. Yet, knowing the saga formula, we also know that he must lose in the end. In one sense, then, the end of the novel is inspiring, for Per Hansa challenged his fate heroically. But, in another sense, the end is indeed tragic and ironic. Because he dies facing west, we are struck by the futility of his dream and the tragic outcome of his pride. He ventures out into the blizzard not necessarily to challenge his fate, but foolishly to prove to himself and to his neighbors that, as Sorrine says, "we all have a feeling that nothing is impossible for you. . . ."[23]

Beret's attitude toward fate is also significant. Until she finds strength in her religion, she has no will to fight her fate, sinking into insanity. At the end, she is the one who survives, but her fanaticism has made her bitter and irrational, for it is she who insists that Per risk his life to bring back a minister for his dying friend, Hans Olsa. Because we know the saga's pre-scription for fate and the heroism implied by challenging fate, the charac-ters of Beret and Per Hansa become more complex. Superficially, Per is the saga-hero battling fate and Beret is morally insufficient because she suc-cumbs to her fate without a fight. But because of Rolvaag's irony and the negative implications of Per's pride and Beret's fanaticism, the character delineation cannot be so easily described. The psychological drama may be for Rolvaag a process of dealing with both the foolishness and the heroicism of challenging fate.

The particular ways in which fatalism is dealt with in Norwegian folklore and literary tradition are salient for any discussion of Rolvaag's novel and the Norwegian elements in the story. Though his use of the saga form may be unconscious, his literary debt to Henrik Ibsen is certain. Indeed, one of the three courses Rolvaag regularly taught at St. Olaf was devoted to Ibsen. In much of Ibsen's work, the individual, though doomed to fail in the end, must nevertheless aspire. In his recent work on Rolvaag, Harold Simonson looks at the author's use of both Ibsen and Sören Kierkegaard to inform the tragedy of his novels. As Simonson argues, "Heroic in his choosing, Per Hansa is fallen in his choice. This is the paradox informing great tragedy. Even the most heroic self-attainment is doomed." The sin is presupposing total human initiative.[24] That these themes are prevalent both in the saga tradition and in Ibsen's work suggests that fatalism tempered by optimism is an important element in the Norwegian cultural worldview.

This dichotomy between optimism and fatalism permeates Norwegian folk tradition. The folk landscape is inhabited by evil trolls, *huldre* (hidden) people, ghosts, and magic. This otherworldly reality offers signs of both destiny and foreboding; it aids the culture in explaining its world. But we must not forget the flipside of fate—what Paul Reigstad calls "a native Norwegian optimism."[25] The most constant motif in Norwegian folktales is the *Askeladd*, or ash-boy, a parallel character to some of the saga-heroes.[26] Though the circumstances differ in every story, the *Askeladd* overcomes his unpromising beginnings and, through his cunning and wit, accomplishes impossible feats and succeeds in fighting off the trolls and winning both the princess and the kingdom, or more commonly the Castle of Soria Moria.[27] The *Askeladd* theme is repeated often in Rolvaag's lectures and essays. He continually uses this folk motif to describe that restless and heroic aspect of Norwegian culture that comes to such full fruition in the character of

Per Hansa. For example, in a lecture on Norwegian immigration history, he tells his students about a "young good-for-nothing sort of fellow, a sort of an *Askeladd*," who goes to America and succeeds in making a great deal of money. He then returns to his village to become "a leader of a whole expedition of immigrants."[28]

Indeed, the tale of *Askeladd* and his battle with the trolls is perhaps Rolvaag's most consistent and sustained allusion to folklore in *Giants in the Earth*. From the very beginning, Per's neighbors speak of him as the most clever among them. At every turn, Per accomplishes something incredible, whether it be producing the best wheat in the neighborhood, fighting his way through a blizzard, or healing a wounded Indian. Per views himself in terms of *Askeladd*, as a hero who must fight the trolls on the prairie to realize his kingdom. When he first sees his quarter-section, he observes with great emotion, "This kingdom is going to be *mine!*" In Norwegian folklore, a large farm is often referred to as a "kingdom," and Per's farm is no exception. He fantasizes about a great farm, "yielding its fruitful harvests," upon which he would build "a royal mansion" for his princess, Beret. All that summer, "Per Hansa was transported, was carried farther and ever farther away on the winds of a wondrous fairy tale—a romance in which he was both prince and king, the sole possessor of countless treasures."[29] But in order to gain his kingdom, Per must battle not only the trolls "in the earth," who unleash drought, pestilence, and loneliness, but also the more powerful trolls within himself and within his wife. Per does not fully lose his battle against nature; he wrests out of the earth the best farm in the community. What he does lose is his struggle against his own pride and against his wife's religious fanaticism. He loses both his life and his princess to the trolls that exist in the "'recesses of heart and brain.'"[30]

In addition to the saga structure and the sustained *Askeladd* references, Rolvaag's novel is permeated with several other folkloric elements. The importance of folklore to Rolvaag's work becomes all the more evident when one looks at the translation of the Norwegian version into English. Rolvaag felt that he could not do justice to American idiomatic expression, so he did not wish to translate the work himself. For various reasons, the novel was translated into English literally by a number of Norwegian-Americans; it then went to author Lincoln Colcord, who knew no Norwegian, for "touching up with a few punches of style."[31] It was sent back to Rolvaag for revision. In a letter from Colcord to Rolvaag, the importance of the author's Norwegian culture to the final version becomes very clear. After reading some revisions made by Rolvaag, Colcord remarks, "The amount of color that you have put into these two pages, in comparison with that in the manuscript from which I worked, is amazing; I am sending the pages I worked from, along with those which you have just done, so that you can run them over and study this point." He then gives some examples, comparing Rolvaag's version to his own:

R: As he now related it all to those so vitally concerned, his narrative caught fire; he grew enthusiastic; his words ringing with a glad exaltation, sounded like a fairy tale that he reveled in.

C: The narrative became loud and merry, and sounded like a fairy tale.

R: As she sat there listening to the wind playing with the darkness her revolt gradually subsided; deep melancholy came instead.

C: As she sat there, the storm within her slowly abated, and deep melancholy came instead.[32]

These passages are indicative of more than "an amount of color." In the first, Rolvaag's language connotes the living performance of folktales, a tradition that is still alive among his immigrant characters. The narrative does more than become "loud and merry"; it catches fire. It doesn't just sound *like* a fairy tale; it sounds like a fairy tale the teller *revels* in. In the second passage, Rolvaag's language personifies nature and gives it magical qualities. The storm is not only "within her," but is in nature itself as the wind plays with the darkness. Both of these folkloristic traits—the sense of performance and the sense that nature has magical qualities—are located in Rolvaag's tradition, but would be impossible for Colcord to evoke within his own. Furthermore, rather than merely providing "local color," when understood, these elements of folklore help to explain to the non-Norwegian reader what appear to be strange or odd reactions to events. And, more importantly, they illuminate the particular ways in which the Norwegians interpret their world—an interpretation relying on both old Norse pagan belief and a pietistic Christianity.

In both the oral and recorded folklore tradition, the physical landscape plays a significant role. Folklorists have demonstrated that there is a dynamic relationship between folklore and landscape. As Timothy Cochrane has observed, "Place influence[s] folklore and folklore influence[s] the experience of place . . . place and folklore [are] mutually interacting."[33]

Environmental geographer Yi-Fu Tuan argues eloquently that "landscape is personal and tribal history made visible. The native's identity—his place in the scheme of things—is not in doubt, because the myths that support it are as real as the rocks and waterholes he can see and touch. He finds recorded in his land the ancient story of the lives and deeds of the immortal beings whom he reveres. The whole countryside is his family tree."[34]

In Norway, not only did the native landscape evoke feelings of rootedness, an organic connection to Norwegian culture, but it also had consequences for specific forms of traditional Norwegian folklore. As Rolvaag biographer Paul Reigstad points out, for example, in Norwegian literature, climbing mountains "frequently symbolizes human aspiration. Forbidding peaks and desolate snowfields inevitably suggest the struggle for attainment." The landscape itself evoked "Norwegian" optimism as well as fatalism. According to Reigstad, as a boy, Rolvaag himself "was steeped in the belief that the world about him was full of living spirits."[35] In his unpublished autobiography, Rolvaag writes that

> all nature was alive with the supernatural. In the barn lived the *nisse*, in the hills the goodpeople, in glens and dales the *huldre*, in the sea the mermaids and the sea serpent, and the *draug*—the most terrible of them all. . . . I needed only to look out our last window to see the Seven Sisters, seven jagged mountain peaks. . . . Sometimes I feared these giant maidens. Trolls they were, trolls turned into stone . . . [on] dark and rainy days in the late fall, they put on wet clothes and wrapped banks of fog about their heads; then they looked forboding in their mighty isolation. They must know terrible secrets.[36]

Foreshadowing both good luck and tragedy, all of these folklore and landscape elements would later permeate *Giants in the Earth*.

The image of physical landscape as a repository of supernatural power is not limited to the Norwegian landscape, however. In the novel, the Norwegian settlers transfer these supernatural beliefs onto the Dakota prairies. The most obvious indication of this transfer is the heading of the last chapter, "The Great Plains Drinks the Blood of Christian Men and Is Satisfied." Here the plains are directly defined as evil trolls; this reference to land and nature as embodied by trolls and living presences is sustained throughout the novel, from its title to its presentation of Per's last battle with the prairie. The imagery is graphic. "Monsterlike, the Plain lay there—sucked in her breath one week, and next blew it out again. Man she scorned; his works she would not brook. . . ." At another point, a coming storm is described as an "apparition" that "writhed and swelled with life." Per and Hans Olsa view the sudden blizzard as "a giant troll [who] had risen up in the west, ripped open his great sack of woolly fleece, and emptied the whole contents of it above their heads." The land even held power over the psyche at certain times. On their first evening together in their settlement, the neighbors become apprehensive about their future out in the wilderness. "A peculiar mood came drifting in with the dusk. It seemed to float on the evening breeze, to issue forth out the heart of the untamed nature around them. . . . It even seemed to rise like an impalpable mist out of the ground on which they sat." Thus, the land becomes for the settlers not only the promise of a future "kingdom," but the embodiment of the evils against which they must battle—drought, storm, loneliness, and fear. Like the heroes in their folktales, they must wage war against these trolls.[37]

As Tuan argues, however, landscape evokes different cultural responses. Spaciousness, for example, can be both exhilarating for a person with Per's temperament and frightening for Beret. Open space as opposed to familiar place can evoke the promise of the open road as well as a feeling of vulnerability. As Tuan puts it, "to be open and free is to be exposed and vulnerable." Per and Beret in many ways exemplify these two perspectives—a typically Western sense of space as boundless wealth, power, and prestige, and a rooted, limited sense of place as "a calm center of established values." While Per feels exhilarated by the vast open space of the frontier, Beret feels extremely vulnerable without the physical and culture boundaries of her Norwegian community.[38]

While, for Per, the land represents his fight to wrest the Castle of Soria Moria from the trolls, for Beret, her images of the land reveal her inner turmoil over her fate as the wife of a pioneer. Early in the novel, Beret views the barren landscape with foreboding, as a place where there wasn't "even one thing to hide behind!" As Rolvaag has written about Beret in another context, "For generations Beret's forebears had lived on the shore of the restless North Atlantic. They had been lulled to sleep by the swash of the sea; they had awakened to the same sound. Small wonder that the song of the sea should live in her blood. And the mountains stood near by. It is only natural that Beret, after coming in the flat, open reaches of Dakota Territory should miss them and experience the feeling of being lost, for there was 'nothing to hide behind.'"[39] Beret believed that the frontier was no place for human beings; they would inevitably become "beasts" there, cut off from organic roots in the Norwegian landscape. The community she had left behind had boundaries within which civilized life went on; out on the prairie, there was no such refuge. One evening when Per was away, Beret had taken the children for a walk. When they returned toward the sod house, "the air of the place had suddenly filled with terror and mystery. The wagons had floated like grey specks in the dusk; and all at once it had seemed as if the desolation of a vast continent were centering there and drawing a magic circle about their home. She had even seen the intangible barrier with her own eyes . . . had seen it clearly . . . had had to force herself to step across it. . . ."[40] To the American reader, this "magic ring" is merely a delusion of a woman in the first throes of imminent insanity. But to the Norwegian reader, the vision resonates with more meaning. In Norse mythology, the inner ring, or *Midgard*, of the cosmological structure represents the knowable self. The *Utgard*, on the other hand, is the outer ring, the home of trolls and giants.[41] For Beret, the magic ring is a conception of the land as an evil spirit. She is no longer living in the human dimension and is trapped by the evil forces in the ring.

When Beret is feeling less lonely and desolate, there is "no magic circle to step across!" But eventually the ring surrounds her almost constantly, a barrier which Per cannot cross. Communication between the two becomes impossible. Later in the novel, when the prairie has taken its toll on Beret's mental health, she has a vision that rises out of the landscape and stays with her through the beginnings of her illness. "Beret was gazing at the western sky . . . her eyes were riveted on a certain cloud that had taken on the shape of a face, awful of mien and giantlike in proportions. . . . Here was the simple solution to the whole riddle. She had known in her heart all the time that people were never led into such deep affliction unless an evil power had been turned loose among them. . . . She sat still as death, feeling the supernatural emanations all around her."[42] The most dreaded apparition in Norwegian lore is the *draug*, a "living dead person," whose appearance portends disaster, usually drowning.[43] This vision in many ways foreshadows the locust plague. Beret dreads what that awful mouth will spit out, and, indeed, it spews out a plague. For Beret, the appearance of this vision is the beginning of her plunge into serious mental illness.

In an alien landscape, Rolvaag's characters often react and respond to their new environment in terms of folklore. References to folk belief are scattered throughout the narrative and are particularly evident at times of crisis when one's most deep-seated cultural beliefs surface. As Lawrence Levine points out in his discussion of African-American folk thought, there is "plentiful evidence" that when people feel a lack of control over their lives, they often turn to rituals, myths, and practices that have become traditional.[44]

For example, one of the first problems encountered by the settlers is the mysterious disappearance of their cattle. The cattle are later found, but the incident causes great distress. Though they do have a rational explanation for the disappearance, the settlers still at times suspect supernatural forces: "for surely the gnomes hadn't taken them underground! . . . The evening brought memories to them—memories of half-forgotten tales which people had heard and repeated long, long ago. . . . It had been known to have actually taken place, that both man and beast would be spirited away by trolls. . . ." In Norwegian lore, *huldrefolk* (hidden people) often punish humans who disturb them be stealing away their cattle. That night, no one could sleep at Per Hansa's house, for "a strange uneasiness had entered there and would not leave. . . ."[45] While on the surface this episode provides little but comic relief, on a deeper level it is part of that unity that ties the episodes together—a foregrounding of imminent disaster.

A second crisis, and one that has much more bearing on the psychological characterization of both Beret and Per Hansa, occurs when Per removes landmarkers placed by previous homesteaders. Though he and his neighbors always had legal right to the land, he did not know this while committing his "crime." His guilt and Beret's knowledge of his act eat away at both of them. For the American reader, Rolvaag footnotes their reactions: "In light of Norwegian peasant psychology, Beret's fear is easily understandable; for a more heinous crime than meddling with other people's landmarks could hardly be imagined."[46] Indeed, in Norwegian lore, a *dieldegast* is a ghost of someone who stole land by moving a neighbor's "boundary stones," someone whose punishment is to wander restlessly after death.

In a third crisis, the settlers' almost irrational reaction to the fact that a family had to abandon their dead child partially buried on the prairie can perhaps be explained more fully by reference to folklore. According to the lore, those not buried in consecrated ground roamed about and wreaked evil upon people.[47] It is perhaps no coincidence that right after the family leaves the settlement, Beret sees her apparition and sinks into insanity. Both the landmarkers and the dead child symbolize for Beret the savage depths to which the settlers have sunk out in the wilderness.

Folklore also helps us understand the crisis that occurs when the locusts make their first appearance. They descend upon a land brimming with promise. "With every day that passed the wheat filled out more and more; the heads grew heavy and full of milk; as soon as the breeze died down in the afternoon, they could tilt toward the setting sun and slowly drop off to sleep, only to dream of the marvellous life that was now stirring within them." Following this idyllic description, the arrival of "a weltering turmoil of raging little demons" is all the more devastating. The settlers react with their native fatalism: it is a plague sent by God, or "Another One" speaking. Per Hansa, the saga-hero, reacts differently to his fate, however. "His utter impotence in the face of this tragedy threw him into an uncontrollable rage; he lost all restraint over himself."[48] He sends his son for the rifle and shoots into the welter, scattering the locusts away from his field, at least for the time being.

On one level, this episode is just another example of Per's rationalism and ingenuity. But for Norwegian readers, the episode may have conjured up other allusions. In the popular tale "The Maid of the Glass Mountain," every Midsummer Night, "when the grass [is] greenest and lushest," a farmer's meadow is completely eaten by a mysterious creature. Each of the man's sons stands watch in the barn in order to surprise and destroy the creature. Of course, the only son to succeed is the clever and ignored *Askeladd*. He throws a piece of steel over the giant horse, which exorcises the animal of its evil.[49] In the struggle with trolls and *huldrefolk*, steel is the most effective weapon in Norwegian lore. The similarity between this fairy-tale and the locust incident is striking. For the reader who knows the tale, it enhances Per's parallel image with the *Askeladd*. Furthermore, it heightens the tension between Christianity and pagan belief. While his neighbor calls Per blasphemous because he is challenging the will of God, Per is struggling against a concept of fate that has other supernatural origins, a concept that encourages aspiration in spite of fate.

These items of folklore in one sense demonstrate that Rolvaag's characters transferred their folk beliefs to a new landscape in an effort to understand and explain the alien environment. But they also serve as a reminder of the difference between Per and Beret's experience of the New World.

Much of Beret's distress arises out of her longing for the Old World and what she sees as the evil of forgetting the old ways. Her grandfather's chest is the most obvious symbol of that longing for the security of her old community. The seventeenth-century chest embodies the deep roots of her family in Norway. She is the one among the settlers who most consciously holds onto the past and reacts most strongly to any changes in the native culture of the settlers.

When their son Peder is born, for example, Per Hansa gives him the second name of "Victorious" (Seier). The name is unusual in Norwegian, though there is evidence that it was used by ancient Danish kings. To Beret, the name is not only foreign, but blasphemous, "not a human name."[50] How could one be "victorious" in this land embodied by evil? This name becomes an obsession with Beret in her illness and a great source of guilt for Per until a minister assures them both that "Victorious" is an entirely appropriate, if not perfect, name. Names again enter the conflict when the families decide to change their names to be more understandable in and consistent with the English language. Instead of being "Hans's Son" in Norwegian, for example, Per's new family name is "Holm." While the settlers choose new names after their places of origin or the farms where they grew up, also a Norwegian custom, Beret sees the change as a sign of disrespect for their fathers, a sign of evil. Her obsession with the past is by this time becoming more and more rigid.

The man who helps to cure Beret of her illness and Per of much of his guilt over his wife's condition is the minister, who in many ways is Rolvaag's spokesman. In preaching to the settlers, the minister at first compares their experiences to that of the Israelites. But he then realizes that the best way to reach these people is to speak to them as Norwegians, out of their own experience. Like the Israelites, "they must remain faithful to the heritage of their fathers," and if they do so the Lord's promises will be fulfilled. Indeed, the settlers, including Per Hansa, are most successful when they "remain faithful to their heritage" and rely on their Norwegian culture to guide their behavior. Per Hansa's idea for his sod house connected to the barn for warmth rises out of a "vague recollection of having heard how people in the olden days used to build their houses in that way . . ."; he relies on his "sailor's instinct" to guide his way through winter storms; and he ingeniously weaves a fishing net to capture ducks, keeping his family fed most of the winter. Per Hansa uses his folk culture to contribute to his growth in the new land. Beret, on the other hand, clings to her religion and the old ways to such a degree that she becomes unyielding and unforgiving. Per's problem arises when he does not acknowledge the costs of emigration and when he neglects to share his clever ideas with his community. His pride rules his ambition to "outdo" his neighbors and gain his "kingdom."[51]

These incidents illuminate Rolvaag's purpose in writing *Giants in the Earth* for his specific audience. According to Einar Haugen, Rolvaag saw his life-mission as the preservation of the cultural heritage of his people: "He argued that the best American was the one who knew the most about the culture of his own group."[52] In his valedictory address as a graduate of Augustana Academy in 1901, Rolvaag's topic was "that a human being cannot deny his own background and inherited culture and remain a whole and true and healthy person."[53] From that point on, Rolvaag devoted himself to the cause of cultural preservation. He was founder of the Society for Norwegian Language and Culture; a leader in Nordlandslaget, an organization of networks between emigrants from northern Norway and those back home; and the first editor of *For Faedrearven*, the publication of a group that promoted Norwegian culture in the Northwest. In 1925, he helped to organize the Norwegian-American Historical Association, whose aim was to collect and preserve Norwegian culture. In his organizational work, his lectures, and his fiction, then, Rolvaag was deeply concerned with the lives of Norwegian emigrants in America. He saw his role as an artist paralleling his role in the historical association. Like his literary hero Ibsen, he viewed the artist as a propagandist who cannot ignore responsibility to others by withdrawing into pure aestheticism. When he first came to America in the 1890s, Rolvaag noted in his diary, ". . . a great pioneering work could be done if one were able to remake the spiritless creatures living here into human beings." Of his early encounters with Norwegians in America, he wrote, "They are dead, dead, living dead! . . . The sense of beauty with which they might perceive the wonders and glories of nature has been killed by the cold hand of materialism." This imagery of the living dead—the worst kind of troll—epitomizes what Rolvaag perceived as the loss of "the intimate spiritual communion between the individual and his people," a loss that occurs when the emigrant gives up common language, customs, and traditions.[54]

But Rolvaag was not a cultural purist. He did not encourage emigrants to live in isolation. In his view, for successful settlement to be achieved, the

Norwegians should put their roots in the new soil. As he told his students at St. Olaf, the most profound contribution the Norwegians could make to their new country would be to cultivate their traditional beliefs and "add" those to American culture. In *Giants in the Earth*, as we have seen, Per Hansa's American successes exploit the customs and practices of the Old World, while Beret's failures come from her tenacious hold on Norwegian culture. Through the minister and the other characters in the novel, particularly Hans Olsa and his wife Sorrine, Rolvaag seems to be arguing for a middle ground between Per and Beret. Indeed, the minister seems to represent a specific brand of Christianity that blends Beret's love and need for the old ways and Per's optimistic hope for the future. While he encourages the Norwegians to remain "true to their race" in the new land, he offers pragmatic, earthly kinds of comfort to Per Hansa and Tonseten, for example, when he assures them that their need to adapt to new circumstances with new modes of behavior is not evil. Beret's fundamental fanaticism makes her too unyielding to embrace what Rolvaag offers. And Per Hansa may be equally unyielding in his optimism by refusing to understand the costs of "empire-building." The minister helps him to realize that some are not meant for such pursuits. Per tells Hans Olsa, "I should not have coaxed and persuaded her to come with me out here. . . . For you and me, life out here is nothing; but there may be others so constructed that they don't fit into this life at all; and yet they are finer and better souls then either one of us. . . ." Overhearing Per's realization, Beret eases out of her madness. But that madness is replaced by the unyielding fundamentalism, and Per loses his battle for his princess.[55]

More than a realistic document of Norwegian settlement on the prairie, Rolvaag's work also engages the dialogue between cultural pluralists and assimilationists in the fierce, nationalistic wake of World War I. This dialogue was particularly strong among the academic community at St. Olaf between those who thought assimilation was perhaps regrettable but inevitable and those like Rolvaag and his close friend Waldemar Ager who fought consistently to hold back that assimilation. In *Their Father's God*, the third book in his trilogy, Rolvaag's minister preaches the antithesis of the melting pot: "If this process of levelling down, of making everybody alike by blotting out all racial traits, is allowed to continue, America is doomed to become the most impoverished land spiritually on the face of the earth; out of our highly praised melting pot will come a . . . dull, smug complacency, barren of all creative thought and effort."[56] Though most apparent in *Peder Victorious* and *Their Father's God*, Rolvaag's promotion of cultural pluralism as a means to counter the "living dead" he saw when he first arrived in America also informs the conflict between Beret and Per Hansa in *Giants in the Earth*.

It was in the context of this tension that Rolvaag wrote his novel. The complex Norwegian codes make it clear that he intended a specific message for the Norwegian-American community. Knowing the crucial place of fatalism in Norwegian culture, it would be difficult to assert that the novel is a paean to the successful pioneer struggle: though Beret survives to carry on, she succeeds because she is not pulled by a restless dream. She sees the frontier not as a vision of future riches but as an earthly place in which she must survive. And, in the context of Norwegian culture, Per's infectious optimism is undercut by the continuous foreshadowing of certain disaster. In this way, at the same time that Rolvaag laments Beret's loss of her cultural community and her sense of place, he critiques the American myth of the frontier and an ever-expanding landscape. In many ways, this strategy can be viewed as a kind of "countermemory" that reconstitutes a dominant, seemingly universal narrative with a localized, historically grounded experience of oppression.[57] Rolvaag addressed the tensions between Per Hansa's attempted enactment of the dominant narrative of American progress and Beret's lived experience of immigrant pain and loss of place. The mythical narrative of modern progress embodied in the atomized individuals on the American frontier contrasted greatly with Rolvaag's own experience as an immigrant and an observer of immigrants within a foreign culture that demanded they relinquish ethnic identity. Using complex cultural codes from Norwegian culture, Rolvaag proposed an alternative version of immigration in the hopes of salvaging an ethnic identity for his community.

NOTES

1. O. E. Rolvaag, *Giants in the Earth* (New York: Harper and Row, 1955), n.p.

2. Robert Steensma, "Rolvaag and Turner's Frontier Thesis," *North Dakota Quarterly* 27 (1959): 100–105. See also Lewis Saum, "The Success Theme in Great Plains Realism," *American Quarterly* 18 (Winter 1966): 579–98.

3. *Giants*, 453.

4. Alan Richardson, *Genesis I–XI: Introduction and Commentary* (London: SCM Press, 1953), 93–95, 120.

5. See, for example, Joseph E. Baker, "Western Man against Nature," *College English* 4 (1942): 19–26; Paul A. Olson, "The Epic and Great Plains Literature: Rolvaag, Cather, and Neihardt," *Prairie Schooner* 55 (1981): 263–85; and Wayne F. Mortenson, "The Problem of the Loss of Culture in Rolvaag's *Giants in the Earth, Peder Victorious,* and *Their Father's God*," *Minnesota English Journal* 8 (1972): 42–50.

6. For a discussion of the debates within the Norwegian-American community about ethnicity and Americanization and the struggle to forge an ethnic identity out of these debates in the 1920s, see April Schultz, " 'The Pride of the Race Had Been Touched': The 1925 Norse-American Immigration Centennial and Ethnic Identity," *Journal of American History* 77 (1991): 1265–95.

7. Orm Overland, "Ole Edvart Rolvaag and *Giants in the Earth*: A Writer between Two Countries," *American Studies in Scandinavia* 13 (1981): 39.

8. O. E. Rolvaag, "Country and Fatherland," translated selection from *Amerika-Breve,* in *American Prefaces* 7 (1936): 110–12 (Rolvaag's italics).

9. Ibid., 110.

10. Immigration History Lectures, 1920–21, Box 20, Rolvaag Papers (Archives of the Norwegian-American Historical Association, St. Olaf College, Northfield, Minnesota).

11. O. E. Rolvaag, "Foreword," in Thomas Job, *Giants in the Earth: A Tragedy in Six Scenes* (Minneapolis: Northwestern Press, 1939), n.p. In 1927, Henry S. Commager noted that Rolvaag was among a group that rejected the romanticism of the frontier and focused rather on the human cost of frontier life. See Commager, "The Literature of the Pioneer West," *Minnesota History* 7 (1927): 319–28.

12. Rolvaag, "Country and Fatherland," 110–11. In 1893, E. V. Smalley identified this problem in "The Isolation of Life on Prairie Farms," *Atlantic Monthly* 72 (1893): 378–82. According to Smalley, "An alarming amount of insanity occurs in the new prairie states among farmers and their wives. In proportion to their numbers, the Scandinavian settlers furnish the largest contingent to the asylums" (380).

13. Rolvaag, *Giants,* n.p.

14. Overland, "Ole Edvart Rolvaag," 5.

15. Halvdan Koht, *The Old Norse Sagas* (New York: American-Scandinavian Foundation, 1931), 17.

16. Peter Hallberg, *The Icelandic Saga* (Lincoln: University of Nebraska Press, 1962), 73–99.

17. Erling Larsen, "The Art of O. E. Rolvaag," *Minnesota English Journal* 8 (1972): 17.

18. Koht, *The Old Norse Sagas*, 14.

19. Hallberg, *The Icelandic Saga*, 73.

20. *Giants*, 208.

21. Koht, *The Old Norse Sagas*, 30.

22. Hallberg, *The Icelandic Saga*, 88, 96.

23. *Giants*, 445.

24. Harold Simonson, *Prairies Within: The Tragic Trilogy of O. E. Rolvaag* (Seattle: University of Washington Press, 1987), 35.

25. Paul Reigstad, "Rolvaag as Myth-Maker," in *Ole Rolvaag: Artist and Cultural Leader* (Northfield, Minn.: St. Olaf College Press, 1975), 52.

26. Jan Brunvand, "Norway's *Askeladden*. The Unpromising Hero, and Junior-Right," *Journal of American Folklore* 72 (1959): 14.

27. According to Brunvand, the *Askeladd* hero has been persistent in Norwegian folklore; since Peter Christen Asbjornsen and Jorgen Moe's popular fairy tale collection was published in 1852, the character has been widely regarded in Norway as "a remarkably complete personification of Norway's national traits." The idea that the *Askeladd* is the "outgrowth of some natural genius of Norwegian peasants has become firmly entrenched"; the dreams of these Norwegian peasants are personified in the *Askeladd*, who is "successful against all odds" (ibid., 14).

28. Immigration History Lectures, 1920–21, Box 20, Rolvaag Papers.

29. *Giants*, 35, 45, 48, 107.

30. Einar Haugen, "O. E. Rolvaag: The Man and His Work," in *Ole Rolvaag: Artist and Cultural Leader* (Northfield, Minn.: St. Olaf College Press, 1975), 20 (quote attributed to Henrik Ibsen).

31. Rolvaag to Lincoln Colcord, 16 September 1926, Box 5, Rolvaag Papers.

32. Colcord to Rolvaag, January 1927, Box 5, Rolvaag Papers.

33. Timothy Cochrane, "Place, People, and Folklore: An Isle Royale Case Study," *Western Folklore* 46 (1987): 2.

34. Yi-Fu Tuan, *Space and Place: The Perspective of Experience* (Minneapolis: University of Minnesota Press, 1977), 157–58.

35. Paul Reigstad, *Rolvaag: His Life and His Art* (Lincoln: University of Nebraska Press, 1972), 3.

36. Rolvaag, "The Romance of Life," *American Prefaces* 7 (1936): 99, translated selections from unpublished autobiography, Rolvaag Papers.

37. *Giants*, 241, 259, 260, 32.

38. Tuan, *Space and Place*, 54. It should be noted that Rolvaag's conception of Per and Beret's different experiences with landscape and their relationship to ethnic identity is very gendered. His characterization of Per as a kind of "American

Adam" and Beret as the repository of tradition perpetuates certain mythologies about gender and deserves fuller treatment in another context.

39. Rolvaag, "Foreword," in Job, *Giants in the Earth: A Tragedy in Six Scenes*, n.p.

40. *Giants*, 29, 56.

41. Steven Hahn, "Vision and Reality in *Giants in the Earth*," *South Dakota Review* 17 (1979): 87–88.

42. *Giants*, 57, 321.

43. Tor Age Bringsvaerd, *Phantoms and Fairies from Norwegian Folklore* (Oslo: Johan Grundt Tanum Forlag, n.d.), 53.

44. Lawrence Levine, *Black Culture and Black Consciousness: Afro-American Folk Thought from Slavery to Freedom* (New York: Oxford University Press, 1977), 62–63.

45. *Giants*, 91–95.

46. Ibid., 120–21.

47. Bringsvaerd, *Phantoms and Fairies*, 47, 53.

48. *Giants*, 323, 332, 334.

49. Ingri D'Aulaire and Edgar Parin, *East of the Sun and West of the Moon: Twenty-one Norwegian Folktales* (New York: Viking Press, 1938), 45.

50. *Giants*, 246.

51. Ibid., 362, 53, 260.

52. Haugen, "O. E. Rolvaag," 18.

53. Ella Valborg Tweet, "Recollections of My Father," *Minnesota English Journal* 8 (1972): 10.

54. Reigstad, *Rolvaag*, 32, 41.

55. *Giants*, 405.

56. Rolvaag, *Their Father's God* (Lincoln: University of Nebraska Press, 1982), 210.

57. On such a definition of countermemory, see George Lipsitz, *Time Passages: Collective Memory and Popular Culture* (Minneapolis: University of Minnesota Press, 1990), 213.

Back Home: Southern
Identity and African-American
Gospel Quartet Performance

RAY ALLEN

"You see people down here, they know how to have
church!" exclaims Jeff Richardson, twenty-five-year-old drummer for the
Brooklyn Skyways, one of New York City's premier black gospel quartets.
"They know how to get down and clap their hands, and shout, and have a
good time without any music [instruments]. Up in New York they just mess
around, until it's time to hear some music and clap their hands." Richardson narrates as we wind down a two-lane country road outside of Sumter,
South Carolina, on a bright August morning. Willie Johnson, leader of the

Skyways, hums an old hymn as he guides the bus toward I-95 and home. The other members of the Skyways and some fifteen friends and relatives sit quietly or doze, still recovering from the busy weekend's activities. Johnson brought the Skyways and company to his hometown of Sumter to sing for his nephew's wedding reception on Saturday evening and to perform at two small church programs on Sunday. Though not a profitable tour, the trip was a joyful homecoming for Johnson and his family, and a chance for the other Skyways to enjoy a relaxing weekend in the "Southland." But now it's Monday morning and the bus hurtles north on its fourteen-hour voyage back to Brooklyn, where most will return to work on Tuesday morning.

"People are very sincere about religion down here," Richardson continues. "They know the way, they came up with it. See, this is the place where everything was really created from—the South. They [rural African-Americans] just moved north to expand. But religion was really based right here, in these woods! Before all these big beautiful church buildings were built, you just had dirt roads and wooden churches. See, this is where it all comes from."

Richardson's impassioned homage to the roots of his southern faith is particularly interesting, for unlike the other Skyways he was not born in the South, but rather in Brooklyn, N.Y. However, like many second- and third-generation northern African-Americans, he spent childhood summers with his grandmother in South Carolina and continues to visit friends and family on a regular basis. Moreover, he is presently considering relocating in Fayetteville, North Carolina. His attitudes are typical of many northern African-Americans, young and old, who maintain strong cultural ties to the South. And for many like him, gospel quartet singing serves as a vital symbolic expression of southern religion and identity.

Folklorists have only recently begun exploring the significance of traditional expressions that reflect regional affiliation for displaced migrant groups in the United States.[1] In the introduction to the *Encyclopedia of Southern Culture*, co-editors Charles Reagan Wilson and William Ferris suggest that the American South "exists as a state of mind both within and beyond its geographic boundaries." They contend that the South, as a cultural mind set, endures among groups of southern migrants, such as African-American Mississippians who settled in south Chicago or white Appalachians who relocated in Detroit.[2] A challenging research problem for folklorists, then, is to discover exactly how such southern migrants make use of traditional folklore in maintaining aspects of their rural, southern "state of mind," while simultaneously forging a modern urban identity in a physical setting far removed from their southern homeland.

This present inquiry focuses on the role of African-American gospel quartet singing in easing the stress of urban acculturation for members of New York City's southern, working-class, black church community.[3] New York City is currently home to the largest and most diverse African-American population in the United States (1.7 million). The majority of this populace is of rural, southern, Protestant extraction—migrants and the descendants of migrants who journeyed to New York during the Great Migrations, which began in the 1910s and, fueled by World War II, continued through the 1950s. A significant number of these working-class churchgoers remain affiliated with the traditional southern, evangelical denominations—Baptist, Methodist, and Holiness/Pentecostal.

Although southern migration into New York City has diminished significantly since the 1960s, the great majority of middle-aged and older members of the black church community were born and reared in the rural South. Most originally hail from the southeastern states of North Carolina, South Carolina, Virginia, and Georgia.[4] And most, despite years of residence in New York, continue to identify themselves as "southern people." Further, individuals and entire families frequently travel to the South several times a year for family homecomings, reunions, weddings, and funerals. This allows family, social, and church networks to remain intact, in spite of the geographical dislocation. A significant number of older urban African-Americans, in fact, consider moving back to the South upon retirement, citing the region's reasonable cost of living, improved race relations (following the lifting of Jim Crow laws), and moderate climate, as well as their desire to be reunited with their extended family and to live in what they perceive as a safer, cleaner environment. The phenomenon of reverse migration is gradually becoming a reality,[5] as Clifford Williams of the Brooklyn Skyways suggests:

> People left the South for better living, for better jobs. But the average
> person still wants to go back home. A lot are doing it, buying houses in
> the South and moving back. Some retire, some move back for a job,
> maybe in a different state or town. Houses are cheaper, and you have

nice land all around. You can buy two or three houses in the South for what you could in New York. Living is better there, it's not as fast as New York. There's lots of fresh air, and clean, beautiful country. You don't have to worry about the hooligans mugging you. You're not all crowded up.[6]

But what of the younger, second- and third-generation, New York–born churchgoers? Many, like Jeff Richardson, appear to retain a strong, self-conscious affiliation with their parents' southern roots, having absorbed a great deal of southern culture firsthand during summer vacations and holidays spent with extended family in the South. They speak with great respect and fondness for the "Southland"—a place, they claim, where people are friendlier and more respectful to one another, families are stronger, crime is less prevalent, the air and water are cleaner, the food is tastier, and the overall pace of life is slower and saner. Most agree that the South is a better place to raise children, citing superior schools and a safer environment relative to conditions in New York City.

For southerners residing within or outside of the region, music, religion, and folk custom play an essential role in constructing and maintaining a mythic vision of the old rural South. For example, in folk and popular music dating back to the nineteenth-century minstrel stage, the old South is portrayed as an idyllic, rural paradise. Robert Cantwell aptly notes that early country and bluegrass songs are filled with nostalgic images of the old southern home place, the beautiful hills, the devoted family, and the old-time religion.[7] He argues that these symbols are especially compelling for southern whites who migrated to the urban centers of the North and Midwest: ". . . the Kentuckian, who left home with his family while still a boy but who nevertheless still dreams of going back, weaving his way through the Detroit traffic on a bleary February morning toward his job on the assembly line, listening on the eight-track auto tapedeck he bought with his handsome salary he cannot give up, to Bill Monroe and the Blue Grass Boys, singing 'I'm Going Back to Old Kentucky.'"[8]

While African-American blues songs rarely demonstrate such overt sentimentality, the impulse to recount and romanticize one's southern past plays a vital role in black gospel performance. But the significance of the old rural South is more complex for African-Americans than for their white counterparts. The South as symbol presents African-Americans—particularly those migrants living in urban areas outside the region—with something of a paradox. Amiri Baraka notes that while the South represents "the incredible fabric of guilt and servitude identified graphically within the Negro consciousness," it also connotes home: "It was the place that Negroes knew, and given the natural attachment of man to the land, even loved. The North was to be beaten, there was room for attack. No such room had been possible in the South, but it was still what could be called home."[9] Gerald Davis ponders this dilemma and concludes:

> At the most fundamental, sensate levels, the South is regarded as "roots," a vaguely perceived but powerful point of reference that secures personality clusters in this geographic region. In a cosmological sense this concept of "roots" also unites African-Americans with a network that has both historical and contemporary significance. Many African-Americans who migrated from the South as long ago as thirty years, as recently as thirty days, regard the region as "backward" and "country," although the South is in many ways more progressive than other areas in the nation. Paradoxically, these same persons, and many thousand others, return annually to the region for high school reunions, church homecomings, family reunions, funerals, and vacations. The South is a secure place of renewal, of contact with humanizing spirits, of communication with the souls of Black Folks.[10]

As Davis and Baraka point out, the nature of this North/South relationship is fraught with ambiguity. On one hand, the rural South signifies a time and place which many African-Americans had to abandon in order to achieve reasonable social and economic status. On the other, it continues to represent a cradle of family, church, and historical roots. In spite of its legacy of slavery, racial oppression, and rural poverty, the South still looms large in the psyches of many urban African-Americans as a mysterious spiritual homeland.

The strong influence of evangelical Protestantism, a hallmark of southern culture since the Great Awakenings of the late eighteenth and early nineteenth centuries, has earned black and white southerners the reputation of being particularly "religious" in temperament. The image of the South as the "Bible Belt" or the heartland of the "old-time religion" is deeply rooted in historical fact and social reality. A strict code of morals tends to be associated with southern religion, as historian Samuel Hill notes:

To be a converted Christian, a saved person, was known to entail appropriate demeanor in gratitude for forgiveness and as worthy of one's new status and identity. Obedience to Christ's teaching was held up as essential. In the context of Southern society, that meant honesty, familial integrity, sociability, and neighborliness on the affirmative side. It also necessitated "abstaining from the appearance of evil," interpreted as cursing, gambling, breaking the sabbath, dancing, and (especially later) drinking. Totalled, the moral impact was toward a disciplined life. One is attentive to what he or she does and does not do, indeed even scrupulous. The instincts of the flesh must be bridled and full run given to the leading of the Spirit. This made for a people who were morally serious about work and secular values as well as about godliness.[11]

Local New York quartet singers constantly express similar attitudes about southern religion and values. They envision the old rural South as a spiritual Mecca where respect for religion, family, hard work, and strict morality form the foundation of social life. These images are contrasted to the evils of contemporary northern urban life, as the following testimonies suggest:

Down South, the most you usually do is to go to church and to go to work. But you take here in New York, there's always a ball game, a card game, a party going on. People forget about going to church, forget about the good strict life, once they hit New York. And sometimes people come here with religion, and when they leave they done lost it! . . . Some people down South never saw lights burning all night. When they go in the house it's dark. But in New York, the ladies' shoe heels hitting the streets all night, these lights burning all night, and some people think it's still daytime. . . . In the Southland, if a person dies, the neighborhood around there, it was silent for a while, very sad for a while. But in New York, before you leave the chapel, people will be laughing and carrying on, just like nothing happened. Here they bury you today, and forget about you before they get you in the ground.

(Charlie Storey of the All Stars)

People in the South were more serious about Christianity than they are up here. In New York, it's dog eat dog. But in the South, the children were brought up to say "yes sir, no sir" to older people. And if my child sasses you out, and you report it to me, I'm going to whoop him. And in school, the teachers use to whoop the kids. . . . So a few years back, a southern kid had good manners toward any older person. But these kids here in New York, three years old—I wouldn't use the words they say, but they'll tell you plain. . . . See, everything wasn't bad in the South. You look back on those times, we were brought up right, we were taught right. Not that we thought so at the time, but it was a better way of life, an easier way of life, than it is now, here in New York.

(Ralph MacLemore of the All Stars)

I think black people in the southern states, they have more respect for themselves than people up here [in New York] do. People here don't have no consciousness, no respect. The kids have no discipline—they were more disciplined in the South. I can tell you about myself, my mother kept me in church, that's number one. And number two was, I was not out late at night, she knew where I was. And number three, I didn't ever disrespect an elder person, if I did I got a spanking. . . . Sometimes I wonder, if I had been raised in New York, I wouldn't be the same person I am now. Because the environment, all the drugs— you've got to be strong to be raised here, in the ghettos. Kids, fourteen and fifteen years old, killing, robbing and stealing, killing their own parents. That is sad. And there is a difference, you don't hear about these things going on in the southern states.

(David Stewart of the Wearyland Singers)

The urban/North versus rural/South oppositions are particularly vivid in these commentaries. The former is viewed in terms of sin and chaos— crime, drugs, prostitution, broken families, and the general decay of religion and morality. By contrast, the traditional southern way of life is still venerated for its emphasis on religiosity, hard work, self-discipline, respect for family and elders, and the practice of strict Christian morality.

Considering the dominant migration patterns, it comes as no surprise that most middle-aged and older quartet singers active in New York today were born and reared in the South. Quantitative demographic figures reflecting the exact makeup of quartet audiences are simply not readily available. However, casual observation and informal conversations suggest that the vast majority of black New Yorkers who attend gospel programs were either born in the South or maintain strong family ties to the region. Several examples underscore the validity of this assumption. The emcee presiding at a large Brooklyn church program in the fall of 1988 stalled for time by asking audience members where they were from. By a show of hands, approximately three-quarters of the five hundred present identified their home states as North Carolina, South Carolina, Georgia, or Virginia. A handful were from Alabama, Mississippi, and Florida. The remainder—less than a quarter of the total, and almost exclusively young—claimed Brooklyn as home. Smaller programs, such as the 1986 anniversary of Reverend Young and the Morning Glories, often take on the ambience of a homecoming or family reunion. At this particular program all seven singing groups were either related to the Reverend Young or were originally from his home community near Columbia, South Carolina. Participants establish and renew social networks with southern friends and family. And it is no coincidence that barbequed chicken, cornbread, collard greens, and other southern style foods are popular dishes at such gatherings.

The conflict between the old, southern religious values and contemporary, northern urban secular life permeates many facets of gospel programs in New York. It is not insignificant that the terms "southern style" and "traditional" still appear on posters advertising gospel quartet programs in Brooklyn, Jamaica, Harlem, and the South Bronx. Such adjectives are used to describe groups who perform in the demonstrative, postwar hard gospel style as opposed to the smoother, contemporary sound that currently dominates the commercial gospel airways and recording industry. Indeed, singers and churchgoers perceive the hard gospel style as being southern in origin and nature. In their minds black religion and music are rooted in the South, so naturally the best gospel soloists, quartet singers, and church singers came, and continue to emerge, from the region. Most church people would agree enthusiastically with Jeff Richardson's contention that in terms of worship and song the rural South is "the place where everything [religion and music] was really created."

In preprogram advertising, nearly all groups mention their home borough or community. Thus, a flyer for an upcoming program might list groups as follows: "The Spiritual Voices of Brooklyn," "The Wearyland Gospel Singers of Corona," "The Golden Jubilees of Jamaica," "The Haynes Singers of the Bronx," and so forth. However, some New York–based groups continue to use their old southern affiliation on advertising and promotional material. A good example is the Brooklyn-based Gospel Crowns. Because several members are natives of Alabama, the group often bills itself as the "Gospel Crowns of Birmingham, Alabama." A Manhattan group consisting of mostly South Carolinians commonly advertises itself as "The Gospel Heavyweights of Sumpter, South Carolina," even though the members have lived in New York City for years. Some groups frown on this practice, claiming their competitors are willfully deceiving gospel audiences by pretending to be from out of town. Those who maintain a southern affiliation, however, explain they are proud of their heritage and simply hope to attract additional fans from their southern hometown or state with such advertising.

Recordings or broadcasts of "southern-style," hard gospel quartet singing can implicitly trigger associations of the South among African-American churchgoers. But the music demonstrates its maximum potential as a signifying agent at live performances involving singers and audiences of common southern heritage. Images of southern family, religion, and traditional life are constantly evoked during many gospel programs. Singers often open their set by announcing their home state or town and asking if anyone else in the congregation is from the area. While the lyrics to songs like "Old Time Religion" mention older ways of southern worship, the chanted narratives that introduce and connect songs provide the most vivid references. Such narratives may remind listeners of their southern roots, evoke sentimental memories of family and childhood experiences, reflect on hardships and burdens, and expound on the need to "get back" to the old southern religion and values that are constantly threatened by the demonic forces of urban secular life. One young singer with the Bronx-based Travelling Sons admonishes his audience not to stray from the old southern-style singing and praying:

> You see we've gotten away,
>   from the old-time religion.
> We don't sing like we used to sing,
>   we don't pray like we used to pray,
>   back down in North Carolina.
> Oh yea—
> Sing with me,
>   words that go like this:
>   [begins song, "I'll Fly Away"] [12]

Singers love to expound upon the hardships they personally faced growing up in the rural South, particularly the lack of basic necessities such as food, clothing, electricity, and adequate shelter. Testimonies lament the difficult times, but always credit God for delivering His people from such conditions. Lee Cloud of the Northernaires introduces a song by reminding his audience that he's just a "country boy" from down South:

> I come up the rough side of the mountain,
>> but look at me tonight church!
> Ain't He [God] good y'all?
> I use to talk about what a hard time we was having—
> Sometimes we would come home from the cotton fields,
>> and not know where our next meal was coming from.
> But let me tell you if you stay with God,
>> the Devil'll leave you alone.[13]

Deacon Jones of the Pilgrim Sounds tells a Brooklyn audience:

> Y'all should take time out a little while,
>> and look where the Lord brought you from.
> I don't know about you,
>> but down in North Carolina,
> I had it ha-a-a-rd,
>> oh yes I did.
> I don't mind letting you know tonight church,
>> that I ain't always had this nice suit of clothes to wear,
> I want you to know tonight church,
>> that I ain't always served God like this.
> Things I use to do,
>> I'm glad I don't do no more,
> Since Jesus,
>> came in my life.[14]

Other narratives romanticize the old-time southern ways of worship. Illustrative is Darrel McFadden's opening to the Golden Sons' rendition of the song "I'm So Glad about It":

I don't know about you tonight,
    but God has been good to me.
Has God been good to you tonight? (Yes He has)
    Let me see the hands of those who know that the Lord has been
        good to you. (Yes He has)
There's a song,
    that we use to sing down in South Carolina.
We use to have what you call the old-time revival meetings,
We use to have what they call the amen corner.
People from miles and miles around,
    would come together and worship the Lord's name.
And I remember,
    back in the hills of South Carolina,
There was an old gray-headed man,
    he got up and testified. (yeah)
And he said:
"I thank God,
    for letting me see a day I never seen before, (well, well, well)
And, ah, I thank God, (I thank God)
    for giving me food to eat, (yeah)
        and bread to drink," (yeah)
And the old man he got happy,
    and he started to sing a song, said:
        [singing begins]
It's another day's journey,
    and I'm glad, (I'm glad about it)
I'm glad, (I'm glad about it)
Said I'm glad. (I'm glad about it)
It's another day's journey,
    church and I'm so glad, (I'm glad about it)
I'm so glad to be here.[15]

It is worth noting that McFadden, in his early 20s, was born in Brooklyn, not in South Carolina. But like Jeff Richardson and many other young singers, he spent his childhood summers with extended family in the South and was thoroughly immersed in southern rural church practices from an early age. Moreover, those singers and listeners who are too young or geographically removed from the South to have personally experienced the "cotton fields" or "old-time revival meetings" have heard them recounted often in family and church oral history. Images of the old South become deeply ingrained in their own cultural psyches, prompting them, like their elders, to respond to such narrations.

Two distinct, though not unrelated pictures of the rural South emerge in these sorts of narratives and song commentaries. One is the South as sacred homeland—a mythic world of gray-haired mothers, hard-working fathers, praying deacons, cotton fields, and old-time revival meetings. Often a specific southern location ("the hills of North Carolina") is cited as the place of the singer's original conversion ("where I first got religion"). Recollections of the sacred homeland are always cloaked in nostalgic, romantic imagery. The other picture portrays the South as a place of hardship suffered/transcended. Here the southern experience is depicted in terms of servitude, harsh conditions, and rural poverty. But it is a beast that can be fought and, with God's help, overcome. The social freedoms and material gains achieved by the singers (and their congregations) stand as proof of the church community's victory over hardship and oppression—"We made it out of the cotton fields, ain't God good, y'all?" Images of the South as a sacred homeland and a place of hardship suffered/transcended are both evident in the following narrative that Marlene Miller of the Biblettes uses to introduce the song "Old Time Religion":

> I'm reminded of
> Georgia where I came from.
> You see, I'm not ashamed,
> to let you know where I came from.
> Back then,
> we used to work all day long in the fields,
> And Lord back then,
> we used to go to revival meetings,
>   til the dawn [. . ? . .]
> We used to go home,
> wash our clothes,
>   had an old tin tub.
> We got in an old tub,
> take a bath,

We didn't have no curly kits, [hair-conditioning products]
    like we do today.
So don't be ashamed,
    of where you come from.
I want you to know,
    God is good to me.
We used to go in the kitchen,
    open up the lard can,
        run some lard around our hair.
See we didn't have no curly kits back then,
    like we do today.
I know we're going to have church tonight,
    I know we're going to have church.
The reason I'm telling you this,
    I want you to go back in revival,
I want you to get something out of this, tonight,
    because God is good to you.
See we didn't have plenty of oil and coal,
    like we have today,
We used to gather in the kitchen,
    we had a wood stove,
And back then we had mules and wagons,
    see I'm not too cute to let you know
    what a mule and wagon is.
We'd go to church in that wagon,
    we used to go down an old, dusty road.
And before we got there,
    the young people would jump up off the wagon,
        so their boy friends and girl friends wouldn't
        see. [that they rode in a wagon]
I know you know what I'm talking about.
I don't care what you got tonight,
    your fancy house,
        your fine car,
You know when you get to church,
    [. . ? . .]

And when you come in the door,
>   you can't hardly say "amen" for Jesus.
If you know what I'm talking about,
>   let me see you wave your hands! [16]

Miller's narration does more than simply venerate the old-time religion, regular church attendance, hard work, and the virtues of rural southern life. Listeners are further instructed not to be ashamed of their southern roots. In fact, the traditional ways of life—working in the fields, washing clothes in an old tin tub, heating with wood, straightening hair with lard, and traveling by mule and wagon—are recalled with a certain degree of pride and respect. Life was difficult in those days, but with God's help the faithful not only persevered, they triumphed over adversity. The narrative further serves to remind the congregation that while they should be happy that God has brought them to a point where they have the conveniences of cars, central heating, curly kits, and comfortable homes, they should never forget the hardships the Lord brought them through. And further, they must never allow themselves to become so sophisticated—so "cute" as Miller says—that they won't say "amen" in church. In short, singers warn their urban congregations not to stray too far from the old-time singing, praying, and religion of their rural ancestors. And if Miller's story and song are delivered with sincere passion, her words may literally take her audience "back in revival" with the invocation of the Spirit and a communal shout.

Narratives are often intended to create reflective moods and subtly ease listeners into nostalgic frames of mind. Ensuing songs, while not necessarily making explicit reference to the South, can touch upon these sentiments. In other words, the correct combination of narrative and song can activate clusters of extramusical associations, transporting southern listeners back in space and time. Individual listeners might be reminded of their family, church, and community back home; of their parents, grandparents, and other loved ones passed on; of the stifling economic and racial barriers they fought (and continue to fight) to overcome; or of their original conversion experience. Spoken and sung texts are layered with these sorts of connotative meanings that are readily apprehended by an audience of southern African-Americans. When Miller quips to her congregation "I know you know what I'm talking about" and is greeted by an enthusiastic "amen," she confirms that all present have personally experienced the struggle, the hardship, and the triumph of which she speaks. A shared history and identity as southern black Christians is clearly implied.

The process that generates these cultural and historical associations is clearly demonstrated in the following performance by Earl Ledbetter and the Wearyland Singers:

[chanted introduction]
We're going to leave you,
> we're going to leave you now.

I got one song,
> that's been bothering me.

I'm back,
> from the hills of North Carolina.

Had a chance to go there and sing,
> for my mother and father one day.

But there was this,
> old deacon there.

He got up from his seat, ha,
> and he began to walk,
>> to the mourning bench. (yeah)

He said,
> I've been here,
>> for seventy-seven long years.

Trying to hold on,
> to God's unchanging hand.

He said I look at the audience,
> I didn't see nobody say amen. (yeah)

But he said God's been good to me,
> He been good to me. (yeah)

Been better to me than I been to my own self.
There's an old song,
> he began to sing,
>> when he walked back to his seat.

Some glad morning,
> when this life is all over,

I want two wings to fly away,
    to be at rest.
Give me, (yeah)
Give me, (yeah)
Two wings, ha,
To fly away,
To fly away, (come on son)
    to be at rest.
And it sounds something like this—
[instruments start steady beat and chords, singing begins]
Oh some, some glad morning, y'all,
    I'm singing when, when this life is over
I,
    will fly away.
Said I'm going, going to a place,
    joy shall never end,
Oh, I,
    will fly,
        away, fly away.
Just, oh just my Lord,
    just a few more, few more—
        weary days and then,
Lord I, yes I will y'all,
    will fly away,
Said I'm going—going to a place,
    Lord I'm going to a place,
    Lord I'm going to a place,
    Lord I'm going to a place,
    Lord I'm going to a place,
        joy shall never end,
Oh, I,
    will fly,
        away, fly away.[17]

Later, reflecting on his performance of "I'll Fly Away," Ledbetter concluded:

A lot of people out there are southern, and these sorts of things bring back memories. That's why David or I talk about the old man [the deacon]. If he had a song, that's what he would sing. "Some glad morning, when this life is over, I'll fly away." It really makes people think about their lives, and how they came up through the years. . . . Memories of the hard times they had, and their parents and grandparents had. And that song, it goes way back to years ago, and everybody knows it. Everybody knows how they used to sing it, and knows we're singing it like this. It's a touching type of thing—it touches them. . . . And by me saying, "I'm back from the Hills of North Carolina," somebody in the audience is from North Carolina, and they'll know what I'm singing about. They know how I feel, because we were brought up in slavery, you know. We didn't have what a lot of people have. And that kind of touches the heart, when you find somebody up there singing gospel from North Carolina. Somebody out there says, "Oh, I know what he's singing about."[18]

In his introduction, Ledbetter sets a sentimental tone by reminding his audience that he and his family are from the rural hill country of North Carolina. Ledbetter knows this will gain the attention of North Carolinians and possibly other southerners in his audience. He hopes to set their minds drifting "back home," as his words elicit memories of their parents, church, and community. Next Ledbetter introduces the venerable old deacon, a man whose seventy-seven-year devotion personifies the steadfast Christian faith. After a brief testimony, the deacon begins to sing an "old song" that foreshadows his death and ascent to heaven. Ledbetter finally collapses the space and time separating the congregation from the imaginary scene by actually singing the deacon's song, "I'll Fly Away." If he has delivered his words convincingly, they will arouse memories of family and church life in the South. The congregation will be "touched" by the song as present and past are fused in one affecting moment. Interestingly enough, there are no direct references to the South, or the family, or any "old-time" ways of life in the lyrics of "I'll Fly Away." They are not needed. Ledbetter's introduction has already placed the song in the necessary historical context to evoke specific extramusical associations and a strong emotional response from his southern audience. As he points out, "that song, it goes way back to years ago, and everybody knows it." Thus, a song such as "I'll Fly Away"—already heavily loaded with connotative references and perceived by church audiences as being old and southern—explodes with deep-seated meaning when prefaced by a sentimental narrative concerning the old South, the old deacon, and the old-time religion.

The Wearyland's performance of "I'll Fly Away" offers further evidence that the meaning of a gospel song cannot be fully comprehended through simple verse/chorus lyrical analysis. Isolating the song text—the sung words beginning with "Oh some, some glad morning"—leads to the erroneous conclusion that the song's primary message is future and otherworldly. Listeners are assured that their earthly struggles, those "weary days," will soon pass, for eventually they will "fly away" to their joyful rewards in heaven. But when the chanted song commentary and the larger sociohistorical context are taken into account, a radically different interpretation emerges. In the setting of a live gospel program with an audience of southern African-Americans, the spoken and sung words communicate referential, extra-musical associations that transcend the denotative lyrical theme of future heavenly reward. Images of the North Carolina hills and the old deacon trigger an emotional response that pulls past into present. The exuberant heavenly joy predicted by the song text may indeed erupt at that moment if the Holy Spirit should choose to descend. In terms of overall meaning, the entire performance is about much more than simply flying away to heaven. It speaks to the struggles of a shared southern past, the joys of present communal fellowship, and the promise of a glorious future. Listeners, young and old, are reminded of who they are, where they (and their families) originally came from, and how they can achieve victory in this world.

Worth noting is the fact that most of the scenes of southern life and worship portrayed in narratives and song commentaries are set in the past. Many narratives are intensely nostalgic; they express a yearning to transcend time as well as space, to travel back to the old-time ways of past generations. Whether the focus is on the South as a sacred homeland or as a place of hardship suffered/transcended, the singer is always looking back in time. He or she longs to recapture the emotional intensity of the old religion, the security of the extended family and small-town community, or to proclaim victory over past tribulations. Today's achievements are always contrasted to yesterday's struggles—"I don't mind letting you know to-night, church, that I ain't always had this nice suit of clothes to wear." By referencing the old South the musicians seek to evoke a shared history that strengthens the sense of present community. That is, nostalgic narratives work as one more strategy that singers use to connect with their audience, to reinforce common bonds, and to move the performance towards *communitas*. This may explain why narratives about the old-time South are also used, on occasion, by professional touring quartets and community-based groups based in the South. For example, the lead singer of the Pilgrim Jubilee Singers (a well-known professional quartet from Chicago) testifies that he grew up in a three-room shack in Mississippi and that his family "didn't have much back then, but we had a family altar." Anthony Heilbut suggests the narration serves "to induce camaraderie that quickly draws together a church full of strangers." [19] On a commercial recording, Louis Jordan of the Swan Silvertones narrates: "Back in the hills of South Carolina where I come from, they used to have what they called a revival there." [20] The performance, Morton Marks surmises, aims to "literally revive an old revival meeting," to "reproduce the South Carolina church when everybody 'got up shouting.'" [21] Glenn Hinson reports that local quartets in North Carolina make reference to childhood hardships and the old ways of worship in order to establish a sense of "co-identity" between themselves and their listeners. [22] Daniel Patterson notes that members of the Golden Echoes, a community-based North Carolina group, often speak of the brutal poverty their parents struggled to overcome. But each time group members mount the stage in their well-tailored matching outfits, they "stand as resplendent embodiments of the material blessings for which the entire community longs." [23] For city and town-based southern singers, "back home" may signify the rural setting and bygone era of one's preurban past. [24]

Sentimental narratives set in the old South connote a shared past and serve to unify gospel singers with fellow listeners who experience the South as a "state of mind," whether the actual performance takes place inside or outside the geographic confines of the South. However, for local New York singers, whose daily experience is shaped by a geographic as well as a temporal separation from their southern home and heritage, imagery of the old South functions as a particularly powerful symbol of community and roots. The nostalgic portrayal of the old rural South by modern gospel quartets,

along with the general popularity of southern-derived gospel quartet singing, appears to be part of a larger movement to revive and sustain traditional southern beliefs and values in the contemporary urban North.[25] Such
"revitalization movements," anthropologists explain, are "associated with
frustrating situations and are primarily attempts to compensate for the frus-
trations of the society's members. The elements revived become symbols of
a period when the society was free, or in retrospect, happy and great. . . .
By keeping the past in mind, such elements help to reestablish and maintain
the self-respect of the group's members in the face of adverse conditions."[26]
The rapid growth of southern-style black religion in the urban North and
the subsequent rise of gospel song and gospel quartet singing in the 1930s
and 1940s, respectively, were certainly responses to adverse social conditions
experienced by dislocated rural migrants. Further, these religious and artistic expressions reinforced self-respect and independence for several generations of black city dwellers. However, the images of southern life being
revived are hardly symbols of a time (or place) when African-American
society was free or great. On the contrary, when gospel singers speak of
hardships suffered/transcended, they refer to centuries of slavery, postbel-
lum segregation, Jim Crow laws, and stifling rural poverty. They are certainly not advocating a return to such conditions. Rather, they are seeking
to revive and perpetuate a southern, religious worldview and core set of
values, which, they believe, assisted past generations of African-Americans
in their ongoing fight against seemingly insurmountable racial, social, and
economic barriers.

This strategy has strong precedent, for historically the southern church
has assumed a central role in the struggle for the survival and liberation of
African-Americans in the United States. More than any other institution,
the church has provided African-Americans with a haven to forge their own
sense of cultural identity.[27] The old-time religion, preaching, and singing
bolstered black southerners in their resolve to overcome slavery and the
institutionalized racism that followed, and in their more recent efforts to
hurdle the barriers of poverty, inadequte education, and social disparity. In
the minds of the southern-born gospel singers, the same religion and values
that delivered their forefathers and mothers in the rural South will assist
them and their offspring in overcoming the hardships of contemporary
urban life. While Satan may manifest himself in new ways in the city—

through drugs, rampant crime, prostitution, gambling, and crowded slum housing—the solution to these problems remains the same. Go to church, work hard, respect your family, live a "clean" moral life, and God will see you through. The fear, of course, is that younger generations will stray from the church and eventually scorn their southern roots and religious upbringing, opting instead for a secular lifestyle. From the churchgoers' perspective, such loss of faith inevitably leads to the decay of moral values and a life fraught with unstable family and love relations, unemployment, crime, drug and alcohol abuse, and so forth.

In conclusion, within the context of ritualized African-American gospel quartet performance, the image of the old-time rural South serves as a metaphor for social, moral, and spiritual salvation. This allows gospel quartets to mediate certain tensions by providing a sort of spiritual/aesthetic bridge between the sacred world of the rural southern migrants and the secular reality of their new urban home. Specifically, quartet performances help to assuage the deep oppositions of sacred versus secular, traditional versus modern, rural versus urban, and southern versus northern (midwestern/western) that lie at the heart of the African-American acculturation process. That is, while community-based quartet singing carries strong southern, rural connotations, elements of urban style and professionalism are clearly evident. Even local groups (who don't depend on singing for a living) dress in carefully matched uniforms, hawk vanity press tapes and records, occasionally travel out of town for special engagements, and often are paid for their services. Further, younger gospel quartets—consisting primarily of New York–born singers—move comfortably between contemporary gospel arrangements complete with "sweet" soul harmonies, funk-style slap bass, rock-inflected guitar breaks, and swirling synthesizer accompaniments and the older hymns and church songs arranged in the traditional, "southern" quartet style.

For both artists and audience members, such performances provide occasions for engaging in a form of urban popular culture that is consciously rooted in southern religious tradition. Or, as the singers like to say, they provide "spiritual entertainment." The local gospel singer may play the social role of the successful, well-dressed, semiprofessional urban entertainer, while remaining true to his or her rural southern heritage and religious beliefs. Aspects of traditional and modern social identity are simultaneously expressed in public performance, as this community of southern, rural church people strives to bring meaningful order to the northern, secular urban environment they now call home.

NOTES

1. American folklorists have had a long-standing interest in regionalism and have produced numerous collections of regional folksongs, narratives, and beliefs. For an introductory overview, see Richard Dorson, *American Folklore* (Chicago: University of Chicago Press, 1957), 74–134. A pioneering folklore study of regionalism and material culture is Henry Glassie's *Pattern in the Material Folk Culture of the Eastern United States* (Philadelphia: University of Pennsylvania Press, 1968).

2. Charles Reagan Wilson and William Ferris, *Encyclopedia of Southern Culture* (Chapel Hill: University of North Carolina Press, 1989), xv. For more on the South as a "region of the mind," see the essays in the "Mythic South" section of the encyclopedia.

3. For more on the history of the African-American church and gospel quartet singing in New York City, see Ray Allen, *Singing in the Spirit: African-American Sacred Quartets in New York City* (Philadelphia: University of Pennsylvania Press, 1991); a portion of this essay is drawn from *Singing in the Spirit*, with the permission of the University of Pennsylvania Press. Readers seeking more background on African-American gospel music should consult Anthony Heilbut, *The Gospel Sound* (New York: Anchor Books, 1985); and essays by Horace Boyer and Mellonee Burnim in Irene Jackson, ed., *More Than Dancing: Essays on Afro-American Music and Musicians* (Westport, Conn.: Greenwood Press, 1985). The best history of black gospel quartet singing is Kip Lornell, *Happy in the Service of the Lord: Afro-American Gospel Quartets in Memphis* (Urbana: University of Illinois Press, 1988).

4. This pattern of heaviest migration from North Carolina, South Carolina, Virginia, and Georgia was well established by 1930. See Gilbert Osofsky, *Harlem: The Making of a Ghetto* (New York: Harper and Row, 1971), 129.

5. The pattern of north to south reverse migration among African-Americans has only recently come to the attention of demographers. The turnabout in the migration pattern evidently began sometime in the mid-1970s; according to Census Bureau figures, nearly 100,000 more blacks have moved into the South than out since 1980. See Kenneth Weiss, "Migration by Blacks from the South Turns Around," *New York Times*, 11 June 1989. A forthcoming work by anthropologist Carol Stack promises to offer further insight on the subject.

6. Personal interview with Clifford Williams, 8/29/87.

7. Robert Cantwell, *Bluegrass Breakdown* (Urbana: University of Illinois Press, 1984), 226–48.

8. Ibid., 245.

9. Amiri Baraka (LeRoi Jones), *Blues People* (New York: William, Morrow and Company, 1963), 105.

10. Gerald Davis, *I Got the Word in Me and I Can Sing It, You Know* (Philadelphia: University of Pennsylvania Press, 1985), 9.

11. Samuel Hill, ed., *Religion in the Southern United States* (Macon, Ga.: Mercer University Press, 1983), 396. See also Hill, *Southern Churches in Crisis* (New York: Holt, Rinehart, and Winston, 1966), 20–39, for more on the unique nature of southern Protestantism.

12. Recorded at the Bethel Baptist Church, Brooklyn, N.Y., 9/28/85.

13. Recorded in Hartford, Conn., 3/17/90.

14. Recorded at St. Anthony Baptist Church, Brooklyn, N.Y., 9/24/88.

15. Recorded at the Triplex Theatre, New York City, 11/11/88.

16. Recorded at LaGree Baptist Church, Harlem, N.Y., 9/21/85.

17. Recorded at Restoration Plaza, Brooklyn, N.Y., 6/27/86.

18. Personal interview with Earl Ledbetter, 9/6/86.

19. Anthony Heilbut, *The Gospel Sound* (New York: Limelight Editions, 1985), xx.

20. Morton Marks, "You Can't Sing Unless You're Saved: Reliving the Call in Gospel Music," in *American Religious Groups and Beliefs*, ed. Simon Ottenberg (Cupertino, Cal.: Folklore Institute, 1982), 326.

21. Ibid., 328–29.

22. Glenn Hinson, "When the Words Roll and the Fire Flow: Spirit, Style, and Experience in African-American Gospel Performance" (Ph.D. diss., University of Pennsylvania, 1989), 331–34. Hinson also notes that references to the South are common during performances by Philadelphia groups.

23. Daniel Patterson, " 'Going Up to Meet Him': Songs and Ceremonies of a Black Family's Ascent," in *Diversities of Gifts*, ed. Ruel Tyson, James Peacock, and Daniel Patterson (Urbana: University of Illinois Press, 1988), 99.

24. Brenda McCallum alludes to this point in her work with early Birmingham quartets: "Birmingham's quartet singers kept alive a continuity with the religious traditions of the rural South; their music was a resource of their faith, and helped fulfill their needs for spiritual solace in a time of social stress." See Brenda Mc-Callum, "Songs of Work and Songs of Worship: Sanctified Black Unionism in the Southern City of Steel," *New York Folklore* 14 (1988): 18.

25. Melvin Williams argues that, through southern-derived church worship, the African-American Pentecostals he studied in Pittsburgh were able to "reestablish their lost values and recast their most precious symbols into a system of communication and solidarity." See Williams, *Community in a Black Pentecostal Church* (Pittsburgh: University of Pittsburgh Press, 1974), 142. See also Arthur

Paris, *Black Pentecostalism* (Amherst: University of Massachusetts Press, 1982), 25–27; and Franklin Frazier, *The Negro Church in America* (New York: Schocken Books, 1966).

26. Ralph Linton, "Nativistic Movements," *American Anthropologist* 45 (1943): 233. See also Anthony Wallace, "Revitalization Movements," *American Anthropologist* 58 (1956): 264–81.

27. For more on the role of the black church in the struggle for liberation and social equality, see Albert Raboteau, *Slave Religion* (New York: Oxford University Press, 1978), 289–318; James Cone, *A Black Theology of Liberation* (New York: Lippincott, 1970); and Gayraud Wilmore, *Black Religion and Black Radicalism* (Maryknoll, N.Y.: Orbis Books, 1984), especially 220–41. The use of sacred black music as an agent of social/political change is discussed in James Cone, *The Spirituals and the Blues* (New York: Seabury Press, 1972); and in Wyatt Tee Walker, *Somebody's Calling My Name* (Valley Forge: Judson Press, 1979).

Texts

Language and the Making

of American Place

I think I could write a poem to be called "Concord." For argument I should have the River, the Woods, the Ponds, the Hills, the Fields, the Swamps and Meadows, the Streets and Buildings, and the Villagers. Then Morning, Noon, and Evening, Spring, Summer, Autumn, and Winter, Night, Indian Summer, and the Mountains in the Horizon. – Henry David Thoreau, Journal, *4 September 1841* [1]

Thoreau's Journal*: The Creation of a Sacred Place*

DON SCHEESE

According to literary historian Frederick Turner, "Until Henry David Thoreau in the middle of the nineteenth century, America had no great literature of place or scarcely even the beginnings of such a tradition." [2] This claim, though useful as a starting point in discussing Thoreau's contribution to the literature of place, and hence to the role of place in American culture generally, requires some clarification. Considering the writings of, for example, William Bartram and J. Hector St. John de Crèvecoeur, both of whom preceded Thoreau with important place-centered works, it is more accurate to state that until Thoreau there had been no one who made it a vocation to write in behalf of the *inhabitation and exploration of a wild place*. Between 1773 and 1777, Bartram journeyed through and rhapsodized over the great southern wilderness from the Carolinas to the mouth of the Mississippi River; in the 1770s, Crèvecoeur homesteaded in lower New York state and celebrated his pastoral (rather than wild) setting.[3] By contrast, Thoreau was the first writer to make a conscious effort to explore and insist on the necessity of wildness *at home*. In fact, as the *genius loci* of Concord, Thoreau is without question the most doggedly lococentric writer in American letters. This is precisely his contribution to the literature of place and to nature writing.

Since American studies and the English profession have devoted little attention to the genre of nature writing, a few explanatory remarks are in order.[4] In its ideal form, nature writing melds autobiography, ecological field observation, environmental history, and a land ethic.[5] Attachment to place is a key characteristic of the genre. Based on this tendency, most nature writing can be broadly categorized as travel or inhabitation literature—either as writing which describes a journey through a landscape or region or as writing which describes residence in a particular place. I focus here on inhabiters. From Gilbert White's *The Natural History of Selbourne* to Annie Dillard's *Pilgrim at Tinker Creek*, many nature writers have devoted significant portions of their lives to living in, studying, and writing about a locale they have chosen to call home.

Inhabiters in effect create a place. They do so by celebrating it in the original sense of the term: they frequent it, they become familiar with a place by participating in its natural and human events.[6] Why such devotion to a particular place? Yi-Fu Tuan offers a useful explanation by way of his term "topophilia," which he defines as "a feeling one has toward a place because it is home, the locus of memories, and the means of getting a livelihood."[7] Inhabiters such as Thoreau make it their vocation to live with a heightened awareness of their natural, cultural, and historical surroundings.

A related term of importance in explaining the meaning of inhabiting is Martin Heidegger's "dwelling": "taking care of and creating that space within which something comes into its own and flourishes. Dwelling is primarily saving, in the older sense of setting something free to become itself, what essentially is. . . . Dwelling is that which cares for things so that they essentially presence and come into their own. . . ."[8] In other words, so intensely do inhabiters frequent a place that they come to cherish it. This feeling then promotes in them a desire to save, to preserve, it. *A* place becomes *the* place: sacred place. The inhabiter becomes a preservationist, meaning one who seeks to keep things as they are.

This inherently entails the preservation of some degree of wildness. The idea of retaining the sense of things the way they existed prior to significant alteration of the natural order develops in the mind of the inhabiter as a key concern. Defining the "natural order" of a place is of course problematic and to some extent arbitrary. But, generally, nature writers hold to the belief that widespread land abuse did not occur in the New World until the advent of Anglo-American settlement.[9] Having witnessed and studied land abuse and its consequences, they seek to restore and preserve the dynamic balance of nature.[10] Inhabiters do so by offering their own lives as a paradigm of how to live on the land.

Walden is typically regarded as an (if not *the*) exemplary work of inhabitation literature.[11] But I choose instead to focus on Thoreau's fourteen-volume Journal, in which he wrote almost daily from 1837 until his death in 1862 and from which he quarried material to produce his published works. Recent scholarship has made a strong case for the Journal itself as Thoreau's great life's work and the most impressive documentation of his credo to be "a world traveler in Concord."[12] As the epigraph of this essay suggests, Thoreau desired to study *all* aspects of his life in and around his home. Throughout each year he passionately recorded data in his Journal, both objective and subjective, natural and cultural, in an attempt to compile a "Kalendar" of Concord.[13]

What follows is an explication of a portion of the Journal. I analyze and put into context Thoreau's attempt to record the natural and cultural significance of a series of discoveries he makes in what might be called the "psychic wilderness" of the nineteenth-century landscape of Massachusetts. It was part of his lifelong effort to create a sacred place, to compose "a poem . . . called 'Concord.'"

ON 30 August 1856, Henry David Thoreau was uncharacteristically indecisive over the direction his daily walk should take. Perhaps it was the weather—an unusually heavy rainfall for a New England summer, he reported at the beginning of the day's journal entry. Yet Thoreau walked in all sorts of conditions and at any time of day or night. In 1851, he took long nocturnal walks to observe moonlit landscapes; at other times he waded naked (but for a hat) in the Concord River on what he called "fluvial walks"; and he caught the cold that ultimately led to his death when examining tree stumps in a recently logged woodlot on a bitterly cold day in December 1860.[14]

So it is unlikely that inclement weather contributed to Thoreau's uncertainty. Nor was it the periodic bouts of illness that occasionally detracted from the spirit of his walks or forced him to remain sedentary for weeks at a time; the Journal for 1856–1857 records few if any health problems. Early in the entry he announces that his destination will be Beck Stow's Swamp, about a mile northeast of Concord. His apparent purpose is to study a small species of cranberry, "which Emerson [George Emerson, a nineteenth-century naturalist] says is the common cranberry of the north of Europe" (9:35).[15] But his resolution quickly dissipates. His quest seems to him futile and unprofitable.

Suddenly Thoreau recovers his resolve. He convinces himself that, in spite of one more visit to a familiar destination, something can be salvaged, some information can be gathered, some moral can be learned, to redeem the experience. Such oscillation in mood from doubt to hopeful certainty is characteristic of Thoreau. He typically transforms adversity into victory, vacillation into resolution. A statement which frequently recurs in the Journal—so frequently it might be considered a refrain—is the truism "It is an ill wind that bodes no one any good."[16]

It is the transcendent possibilities of place that lure Thoreau out-of-doors. His walks follow an archetypal pattern in literature in general and nature writing in particular, what Joseph Campbell in *The Hero with a Thousand Faces* describes as Separation, Transformation, and Return.[17] The excursion to Beck Stow's Swamp traces a transit from society to the wild, where Thoreau experiences a multifaceted spiritual Transformation, followed by a Return to Concord. His daily walk is a kind of vision quest and is his mode of self-culture.

Thoreau also experiences therapeutic value in exploring a wild place. He effects a Separation from society in part because he hopes to put out of his mind some sordid contemporary affairs: the debate over slavery. "For only absorbing employment . . . drives Kansas out of your head, and actually and permanently occupies the only desirable and free Kansas against all border ruffians" (9:36), Thoreau writes. He goes to nature to create another border of sorts, a physical and mental buffer zone between himself and the quiet and unquiet desperation of society.

Thoreau seeks Separation for yet another reason. He embarks on daily walks because he is alienated in a more personal sense. Here he takes great pride in being unconcerned with pecuniary profit while pursuing his vocation of poet-naturalist. He feels richer wading in the swamp with his pockets full of inedible cranberries, "treading on wonders at every step, than any farmer going to market with a hundred bushels which he has raked, or hired to be raked" (9:40). The value of the cranberries in his pockets lies in their *apparent* unprofitability. Repulsed by what he described in *Walden* as the "restless, nervous, bustling, trivial Nineteenth Century,"[18] Thoreau is prompted to moralize: "Let not your life be wholly without an object, though it be only to ascertain the flavor of a cranberry . . ." (9:37).

Now, part of Thoreau's smugness and self-defensiveness is attributable to his attitudinizing, his heroic self-concept in reaction to the alienation he felt while living in Concord. After all, this was a man who was ridiculed by his fellow townspeople for failing to find a steady occupation and who was vilified as "the woodsburner" for accidentally setting fire to several hundred acres of local forest.[19] I devote some attention to this posturing on Thoreau's part because it is representative of a pattern often found in nature writing. Because they are alienated, inhabiters and travelers often separate themselves from society and seek transcendence in the natural world. The contrast between the despair of the nature writer in civilization and his or her elation when experiencing Transformation in the wild is striking.[20]

Thoreau wades barefoot through the clammy waters of the swamp for nearly an hour, ignoring the American species of cranberry already harvested and bagged. In a peculiar reversal the ordinarily nationalistic Thoreau prefers the European species because the latter demands a careful eye if it is to be detected. His preference for obscure things is characteristic, and it demonstrates his attention to the particulars of place. Thoreau was fond of quoting Linnaeus on these occasions: "In minimis Natura praestat" (Nature excels in the least things).

His discovery of the cranberry's otherwise overlooked value and the attendant wonders of the swamp results in a remarkable realization. Thoreau feels effectively isolated from society, which enables him to achieve solitude and Transformation but a short distance from town. "What's the need of visiting far-off mountains and bogs," he asks, "if a half-hour's walk will carry me into such wildness and novelty? . . . Is [Nature] not as primitive and vigorous here as anywhere?" (9:42) He goes on to claim: "I see that all is not garden and cultivated field and crops, that there are square rods in Middlesex County as purely primitive and wild as they were a thousand years ago, which have escaped the plow and the axe and the scythe and the cranberry-rake, *little oases of wildness in the desert of our civilization*" (9:44; emphasis mine).

This realization marks a historic moment in the development of nature writing and American culture. Thoreau was among the first writers to seek and praise wildness as a necessary complement to civilization. According to environmental historians, we can trace the creation of national parks—one of America's great contributions to world culture—to Thoreau's calls for wilderness preservation.[21] In *A Week on the Concord and Merrimack Rivers* he declares, "There is in my nature, methinks, a singular yearning toward all wildness." In *Walden* he expands his frame of reference, arguing, "Our village life would stagnate if it were not for the unexplored forests and meadows which surround it. We need the tonic of wildness. . . ." And in "Walking," generally regarded as his manifesto for wilderness preservation, he issues his now-famous proclamation: "In Wildness is the preservation of the World."[22]

The significance of the above Journal passage is that Thoreau now has come to associate wildness with a particular place—in this case, Beck Stow's Swamp. His unique achievement is to point out that wildness can be found almost anywhere; one need not venture to far-off lands in order to find "true" wilderness or, alternately, despair over its absence. He discovers and is nurtured by wildness in plots of land only 16.5 feet square—and in spite of the fact that such plots have already been "civilized" by commercial cranberrying![23]

Thoreau's Transformation, then, involves recreation—or, as he might have said in his day, *re-creation*.[24] In his own imaginative version of nineteenth-century homesteading Thoreau seeks to be at home, to be in place; he seeks, in contrast to the typical pioneer, to live *with* rather than *against* the land. In gaining the satisfaction of coexisting with nature he realizes spiritual renewal.

Transformation also entails a way of seeing the world from a different angle of vision. In his Journal Thoreau writes that "there is no such thing as pure *objective* observation. Your observation, to be interesting, *i.e.* to be significant, must be *subjective*" (6:236–37). As H. Daniel Peck observes in a recent study, this matter of perception was an issue "of deep perplexity to the nineteenth-century romantic mind."[25] Always self-conscious of examining the Not-Me, Thoreau comes to the realization as he wades in the swamp that one cannot find wildness *without* unless it exists *within.* Ralph Waldo Emerson writes in *Nature* that "particular natural facts are symbols of particular spiritual facts."[26] Here Thoreau reverses the theory of correspondence. "It is vain to dream of a wildness distant from ourselves," he writes. "There is none such. It is the bog in our brain and bowels, the primitive vigor of Nature in us, that inspires that dream. I shall never find in the wilds of Labrador any greater wildness than in some recess in Concord, *i.e.,* than I import into it" (9:43). By exploring the undiscovered country of the self Thoreau transforms the local countryside into *terra incognita.* "Is not our own interior white on the chart?" he asks in *Walden.*[27] He demonstrates that for the nature writer what takes place in mental or verbal space is as important as what occurs in physical space. There is a profound connection between place and perception.

Concord's long history of human settlement by both American Indians and Anglo-Americans would seem to undermine Thoreau's assertion of the land's wildness. But it did not. Ordinarily Thoreau delighted in immersing himself in the historical geography of a place (*A Week on the Concord and Merrimack Rivers* is a good example of his interest in this discipline).[28] An unusual feature of the swamp is its apparent lack of human history. "Has any white man ever settled on it?" he asks. "Does any now frequent it? Not even the Indian comes here now" (9:42). Ignoring the fact that the swamp is the site of commercial cranberrying, Thoreau declares that no vestiges of culture remain. Not even the projectile points he was known to find in the "arrowheadiferous" soil around Concord are present. To chronicle the swamp's past is thus truly to write a *natural* history.

This further realization and Transformation are followed by an explanation of Thoreau's attachment to the local landscape. He may have often denigrated the townspeople of Concord for their provinciality and narrow-mindedness. Yet the irony is that he is the provincial *par excellence.* He praises his locale for its proximity to both culture and nature. While wading in the swamp he feels as if he were in an Arctic bog, and the sense of remoteness he derives near home saves him the trouble of venturing to the

Far North. He boasts that "I could be in Rupert's land and supping at home within the hour! This beats the railroad" (9:43). Thoreau's imagina- tin annihilates time and distance. As a result, *a place* is transformed into *other places*.

Near the conclusion of the Journal passage under consideration, Thoreau comes to reverence the swamp. Like Rupert's land, it is forsaken country. Like the small inedible cranberries he favors, the very fact of its neglect transforms it into something sacred. Perhaps as he waded in the swamp Thoreau had in mind a lecture entitled "The Wild" he had delivered five years earlier. "When I would recreate myself," he said then, "I seek the darkest wood, the thickest and most interminable and, to the citizen, most dismal swamp. I enter a swamp as a sacred place, a *sanctum sanctorum*."[29] Beck Stow's Swamp, where there exists "terrene, titanic matter" (9:45), thus becomes a place of worship. "Titanic" was a word of great resonance for Thoreau, one he chose to use sparingly. It appears in "Ktaadn" in tell- ing of the awe he felt while attempting to climb Maine's tallest mountain. The fact that he employs it here suggests the powerful feelings the swamp evokes in him.[30]

The explorers Martin Frobisher and John Charles Frémont (whom Tho- reau mentions frequently in his writings) busied themselves in search of the marvelous. Thoreau's aim, following Emerson's dictum in *Nature*, was to find the marvelous in the commonplace.[31] In doing so he created for himself a place of pilgrimage where he could continually reenact his vocation of inhabiter. "When we are lifted out of the slime and film of our habitual life, we see the whole globe to be an aerolite [meteor], and reverence it as such, and make pilgrimages to it . . ." (9:45). Little did he realize that his modest surroundings would become a sacred place in American culture, a Mecca luring over 400,000 pilgrims annually.[32]

Thoreau concludes the excursion by a Return to Concord, as was his custom, writing up the experience in his Journal the following morning. The remainder of his life he made further trips to the swamp and of course to other "little oases of wildness" about the countryside.

I WISH to conclude with some observations about current trends in schol- arship within the discipline of American studies. A search of the table of contents of the last decade of *American Quarterly*, the leading journal in our field, reveals that we have shifted attention from nature to other topics.

The result is that the discipline of environmental history has in effect co-opted American studies. Articles such as Roderick Nash's "The American Invention of National Parks," which once regularly appeared in *AQ*, are now published in journals such as *Environmental Review* and *Forest & Conservation History*.[33] In part this trend represents the rightful rejection of early "classic" works of American studies for their monolithic interpretation of America's complex and diverse relationships with the land. Indeed, the very titles of some of these works—*The American Adam, Virgin Land, Nature and the American, Wilderness and the American Mind*—belie the heterogeneity of our national experience.[34]

But as nature writing continues to grow in popularity and as our ecological crisis worsens, we would do well to reconsider as a subject of inquiry the fundamental relationship between nature and culture, the profound connections between people and place. I suggest that nature writing is worthy of serious discussion by scholars in American studies. For nature writers both oppose and affirm essential American myths and values. They question the very basis of the American dream because they feel that the work ethic has often flourished at the expense of a land ethic. But they also speak for values that are—or at least used to be—majoritarian: self-reliance, rugged individualism, a life lived in close contact with the land. As secular prophets in the modern religion of environmentalism, nature writers are important to the study of American culture—and all cultures—because they have recognized and preach an essential truth: that to remain viable and vibrant a society must not undermine its natural foundation. They are radical conservatives calling for the preservation of our cultural roots.

NOTES

1. Henry David Thoreau, *The Journal of Henry David Thoreau*, ed. Bradford Torrey and Francis H. Allen, intro. by Walter Harding, 14 vols. (1906; Salt Lake City: Gibbs M. Smith, 1984) 1:282. Future references to the *Journal* are to this edition and appear parenthetically in the text.

2. Frederick Turner, "Literature Lost in the Thickets," *New York Times Book Review* 15 February 1987: 1. See also Turner, *Spirit of Place: The Making of an American Literary Landscape* (San Francisco: Sierra Club Books, 1989), which includes a chapter on *Walden* and *The Maine Woods*.

3. William Bartram, *The Travels of William Bartram: Naturalist's Edition*, ed. Francis Harper (1791; New Haven: Yale University Press, 1958). J. Hector St. John de Crèvecoeur, *Letters from an American Farmer and Sketches of 18th-Century America*, ed. Albert E. Stone (1782; New York: Penguin, 1981). Two good recent discussions of the pastoral theme in American literature are Leo Marx, "Pastoralism in America," in *Ideology and Classic American Literature*, ed. Sacvan Bercovitch and Myra Jehlen (Cambridge, Eng.: Cambridge University Press, 1986), 36–69; and Lawrence Buell, "American Pastoral Ideology Reappraised," *American Literary History* 1 (1989): 1–29.

4. To illustrate the popularity of nature writing and its neglect by the academy, consider that within the last decade a dozen anthologies of the genre have appeared—but no MLA divisions on nature writing or articles in the leading journals such as *PMLA, American Literature*, or *American Quarterly*. The Modern Language Association has published *Teaching Environmental Literature: Materials, Methods, Resources*, ed. Frederick O. Wagge (New York: Modern Language Association of America, 1985). A hopeful sign of the genre's "canonization" is the appearance of *The Norton Book of Nature Writing*, ed. Robert Finch and John Elder (New York: W. W. Norton, 1990).

5. Few definitions of the genre exist. See Philip Marshall Hicks, *The Development of the Natural History Essay in American Literature* (Philadelphia: University of Pennsylvania Press, 1924); Joseph Wood Krutch, introduction to *The Best Nature Writing of Joseph Wood Krutch* (New York: William Morrow, 1969), 13–27; Ann Ronald, introduction to *Words for the Wild: The Sierra Club Trailside Reader* (San Francisco: Sierra Club Books, 1987), xi–xviii; Thomas J. Lyon, introduction to *This Incomperable Lande: A Book of American Nature Writing* (Boston: Houghton Mifflin, 1989), 3–91; and Don Scheese, "Nature Writing: A Wilderness of Books," *Forest & Conservation History* 34 (1990): 204–8.

6. For a useful discussion of the term "celebrate," see Robert Finch, "The Once and Future Cape," *Orion Nature Quarterly* 7 (1988): 24–28.

7. Yi-Fu Tuan, *Topophilia: A Study of Environmental Perception, Attitudes, and Values* (Englewood Cliffs, N.J.: Prentice-Hall, 1974), 93.

8. Martin Heidegger, quoted in *Deep Ecology: Living As If Nature Mattered*, ed. Bill Devall and George Sessions (Salt Lake City: Peregrine Smith, 1985), 98–99. Also valuable to my understanding of place is Sherman Paul, "Thinking with Thoreau," *Thoreau Quarterly* 14 (1982): 18–25, and "From Here/Now: Mostly on Place," *Witness* 3 (1989): 107–15.

9. This belief is confirmed by environmental historians today. See, for example, William Cronon, *Changes in the Land: Indians, Colonists, and the Ecology of New England* (New York: Hill and Wang, 1983).

10. The term "dynamic balance" reflects the current view of ecologists who have rejected previous notions of nature as a steady-state or climax community.

11. See, for example, Lawrence Buell, "The Thoreauvian Pilgrimage: The Structure of an American Cult," *American Literature* 61 (1989): 175–99.

12. Recent studies which focus primarily or significantly on the Journal are William Howarth, *The Book of Concord: Thoreau's Life as a Writer* (New York: Penguin, 1983); Sharon Cameron, *Writing Nature: Henry Thoreau's Journal* (New York: Oxford University Press, 1985); Joan Burbick, *Thoreau's Alternative History: Changing Perspectives on Nature, Culture, and Language* (Philadelphia: University of Pennsylvania Press, 1987); and H. Daniel Peck, *Thoreau's Morning Work: Memory and Perception in "A Week on the Concord and Merrimack Rivers," the Journal, and "Walden"* (New Haven: Yale University Press, 1990). In 1859, Thoreau advised a correspondent to "live at home like a traveller." See *The Correspondence of Henry David Thoreau*, ed. Walter Harding and Carl Bode (New York: New York University Press, 1958), 538. John Aldrich Christie treats this theme in *Thoreau as World Traveler* (New York: Columbia University Press, 1965).

13. The term "Kalendar" derives from Sherman Paul, *The Shores of America: Thoreau's Inward Exploration* (Urbana: University of Illinois Press, 1958), 394–400. See also Peck, *Thoreau's Morning Work*, 47–48, 173.

14. On Thoreau's nocturnal walks, see Walter Harding, introduction to *The Journal of Henry David Thoreau*, 2:vii, and the *Journal*, 2:234–39, 2:248–61. On Thoreau's "fluvial walks," see Harding, introduction to the *Journal*, 4:vi, and the *Journal*, 4:211–15, 3:7–9, and 4:320–21. On the facts surrounding the events leading up to Thoreau's death, see Walter Harding, *The Days of Henry Thoreau* (New York: Dover, 1982), 441.

15. Donald Worster in *Nature's Economy: A History of Ecological Ideas* (Cambridge: Cambridge University Press, 1977) calls Emerson's work "one of the neglected delights of nineteenth-century natural history" (68–70).

16. The continual shifts in mood recorded in the Journal have led to conflicting interpretations. Sherman Paul was the first to argue that in the post-Walden years Thoreau suffered a spiritual declension (*Shores*, 256, 260, 274, 395–96). Harding in the standard biography of Thoreau emphasizes his optimism. Most recently, Frederick Garber in *Thoreau's Fable of Inscribing* (Princeton: Princeton University Press, 1991) holds that someone so self-conscious and self-questioning as Thoreau could never truly feel at home.

17. Joseph Campbell, *The Hero with a Thousand Faces* (Princeton: Princeton University Press, 1949). Lyon comments in *This Incomperable Lande* on the "ubiquity" of this pattern in nature writing generally (477).

18. Henry David Thoreau, *The Illustrated "Walden,"* ed. J. Lyndon Shanley (Princeton: Princeton University Press, 1971), 329.

19. Harding, *The Days*, 160–62. For a good discussion of Thoreau's alienation from Concord, see Leon Edel, *Stuff of Sleep and Dreams: Experiments in Literary Psychology* (New York: Harper and Row, 1982), 47–65.

20. A representative modern example of a nature writer retreating to the wilderness to escape what he calls "syphilization" is Edward Abbey, *Desert Solitaire: A Season in the Wilderness* (New York: Simon and Schuster, 1968).

21. See, for example, Hans Huth, *Nature and the American: Three Centuries of Changing Attitudes* (1957; Lincoln: University of Nebraska Press, 1972), 91–100; and Roderick Nash, *Wilderness and the American Mind*, 3rd ed. (1967; New Haven: Yale University Press, 1982), 84–95. Perhaps the earliest call for wilderness preservation came in 1832 when the artist George Catlin in a newspaper article called for "a *Nation's Park*" in the Great Plains to preserve the resident Indian tribes and the bison upon which their culture depended so heavily. See Nash, *Wilderness*, 100–101. Thoreau made his call for preservation in "Chesuncook" of *The Maine Woods*, first published in the *Atlantic Monthly* in 1858, when he wrote: "Why should not we, who have renounced the king's authority, have our national preserves, where no villages need be destroyed, in which the bear and panther, and some even of the hunter race, may still exist, and not be 'civilized off the face of the earth'. . . ?" (*The Maine Woods*, ed. Joseph J. Moldenhauer [Princeton: Princeton University Press, 1970], 156). Thoreau appeared to arrive at his call for preservation independently, for, according to Robert Sattelmeyer in *Thoreau's Reading: A Study in Intellectual History* (Princeton: Princeton University Press, 1988), he did not read Catlin's *Letters and Notes on the Manners, Customs, and Conditions of the North American Indians Written during Eight Years' Travel amongst the Wildest Tribes of North America* (first published as a book in 1841).

22. Henry David Thoreau, *The Illustrated "A Week on the Concord and Merrimack Rivers,"* ed. Carl F. Hovde, William L. Howarth, and Elizabeth Hall Witherell (Princeton: Princeton University Press, 1980), 54; *The Illustrated "Walden,"* 317; and "Walking," in *The Natural History Essays*, ed. Robert Sattelmeyer (Salt Lake City: Peregrine Smith, 1980), 112.

23. A contemporary writer who has made the exploration of wildness in one's backyard in New England the theme of his work is John Hanson Mitchell, *Ceremonial Time: Fifteen Thousand Years on One Square Mile* (New York: Doubleday, 1984), and *Living at the End of Time* (Boston: Houghton Mifflin, 1990).

24. See the conclusion of "Chesuncook," 156.

25. Peck, *Thoreau's Morning Work*, 104.

26. Ralph Waldo Emerson, *Emerson's "Nature": Origin, Growth, Meaning*, ed.

Merton M. Sealts, Jr., and Alfred R. Ferguson, 2nd ed. (Carbondale: University of Southern Illinois Press, 1979), 15. The best study of Emerson's theory of correspondence is Sherman Paul, *Emerson's Angle of Vision: Man and Nature in American Experience* (Cambridge: Harvard University Press, 1952).

27. *Walden*, 321.

28. Paul comments on Thoreau's interest in what is now called historical geography in *Shores*, 229–30.

29. The lecture "The Wild" was later combined with another entitled "Walking," and an essay by the latter title was published posthumously in the *Atlantic Monthly* in 1862. See Harding, *The Days*, 315, 469. The quotation from "Walking" is taken from *The Natural History Essays*, 116.

30. See "Ktaadn," in which Thoreau writes of the terrain near the summit as "vast, Titanic, and such as man never inhabits" (*The Maine Woods*, 64).

31. *Emerson's "Nature,"* 35.

32. *New York Times* 29 November 1987.

33. Roderick Nash, "The American Invention of National Parks," *American Quarterly* 22 (1970): 726–35.

34. R. W. B. Lewis, *The American Adam: Innocence, Tragedy, and Tradition in the Nineteenth Century* (Chicago: University of Chicago Press, 1955); Henry Nash Smith, *Virgin Land: The American West as Symbol and Myth* (1950; Cambridge: Harvard University Press, 1970); Huth, *Nature and the American*; and Nash, *Wilderness and the American Mind*. For telling critiques of some of these studies, see Bruce Kuklick, "Myth and Symbol in American Studies," *American Quarterly* 24 (1972): 435–50; and R. Gordon Kelly, "Literature and the Historian," *American Quarterly* 26 (1974): 141–59.

Language
is not a vague province. There is a poetry
of the movements of cost, known or unknown
– Paterson *(III.i.109)*[1]

Possessing America: William Carlos Williams's Paterson *and the Poetics of Appropriation*

KINERETH MEYER

"I felt from earliest childhood," wrote William Carlos Williams in 1939, "that America was the only home I could possibly call my own. I felt that it was expressly founded for me, personally, and that it must be my first business in life to possess it, that only by making it my own from the beginning to my own day, in detail, should I ever have a basis for knowing where I stood." Williams's desire to make possessing America his "first business" may be read as deriving from Ralph Waldo Emerson's claim that the poet is the "true land-lord! sea-lord! air-lord!" of the landscape, the rightful "owner" of "that wherein others are only tenants and boarders."[2] As the language of commodity and acquisition throughout Emerson's writings suggests, he was advocating more than self-reliance; he was also advocating economic self-interest. Thus, Myra Jehlen has recently characterized the self-reliant American individualist as both "Capitalist and Poet": insisting on the purely figurative nature of his possession of the American landscape, the American individualist also believes that "a man's value manifests itself in material possession."[3]

In this context, Williams, intending to possess America, reads America's "primal scene"—"Columbus arriving on an unknown shore"[4]—as a primal geography to be recovered and reclaimed. Although this desire to set up an economy of repossession can be traced throughout his work, his long poem *Paterson* suggests the inevitable belatedness of such a poetics of appropriation with particular force. Like other American texts, *Paterson* attempts to recover the priority of discovery; it is, however, a coming after which both marks the landscape for proprietorship and fails in the attempt. Belatedness functions spatially, as well as temporally, in *Paterson*, as a distance to be overcome, as well as a time lapse to be filled. Williams's appropriation of a city in New Jersey (name, geography, and history) as the title for his poem is a synecdoche of the kind of "spatial belatedness" enacted by the poem. Like Walt Whitman in *Song of Myself*, Paterson (man and city) is both center and periphery, the whole and its segmentation. However, whereas the language of Whitman ("one of that centripetal and centrifugal gang") sustains center and periphery in a mutually supportive tension or balance, the language of *Paterson* both seeks a center and questions the viability of that center.[5] In contrast to Whitman's project in *Song of Myself*, Williams's effort to overcome distance through the establishment of the self as center is qualified, not sustained, by the accretion and incursion of physical and historical particulars.

In eighteenth- and nineteenth-century American texts, the desire to overcome belatedness through a kind of verbal control closely parallels the expansionist push of Euro-American settlement; writers sought to possess figuratively the land that new settlers sought to possess materially. The Puritans zoned and mapped out the landscape just as they mapped out everything from the cosmos to their own souls: the town was designated the place of social order and control; the unchartable forest, the dwelling place of Satan. Translating Emersonian self-sufficiency into "real" estate, squatter

Thoreau claimed in *Walden*, "Wherever I sat, there I might live, and the landscape radiated from me accordingly."

As Williams's declaration of his "first business" indicates, twentieth-century writers continue in this acquisitive mode. At the same time, however, increasingly sensitive to the complexities of representation on the one hand, and to the social, political, and environmental abuses of imposed settlement on the other, their writing struggles with its ability to "own" meaning.[6] In terms of American literary history, this struggle elicits repeated (failed) attempts to re-evoke a "virgin" (unrepresented) land as yet unpossessed by the artist, thus highlighting the inherent sexual dimension of possession. Although this struggle does not always overtly draw on the kind of macho hype which typified the rhetoric of Manifest Destiny and other expansionist movements, it enacts a desire for landscape as both whore and virgin—the eternally possessible and the eternally unpossessed.[7]

The following essay suggests that *Paterson* enacts this struggle between possession and nonpossession by involving the reader in a general problematics of representation. *Paterson* grapples not only with the belatedness of a twentieth-century effort to repossess the already named and possessed landscape, but with what is conceived of as an inevitable belatedness of word to thing. Throughout the poem, Williams tests the sufficiency of language; like Emerson's American Scholar, Williams/Paterson "stammers in his speech," not because as an American, he has something new to say, but because he questions the adequacy of saying. "The / language stutters," he says in book I (I.ii.22). Echoing Wallace Stevens, Williams questions the ability of language to ever achieve "that radiance / quartered apart, / unapproached by symbols" (III.i.10B). Because of the insufficiency of the word, the poet can only gain what Williams calls a "partial victory": "So you think because the rose / is red that you shall have the mastery?" (I.iii.30) he queries, mocking his own representational activity (and that of the countless poets who have written rose poems). The much-quoted exhortatory refrain "no ideas but in things" similarly (and paradoxically) insists on the need to remove the veil of verbal mediation in order to represent the "virgin" land.

Johannes Fabian's recent comments on the nature and function of current anthropological writing bear wide implications for theories of literary representation in general and for the representation of the American landscape in particular. In discussing the ways in which ethnographic studies relate to the Other, Fabian distinguishes between "representation*s*" as "entities, products of knowledge or culture" and "representation" as praxis or transformation. According to Fabian, representation*s* derive from a "hegemonic," or "imperial" epistemology (we know the Other by mirroring or reproducing it); representation from a "processual," "productive," and "performative" epistemology (we know the other by transforming, fashioning, and creating it).[8]

Like Walter Ong and Michel Foucault, Fabian examines representation within a "context of power," a particularly apt consideration in any discussion of an American poet's relation to the landscape. My reading of *Paterson* suggests that by pointing to, and thus "possessing," historical, geographical, and material referents, the language of the poem performs, rather than merely thematizes, the interaction in American literature between aesthetics and an ideology of power.[9] At the same time, by blocking the recovery or appropriation of these same referents, this language forces the reader to question those assumptions which posit the power of language to "own" reality. *Paterson*, in other words, enacts a struggle between the nominal and verbal senses of "representation": the poem attempts to make language "fit" the landscape and, concurrently, performs and dramatically communicates the (belated) *activity* of re-presentation.

In the "Author's Note" accompanying the poem, Williams states that his goal was "to find an image large enough to embody the whole knowable world about me. The longer I lived in my place, among the details of my life, I realized that these isolated observations and experiences needed pulling together to gain 'profundity.' I already had the river" (iii). The poet's words here indicate that he has apparently already begun to implement his plan to embody the whole "knowable" (that is, capable of being mastered, possessed) world: "I already *had* the river," he says (my emphasis). The words Williams chooses to describe this possessing or "having" are significant: *Paterson* is not only an "embodiment"; it is a "pulling together," or, as he says at the beginning of book I, a "gathering up," a "taking up of slack," "by multiplication a reduction to one." However, while the poem may be seen as a twentieth-century transformation of the Emersonian impulse to find the "one" by subsuming the whole of the knowable world into the "I," it also suggests a postmodern explosion of stasis and univocality. *Paterson*, Williams continues, is a "celebration" of multiplicity, a carnival of possibility and change which strongly qualifies the canonizing force of poetic appropriation: *Paterson*, writes Williams, is "a dispersal and a meta-morphosis" (2).

In simultaneously "embodying" and "gathering up" the whole knowable world in its words, while at the same time "dispersing" the world in the for-ever unfinished act of representation, *Paterson* is a poem that struggles with its own discourse. Nowhere is this struggle more evident than in the poem's reshaping of the topography of Paterson, New Jersey, into human form:

> Paterson lies in the valley under the Passaic Falls
> its spent waters forming the outline of his back. He
> lies on his right side, head near the thunder
> of the waters filling his dreams!
>
> (I.i.6)

Paterson is the man as city, both past and present; his "wife" is the moun-tain, whose "head" is formed by Garret Mountain Park:

> And there, against him, stretches the low mountain.
> The Park's her head, carved, above the Falls, by the quiet
> river; Colored crystals the secret of those rocks;
> farms and ponds, laurel and the temperate wild cactus,
> yellow flowered . . facing him, his
> arm supporting her, by the *Valley of the Rocks*, asleep.
>
> (I.i.8)

Williams's search for a discourse of the local seems to demonstrate Leo Marx's astute observation that many of the central figures in American texts "tend . . . to connect the recovery of self with the recovery of nature, and to represent their deepest longings in numinous visions of landscape."[10] But Williams's recovery of the self through landscape takes him one step beyond representation—to the absorption of the landscape into the body. Human "ownership" of meaning has become human *as* meaning.[11] As cul-tural geographer Yi-Fu Tuan has convincingly argued, the attempt to un-derstand, or stabilize, the self by giving it topographical shape (and vice versa) has mythic analogues in a variety of cultures. In American texts, I would add, this shaping is informed by a history of territorial appropri-ation, thus preventing any "innocent" consideration of figurative bodily imposition, divorced from ideology. By subsuming the landscape into the human body, Williams attempts figuratively to do the same thing that the first settlers of Paterson did materially: shape the wild landscape in their own idealized image.[12]

In its failure to recover an Edenic state, *Paterson* may be seen as an American pastoral.[13] Jay Gatsby and Ike McCaslin are only two well-known examples of how, in American texts, any attempt to repudiate the responsibilities of history in order to recover the "fresh, green breast of the new world" will inevitably fail. If America's primal scene is Columbus arriving on an unknown shore, then the ethos reflected by American writers—Williams among them—can only be ambiguous: while they long to duplicate Columbus's discovery of an untouched (prelapsarian) land, they also relive the Fall of appropriation (both material and poetic) again and again.

Interestingly, Williams's only direct use of pastoral conventions in *Paterson* seems to be designed to overturn them. The *dramatis personae* he sets up in book IV—Dr. P. (Paterson as rejected swain?), Corydon, and Phyllis (two lesbians)—are apparently meant to show how modern urban life has turned an idyllic space into "this / swill-hole of corrupt cities." The simple, unlettered Phyllis is an especially acute instrument in this modernist recasting of the pastoral. In a letter to her father, she deflates Corydon's pastoral idealization of the landscape (in effect, a thinly veiled seduction):

> But she's a nut, of the worst kind. Today she was telling
> me about some rocks in the river here she calls her three
> sheep. If they're sheep I'm the Queen of England. They're
> white all right but it's from the gulls that crap them up
> all day long.
>
> (IV.i.152)

The pervasive pastoralism of the entire poem, however, undoes this more obvious overturning: *Paterson* seeks to recover the memory of prerepresentational innocence, of:

> A
> world lost,
>   a world unsuspected
>   beckons to new places
> and no whiteness (lost) is so white as the memory
> of whiteness   .
>
> (II.iii.78)

Although it is not structured according to the specific conventions of piping shepherds, peaceful flocks, and green swards, *Paterson* does set up an idealized or hallowed landscape as a contrast (retreat) from the pressures of modern urban life, particularly in book I. Like Theocritus, Williams/ Paterson is a city-dweller "yearning for greener pastures," and like the herdsman, he is a liminal figure, moving back and forth between nature and civilization.[14] As in the traditional pastoral (see, for example, Theocritus, *Idyll I*, or Virgil's *Eclogues*), the ugly, the bent, and the environmentally abused ("cylindrical trees / bent, forked by preconception and accident— / split, furrowed, creased, mottled, stained") are all subsumed into this sacred space, "into the body of the light!" while the Passaic River crashing "in a recoil of spray and rainbow mists" (I.i.6–7) evokes an almost biblical apotheosis. Moreover, the pronounced elegiac tone of some of the passages suggests that we may be looking at an elegy upon the death of American pastoral innocence; physical reminders of loss abound, making the poem a kind of American *Et in Arcadia Ego*.

Thus, while the words of *Paterson* may master and "possess" the scene by "embodying" it in known forms, at the same time they also test, explore, and perform the praxis of representation:

> Jostled as are the waters approaching
> the brink, his thoughts
> interlace, repel and cut under,
> rise rock-thwarted and turn aside
> but forever strain forward—or strike
> an eddy and whirl, marked by a
> leaf or curdy spume, seeming
> to forget
> Retake later the advance and
> are replaced by succeeding hordes
> pushing forward—they coalesce now
> glass-smooth with their swiftness,
> quiet or seem to quiet as at the close
> they leap to the conclusion and
> fall, fall in air!
>
> (I.i.7–8)

The pronoun "his" ("his thoughts") refers to Williams/Paterson in the *act* of representing. The strain of confronting the real and potential violence of the scene and the lack of closure resulting from wave after wave of clashing perceptions make it all but impossible for him to embody the knowable world in a completed image. Although in these words Williams seems to "have" the falls in the form of an implicit metaphor—fish (fertility, creativity?) blindly crowding and pushing ever forward toward their spawning grounds—the striking verbality of this and the following section also functions by undermining the stasis of figurative representation. Verbs such as "interlace," "repel," "cut under," "turn aside," "strain forward," "fall," "split apart," and "rebound" involve both Paterson and the reader in the dispersal and metamorphosis of the landscape.

Williams's attempts to read and interpret the landscape and, similarly, the reader's attempts to recover the poet's representation are "rock-thwarted." This is an interesting variation on what Marx has called the "interrupted idyll," an episode that recurs repeatedly in the American pastoral. According to Marx, the interrupted idyll is usually presented as a scene of serenity and joy which is suddenly interrupted by the machine or by some other token representation of modern technology. Here the raw power of the scene is more sublime than serene, but it is still interrupted, if not by the machine, then more remarkably, perhaps, by the very objects of the poet's perception. Moreover, just as the tumultuous words of the poem communicate the poet's inability to finally possess these objects, they also may block the *reader*'s recuperation of the objects of perception into a "whole": our responses do not coalesce into "meaning" (mastery), but rather clash and "cut under" in a kind of interpretive anarchy as they try to possess the already possessed (represented) landscape. Though our thoughts, like those of the poet, "strain forward" toward some ultimate mastery, these thoughts are "marked" both by absence and by an over-determined presence. On the one hand, gaps in the text of both landscape and poem ("wild cactus, / yellow flowered . ."; "seeming / to forget ") invite interpretive completion, a poetic remembering. On the other hand, these gaps prevent totalization by refusing to be filled or recalled. At the same time, "succeeding hordes" of verbal stimuli (visual and auditory) seem to crowd out poetic or interpretive closure.

It is important to remember that the grammatical subject of this entire section is "thoughts," a word which (mis)leads us back to those "ideas" the poem seems to want to avoid, in the effort to reach those "things" beyond the obfuscating veil of language. And it is in fact the poet's thoughts (ideas) that "leap to the conclusion" in order to generate, match, and complete the vibrancy of the physical scene—"connotative of the equal air, coeval / filling the void" (I.i.8). As we have seen, however, Williams's performance of the difficult, potentially dangerous, and forever unfinished *act* of representation runs counter to his possession and mastery of the landscape in verbal representation*s*. Like Sam Patch, an old-time resident of Paterson who won his fame by jumping into the chasm under the Passaic falls, the poet must risk leaping into the dark "eddy and whirl" (I.i.16–17) in order to undergo a necessary Fall. Patch made a career of leaping until 1829, when he jumped 125 feet into the Genesee River after making a short speech. "Speech failed him," writes Williams. "He was confused. The word had been drained of its meaning." Patch was fished out the next day, "frozen in an ice-cake." Failure is built into such leaping, not because of lack of skill, but because the components of the landscape—stream, ice, falls—"forever surpass" speech; they "have no language" (I.i.24).

The "ravished park" in book II further reenacts the violence of possession and the drama of "a world lost": far from being a hallowed place, the park is "subject to . . . incursions" (II.i.43), interruptions, penetrations. Williams tells us that the "picturesque summit," the "dens of sweet grass," the "ground gently sloping" (II.i.5) are

> Blocked.
> > (Make a song out of that: concretely)
> By whom?
> > > (II.ii.62)

Among the numerous blocking agents, Alexander Hamilton stands out in particular, not because he is a well-known historical figure, but because his actions, in relation to those of the poet, highlight the performance of the poem's struggle with its own discourse.

Hamilton is first introduced early in book I, where he is the focal point for a description of the early demographic composition of Paterson, New Jersey (I.i.10). The population statistics in this section of the poem signify Hamilton's interest in production output, whether the subject is people or goods. This emphasis is taken up more at length in book II, where Hamilton functions as a synecdoche for the economic and industrial visionaries who shaped America.

Williams/Paterson is clearly critical of the results of their "vision," as in the Poundian castigation of the Federal Reserve System as a "Legalized National Usury System" (II.ii.74): "THE WHOLE NATIONAL DEBT IS MADE UP ON INTEREST CHARGES. If the people ever get to thinking of bonds and bills at the same time, the game is up." For Hamilton (as for Paterson), the landscape is nothing less than inspirational; his interpretation of the landscape, however, is solely in terms of acquisition and power:

> Even during the Revolution Hamilton had been impressed by the site of the Great Falls of the Passaic. His fertile imagination envisioned a great manufacturing center, a great Federal City, to supply the needs of the country. Here was water power to turn the mill wheels and the navigable river to carry manufactured goods to the market centers: a national manufactory.
>
> (II.ii.69)

In accusing Hamilton of shaping and molding the city to his own expansionist design, Williams/Paterson is once again recycling the pastoral, whose code particularly proscribes "cupidity and avarice, the yearning after property and prosperity, the desire for affluence and opulence, for money and for precious things."[15] Yet the language of *Paterson* also suggests that Williams may be guilty of the same "crime"—the remaking of the city in his own image, through an economy of appropriation. Williams, it seems, cannot divorce himself from the American acquisitive ethos, which sees the "pursuit of happiness" as both a moral and a material imperative. Nor can he "build his own world" in an Emersonian sense—and become the "true land-lord!" of the landscape—without appropriating the landscape as a vehicle for solipsism.

In this light, it seems clear that pastoral is not the only genre which is overturned; *Paterson* also explodes the norms of the lyric, where a single perceiving eye orders, arranges, and controls the outside scene. More specifically, *Paterson* enacts a tension between what Mikhail Bakhtin has described as the monological and the dialogical orientations of discourse. According to Bakhtin, "the poet is a poet insofar as he accepts the idea of a unitary and singular language and a unitary, monologically sealed-off utterance."[16] In contrast, the dialogic orientation is, in fact, an "inter-orientation" with an "elastic environment" of "other alien words" (276). Clearly valorized by Bakhtin, dialogism finds its "fullest and deepest expression" in the novel, the only genre seen as capable, through "heteroglossia," of evoking our condition as historical, social beings. Only the "mythical Adam," notes Bakhtin, "who approached a virginal and as yet verbally unqualified world with the first word, could really have escaped from start to finish this dialogic inter-orientation with the alien word that occurs in the object. Concrete historical human discourse does not have this privilege . . ." (279).

Although Bakhtin seems here to be setting up mutually exclusive categories, he does acknowledge (though he fails to adequately develop) the difficulty of sustaining a monologically hermetic discourse, even in poetry. "More often than not," he continues, "we experience a profound and conscious tension through which the unitary poetic language of a work rises from the heteroglot and language-diverse chaos of the literary language contemporary to it" (298). These words are, to my mind, an apt commentary on the performance of *Paterson*. In questioning the adequacy of language to represent the "things" of this world figuratively, Williams is in fact trying to evoke an Adamic, or "as yet verbally unqualified world"— Columbus arriving on an unknown shore. In reenacting this scene, he sets himself up as sole (monological) owner and proprietor. Through his inevitable entanglement with the "heteroglot world" (285), however, he becomes a historical being, open to the language of the alien other:

> (He hears! Voices   .   indeterminate! Sees them
> moving, in groups, by twos and fours—filtering
> off by way of the many bypaths.)
>
> (II.i.45)

Bakhtin's distinctions may help illustrate the ways in which *Paterson* is a poem of incursion, where multiple registers and discourses—a "language-diverse chaos"—of reportage, history, economics, and personal letters clash and intersect, making any monolithic, transhistorical concept of "lyric" obsolete.[17] As "Mr. Williams" says in the famous interview in book V, "Anything is good material for poetry. Anything. I've said it time and time again" (V.ii.225). In *Paterson*, this sycretizing or "gathering up" impulse is continually interrupted by a modernist, almost Poundian, plethora of the Other, the specific and incontrovertible *out there.*[18] The poet as the voice declaiming (bragging "as lustily as chanticleer in the morning?") a self-sufficient and self-generating (Pater—son) center makes way for the poet as one voice among many, performing within a "dialogically agitated and tension-filled environment of alien words" (Bakhtin, 276).

The American poet may try to set himself up as the sole owner of "that wherein others are only tenants and boarders" (namely, the American landscape), but his language is entangled, "shot through" with "shared thoughts, points of view, alien value judgments and accents" (Bakhtin, 276). Echoing Whitman in book III, Williams/Paterson asks:

> What language could allay our thirsts,
> what winds lift us, what floods bear us
> past defeats
> but song but deathless song?

The answer to this request is a lyric that gives the American landscape its voice:

> The rock
> married to the river
> makes
> no sound
>
> And the river
> passes—but I remain
> clamant
> calling out ceaselessly
> to the birds
> and clouds
> (listening)
> Who am I?
>
> —the voice!
> (III.i.107)

However, this passage of poetic assertiveness through univocal presence, like similar passages throughout the poem, is inevitably interrupted. "The voice!"—gathering up, giving form and meaning to, both "clamant" and claimant—is just one among many others that insist on the separateness of the individual and the world. In this context, the geographical exactitude of the poetry of Ezra Pound provides interesting analogues. As several critics have noted, the best guide to some of Pound's poems is often a set of Michelin maps.[19] One may almost say the same of *Paterson*,[20] with the important difference being that while the historical and geographical referents of *Paterson*, like "Provincia Deserta" and "Near Perigord," exist "out there" in solid, extratextual reality, they also exist as part of a self-referentiality that sees the land as "expressly founded for me, personally."[21]

Interestingly, the voice of Pound appearing in *Paterson* (quoted from a letter to Williams written at St. Elizabeth's) seems to communicate a double message. First, ever the *miglior fabbro*, Pound suggests a proper reading list:

> re read *all* the Gk tragedies in
> Loeb.—plus Frobenius, plus
> Gessell   plus Brooks Adams
> ef you ain't read him all.—
> Then Golding 'Ovid' is in Everyman lib.
>
> (III.iii.138)

but he simultaneously warns: "don't / go rushin to *read* a book / just cause it is mentioned," as if to send Williams away from a world of words and out into the exactitudes of place. And, in fact, the voice that subsequently interrupts the words of Pound's letter is that of a geological analysis of the substratum found at the Passaic Rolling Mill (III.iii.139). For Williams, such geographical precision extends to the "shaly sandstone" at 2,100 feet and to questions of the economic value of its composition. This passage is not only (quite literally) ground—what Williams calls, in a marvelously original essay on Poe, the "sullen, volcanic inevitability of the *place*"—but a personal *grounding* in this locality. In the light of our reading of *Paterson*, his comments on Poe's writing are revelatory: "Either the New World must be mine as I will have it, or it is a worthless bog. There can be no concession. His attack was *from the center out.* . . . It was a wish to HAVE the world or leave it."[22]

For Williams, as for Poe, the desire for an absolute possession of the landscape contains within it the ever-present possibility of possession *by* the landscape; Pater-son as "the voice!"—the eternally prior discoverer of

America—must contend, above all, with "Earth, the chatterer, father of all speech . . . ." (I.iii.39).

NOTES

1. William Carlos Williams, *Paterson* (New York: New Directions, 1963). All references to *Paterson* are to this edition; book, section, and page numbers are included in the text. For a concise account of the publication history of *Paterson*, see Benjamin Sankey, *A Companion to William Carlos Williams's Paterson* (Berkeley: University of California Press, 1971), 227.

2. Williams's comment is from a letter (22 July 1939) to Horace Gregory. See *The Selected Letters of William Carlos Williams*, ed. John C. Thirlwall (New York: McDowell, Obolensky, 1957), 185. The Emerson reference is to his essay "The Poet." See *Selections from Ralph Waldo Emerson*, ed. Stephen E. Whicher (Boston: Houghton Mifflin, 1957), 240–41.

3. Myra Jehlen, *American Incarnation: The Individual, the Nation, and the Continent* (Cambridge, Mass.: Harvard University Press, 1986), 4. It is noteworthy that Jehlen notes "a *man's* value" (my emphasis), since economic advancement was historically seen in America as a supremely masculine venture.

4. Ibid., 2.

5. See also Williams's comment in an early essay: "Lost, in this . . . [emptiness] as in a forest, I do believe the average American to be an Indian, but an Indian robbed of his world—unless we call machines a forest in themselves." Williams goes on to trace this loss: "From lack of touch, lack of belief. Steadily the individual loses caste, then the local government loses its authority; the head is more and more removed. Finally the center is reached—totally dehumanized, like a Protestant heaven" ("Pere Sebastian Rasles," in *In the American Grain* [1925, 1933; London: MacGibbon and Kee, 1966], 128).

6. This tendency is also present in earlier texts, although it is not as evident there as in twentieth-century texts. On this subject, see Cecilia Tichi, *New World, New Earth: Environmental Reform in American Literature from the Puritans through Whitman* (New Haven: Yale University Press, 1979); and Kinereth Meyer, "Ekphrasis and the Hermeneutics of Landscape," *American Poetry* 8 (1990): 23–37. See also Michael Holquist's important essay on "The Politics of Representation," in *Allegory and Representation*, ed. Stephen J. Greenblatt (Baltimore: Johns Hopkins University Press, 1981), 163–83.

7. See, for example, some of the speeches of Teddy Roosevelt. Before the 1898 war against Spain, Roosevelt confessed himself "a good deal disheartened at the

queer lack of imperial instinct" in the American people, a trait he continually connected with "manliness." See Alfred Kazin, *A Writer's America: Landscape and
Literature* (New York: Knopf, 1988), 101. In this light, it is also interesting to compare American landscape poems written by women. The differences are striking,
not only in the range of their perceptions, but in their overwhelming refusal to
"possess" the landscape. I am presently engaged in an examination of women's
landscape poems in American literature. For an interesting commentary on this
subject, see Annette Kolodny, *The Land before Her* (Chapel Hill: University of
North Carolina Press, 1984).

8. See Johannes Fabian, "Presence and Representation: The Other and Anthropological Writing," *Critical Inquiry* 16 (1990): 753–73.

9. Ibid., 767. On aesthetics and power, see, among other texts, Walter Ong, *The
Barbarian Within* (New York: Macmillan, 1962), and *Fighting for Life* (Ithaca: Cor-
nell University Press, 1981); and Michel Foucault, "The Order of Discourse," in
Untying the Text: A Post-Structuralist Reader, ed. Robert Young (Boston: Rout-
ledge and Kegan Paul, 1981), 48–78. See also the essays in *Ideology and Classic
American Literature*, ed. Sacvan Bercovitch and Myra Jehlen (Cambridge, Eng.:
Cambridge University Press, 1986).

10. Leo Marx, "Pastoralism in America," in Bercovitch and Jehlen, *Ideology*, 54.

11. On this subject, see *Literature and the Body: Essays on Populations and Persons*, ed. Elaine Scarry (Baltimore: Johns Hopkins University Press, 1988). Fabian,
"Presence and Representation," 756, notes that the need "to go *there*, . . . is really
our desire to be *here* (to find or defend our position in the world)."

12. See Yi-Fu Tuan, *Topophilia: A Study of Environmental Perception, Attitudes,
and Values* (Englewood Cliffs, N.J.: Prentice-Hall, 1974), especially 142–44.

13. On failure in the American pastoral, see Marx, "Pastoralism," 59–60.

14. On the conventions of the pastoral in general, see Renato Poggioli, *The Oaten
Flute: Essays on Pastoral Poetry and the Pastoral Ideal* (Cambridge: Harvard University Press, 1975). See also Marx, "Pastoralism," 43, and his book *The Machine
in the Garden: Technology and the Pastoral Idea in America* (New York: Oxford,
1964).

15. Poggioli, *Oaten Flute*, 4.

16. Mikhail Bakhtin, *The Dialogic Imagination*, ed. Michael Holquist (Austin:
University of Texas Press, 1981), 296. My references to Bakhtin are taken from the
section entitled "Discourse in Poetry and Discourse in the Novel," 275–300 (page
numbers are included in the text).

17. On the lyric, see Kinereth Meyer, "Speaking and Writing the Lyric 'I,'"
Genre 22 (1989): 129–49.

18. On this subject, see Marjorie Perloff's important essay, "Pound/Stevens:

Whose Era?" *New Literary History* 13 (1982): 485–514. See also Hugh Kenner, "The Possum in the Cave," in Greenblatt, *Allegory and Representation*, 128–45.

19. In addition to the essays by Perloff and Kenner, see Donald Davie, *Ezra Pound: Poet as Sculptor* (New York: Oxford, 1964), 176–77, 181.

20. Critics such as Sankey and George Zabriskie, "The Geography of 'Paterson,'" *Perspective* 6 (1953): 201–16, have provided important information regarding the physical details of Williams's poem. They do not, however, draw any conclusions as to his representational practice.

21. Thus Perloff, "Pound/Stevens," 506, sees Williams as both "Last Romantic" and "First Modern," bridging the gap between the continued romanticism of Wallace Stevens and the rupture of modernism found in the "encyclopedic" work of Ezra Pound.

22. *In the American Grain*, 219–20.

"Roots, Aren't They Supposed to Be Buried?": The Experience of Place in Midwestern Women's Autobiographies

KATHLEEN R. WALLACE

In his essay in this volume, Yi-Fu Tuan emphasizes the human need to see pattern and coherence. According to Tuan, this tendency often forces us to overlook fissures that characterize a seemingly coherent group. Research in regionalism has focused largely upon such groups. As in the literary canon, the very notion of regionalism and regional identity depends upon shared definitions and values. The Upper Midwest, for instance, has enjoyed for some time a relatively stable regional identity, one that has been aligned with the dominant white culture and patterned primarily on the ethnic heritages of northern European immigrants.[1] Breaks in this dominant narrative are beginning to erupt with increasing frequency as the region's nonwhite population continues to grow and demand recognition.[2]

Autobiographies offer an opportunity to understand alternative visions of popular regional images. In these personal narratives, place appears as a physical phenomenon *and* as a site for meaning. Since socially determined gender roles have historically been used to exclude women from full participation in the creation of regional and cultural narratives, women's autobiographical writing often reveals gaps in regional identities that seem well-established and unassailable wholes. In personal narratives by Patricia Hampl, Brenda Ueland, and Toyse Kyle, Minnesota and the Twin Cities of Minneapolis and St. Paul appear as a complex web of cultural, emotional, and economic constructions that disrupt Minnesota's image as a "northern utopia."[3]

Much research in literature, geography, and American studies has ignored gender as a variable in the experience of place, although recent feminist scholarship, in its attention to gender, has highlighted the fissures latent in traditional notions of the canon or culture. I apply this critique to regionalism, thus complicating simplistic and monolithic definitions of "place." To further expand upon more traditional notions of place, I also adapt the concept of mental mapping from human geography to examine women's strategies for navigating and negotiating natural, built, and psychological environments. As I clarify later, "place" can refer to notions of women's roles (i.e., "women's place") in addition to physical locations.[4]

Over the past thirty years, perception studies in geography have moved from "objective" assessment of geographical areas to an understanding of how perception influences human behavior. In short, as Robin Haynes writes, "What matters is not objective reality, but how it is perceived."[5] Research in mental mapping has concentrated upon *visual* representations of various environments, a predilection some scholars have come to realize may not fully describe how human beings create and respond to environments. In his work on regionalism, Clarence Mondale writes that "[perhaps] nothing so intimately connects culture to place as language."[6] Mondale refers, in particular, to the work of linguists who have mapped regional dialects and speech patterns. But the importance of language also lies in its ability to narrate and create story. Language has the power to create, shape, sustain, and/or disrupt "objective realities" that can form powerful, life-defining mythologies. In this study, I adapt mental mapping by attending to the way language structures and articulates experiences of place.

Popular appreciation of regionalism as a system of categorization relies upon identification with visual images, but the real power behind these images relies upon their ties to language and narrative.[7] Because language is intimately linked to issues of identity, when identity is threatened language is threatened. When academics and social commentators worried that the United States was losing its regional distinctions through the homogenizing effects of mass communications, one of the regional characteristics slated for preservation by folklorists and linguists was dialect. Yet variations in language and other regional characteristics continue to thrive in the latter part of the twentieth century in part *because of* mass communications. The pervasiveness of midwestern speech on network television newscasts, for instance, has not erased regional drawls or twangs. Rather than creating absolute national uniformity, mass communications are prone to promoting regional images that are little more than stereotypes. These images and the rhetoric used to describe them tend to be static, reinforcing boundaries that can limit participation in defining regional identity.

The success of Garrison Keillor's "A Prairie Home Companion" on National Public Radio, for example, is tied to its ability to support the dominant midwestern narrative, a regional myth that concerns itself primarily with satisfying images of hard work, solid values, and friendly folk who live in small towns. As Judith Yaross Lee points out in the first book-length study of Keillor's work as a writer and radio performer, Keillor regularly revealed Lake Wobegon—the setting for his weekly monologues—as a fiction. Nonetheless, Lake Wobegon's attraction was such that fans and critics often missed Keillor's irony, which undercut the nostalgic and sentimental veneer. Some fans "became co-conspirators in the Lake Wobegon fantasy . . . only to lose sight of the basic lie."[8]

When Keillor announced that "A Prairie Home Companion" would end in June 1987, former vice-president Walter Mondale captured the secret of the show's success. He wrote that Lake Wobegon appealed to "rural nostalgia. For millions of us small-towners, Keillor is important because he understands us. He is our youth, our values, our past; he understands our humor and our purpose. This is especially true for those of us who are from small towns *and* are Norwegian."[9]

The words "our" and "us" surface repeatedly in Mondale's commentary. As is evident in his choice of words, Mondale assumes that his (and Keillor's) audience shares this vision of the Midwest and small town life. The possessive pronoun particularly reinforces the cohesiveness of this vision for those who see their roots reflected in it. In short, Lake Wobegon's appeal relies upon a sophisticated relationship between the "truth" in Keillor's seemingly autobiographical monologues and Lake Wobegon's fictional status (a fact disputed by an ad for "APHC" products that describes Lake Wobegon as "that not-so-mythical Camelot of Minnesota"). Because it obscures the boundaries between the mythical and not-so-mythical, Lake Wobegon came to represent Minnesota on the national stage during its thirteen-year run.

Over the past several years, however, the local media have devoted significant column inches and air time to discussing a "new" Minnesota populated with increasing numbers of Native Americans, Asian immigrants, African-Americans, and Hispanics—all populations who don't live in Lake Wobegon, Minnesota's mythological city for Norwegians.[10] Through the recognition now being accorded these other populations, the dominant regional image is gradually being revealed for what it is—a constructed identity.

While current squabbles and, at times, open hostility point to real complexity in the upper midwestern regional identity, scholars and purveyors of mass communications continue to present the situation in confrontational terms, as us (insiders) versus them (outsiders). In the chapter "Ethics of Wholesome Provincialism," Werner Sollers criticizes the limits of such dualisms, which ignore Americans' historical tendency "to create complicated and unsystematically overlapping forms of particular regional, ethnic, and religious identities." Sollers's argument hinges upon his understanding of how theoretical considerations of diversity rely upon seeing all ethnic and racial groups as "homogeneous units." The way around this rigid configuration is, according to Sollers, "to turn to the individual [who] provides discussions of regionalism and ethnicity with pervasive metaphors."[11]

By reconfiguring "the American self as region and ethnic group," Sollers sees autobiographies as capable of representing both "individuality and American identity."[12] While Sollers concentrates upon immigrant autobiographies, women's personal narratives also reveal these negotiations. As I discuss later, autobiographies contribute much to our understanding of issues of place by revealing the multiple, interrelated layers of regional identity.

Despite media attention to rapidly changing demographics, Minnesota's popularized identity has proven to be remarkably tenacious. How and why, then, do such homogeneous mythologies of place retain their pull? Myths provide stories and explanations; they help simplify reality. Yet, in doing so, myths also exclude realities; they ignore stories that do not "fit." Patricia Hampl's memoir *A Romantic Education* (1981) is one such dissonant story, operating within the tension created when one's experiences do not correspond completely to the dominant regional myth.

The grandchild of Czech immigrants, Hampl has lived long enough in Minnesota to identify with some of its regional peculiarities. Her identity as a Minnesotan and her sense of personal and familial history, however, have been compromised by her family's ethnic memories. Hampl's memoir oscillates between her "pride in [Minnesota's] wretched weather" and an immigrant's "ache for history." Like many upper midwesterners who relish the region's cold weather folklore, Hampl's family celebrates "the ice cube [as] the supreme artifact of civilization. And like a small nation, we hardly cared among ourselves that the myths and legends, the peculiar rites of the land, were unknown and undervalued elsewhere, as long as we could edify ourselves again and again with the stunning statistics that constituted our sense of ourselves: the weather, the god-awful winters, which were our civic, practically our cultural, identity." [13]

But as a child, Hampl suffered from what she calls midwestern "provincial anguish" and a sense of historical emptiness, fearing that her grandmother "had immigrated to Nowheresville." Hampl and her family have learned to love Minnesota, but her grandmother's vagueness about the Old World leaves Hampl desiring a deeper tie to the past. "We didn't have a sense of history, but an ache for it that had to be assuaged by an act of the imagination—for there, at the head of the family where history should have been with its culture intact, its relation to the nation assumed, was my grandmother, the rootless wonder, our oak that lived in air, not earth. Our immigrant" (23).

The idea and mystery of history, of connectedness, color Hampl's image of her Czech grandmother as the "rootless wonder." Hampl acknowledges that her grandmother *was something. And she knew what she was* (44). She simply could not articulate, to Hampl's satisfaction, what that something was. Hampl eventually travels to Czechoslovakia searching for history and personal identity. Her purpose there is less a quest for genealogy than it is an opportunity to discover that "the country itself becomes the lost ancestry and, one finds, the country is eloquent. Its long story, its history, satisfy the instinct for kinship in a way that the discovery of a distant cousin could not. For it is really the longing for a lost culture that sends Americans on these pilgrimages" (148).

Prague is ultimately satisfying to Hampl because it "demands relation" (211). The city and its inhabitants are "genuinely mythic" (209). Prague, Hampl writes, "stopped [her] tourism flat" (146). The city satisfies Hampl's "instinct for kinship" in a way that most tourism excursions cannot. She experiences connectedness to a place, to ancestry, to culture, and thus to history. In Prague, Hampl is no longer on the outside looking in. She describes Prague as a "real-life-in-dream . . . a quality that salves conscious and sleeping mind, creating harmony" (208). In many ways, Hampl's description of a "real-life-in-dream" is an apt definition of myth. Myths "salve"; they create harmony. Her awareness of Prague's "ancient grime" works for Hampl because it centers her within a culture and a history. Its ancient grime is a place in which her roots can be buried (146).

Centering, as an image of creating or finding one's place, surfaces repeatedly in Brenda Ueland's memoir *Me* (1938). The dominant mythology of Minnesota-as-Lake Wobegon also appears in *Me*, but not without significant alterations. After several years in New York and after the dissolution of her marriage, Ueland returns with her daughter to live in her childhood home on Lake Calhoun in Minneapolis. Place, for Ueland, operates concretely on two levels: geographic and cultural. A second-generation Norwegian immigrant, Ueland does not dwell upon her ethnic homeland. Rather, Ueland participates fully in the Minnesota myth: she lives on a lake, she swims in it or walks around it every day. Furthermore, as a Norwegian, Ueland is a member of the regional ethnic group that enjoys the most popular exposure.

Ueland's autobiography depicts her "rootedness" in a Minnesotan landscape that clearly nourishes her. Raised, as she says, by a mother who was "naturally feminist" and who "made no distinction between [boys and girls] in actions, freedom, education, or possibilities,"[14] Ueland nonetheless confronts her struggle to place herself in a culture that encourages women to be self-sacrificing. Ueland, who writes from a relatively secure place, also struggles with the tension between psychically and socially constructed boundaries for women's roles. In negotiating these boundaries, she chronicles her attempts to "get inside herself" and see herself as "at the center." Centering operates as Ueland's primary metaphorical device for her discussions of how women might gain power in a culture that has continually forced their contributions to the margins. She writes: "If one can only find the center, what force! what unflinching bold freedom there would be!" (341). For Ueland, writing an autobiography entitled *Me* is in itself a powerful act of centering because it makes the self paramount, a creative act she recognizes many women have not been encouraged or allowed to make. Near the end of her memoir, she discusses a dream that, like Hampl's "real-life-in-dream," creates for her a mythic vision of a centered life:

> [William] Blake was thundering to me to be a wild lonely galloping horse, compact in myself, in my life and my work; not to be just a tenderly loving woman, being bled of anxious love by others and encouraging and nursing them, particularly men who like me. No, I must be compact in myself, in my own thundering, exploding, blazing work. . . . One can only have power and do good for others, if one is an integral center of power oneself. . . . (333–34)

Power, as Carolyn Heilbrun describes it in *Writing a Woman's Life*, "is the ability to take one's place in whatever discourse is essential to action and the right to have one's part matter."[15] Her definition of power, as it helps illuminate women's responses to environments, emphasizes language as a means toward taking one's rightful place. But power, of course, privileges some voices over others. In Minnesota, a state that is overwhelmingly white (95.3 percent), voices that challenge or disrupt civic boosterism of "the good life" in Minnesota are often silent if not absent. While the Minnesota mythology can be off limits to people because of their gender, race, or economic standing, alternative "mental maps" or mythologies of place continue to emerge and struggle for expression.

Toyse Kyle's essay "Minnesota Black, Minnesota Blue" explicitly counters the image of a utopic Midwest. She begins by describing the 13 August 1973 *Time* magazine cover photo of then Minnesota governor Wendell Anderson. Governor Anderson, smiling, holds up a northern pike. The caption reads: "The Good Life in Minnesota." As an African-American, Kyle identifies with the fish, caught in a regional mythology that does not correspond to her experiences. She asks, "Why did I identify with the fish in that photobit of the time of our lives? How did the Minnesota utopia help to shape me as black woman, mother, student, teacher? What's fishy in this picture? Am I crazy? Is this society crazy? Or are we all happy as motorboats in the land of the sky-blue laughing waters?" (169).

These questions, and the very act of questioning, show the split between the white world of flannel shirts and full stringers and Kyle's childhood spent in a "mixed" neighborhood where she was constantly reminded of her "difference." The profound differences between her life and those of her white classmates come to her over time, in quick, startling revelations. As a child, Kyle remembers daydreaming, wanting to be like Dick and Jane; she remembers cheering at a local theater "as Tarzan and the great white hunters beat off vengeful black 'savages'" (189). Both instances mark the pervasiveness and persuasiveness of white culture. Without representative images reflecting her experiences, Kyle finds herself in the curious position of cheering *against* the only expression of her blackness she encounters in mass culture, the stereotypical "black savage."

Little in the promised land of Minnesota supported the developing self-identity of a black girl. Unlike Ueland, who listened to thunder rumble over the lake and took pleasure in the dramatic sounds because they highlighted her security, Kyle heard noises of overcrowded urban housing and poverty. She listened for "the little noises and scratching sounds below the surface at night which signaled that mice or rats were making new holes for entrances into our territory" (187). Kyle learned to stay up after dark to tune the radio to black sounds from Little Rock, Atlanta, and Memphis. Ueland's and Kyle's mental maps are skewed in different directions although they lived within thirty city blocks of each other. Minnesota turns out to be "a bit of a 'trip'" for Kyle, who moved to Minneapolis as a 10-year-old in 1948. In an alien environment filled with white people, Kyle felt "very black . . . and the feeling was hard to live with in those days before black was beautiful" (177).

Listening south for sounds that support her blackness, Kyle learns to operate within what W. E. B. DuBois characterized as a double consciousness. She learns the Minnesota dialect to avoid white people's laughter, but her grandmother down "home" in Kansas City is both amused and irritated at what she sees as Kyle's attempt to act white: "Don't come around here trying to act like no white girl . . . you ain't no Miss Anne . . . you home-folks just like the rest of us" (176). Yet mastering the regional dialect does not guarantee access to the "northern utopia." Kyle's attempts at revising her speech to fit social standards highlight the disparity between her experience and the utopic vision. In addition, Kyle's newly acquired ability to use language to avoid social stigma also threatens to separate her from her family. She learns how to function as a member of the African-American community *within* the community articulated by the Minnesota regional identity—at the risk of her personal identity.

Social stigma and racism also separate Kyle from experiences glorified in Minnesota's national identity as the Land of 10,000 Lakes. Significantly, Kyle never visited a lake with her family. "We didn't have carfare enough or . . . our clothes were not 'good' enough to wear on a streetcar or at a beach where white people might see us" (189). The dominant image of Minnesota is clear enough in Kyle's memoir. The difference between her interpretation and Ueland's is the inaccessibility of that image for blacks in Minnesota in the mid-twentieth century.

In the end, Minnesota leaves Kyle black and blue as she struggles to find her reality in the environment and imagery that surrounds her. "But even in Minnesota—this northern utopia—life goes on below the surface of what most people are willing to see. Moreover, those who wrench themselves to the surface, or who at least manage to delude themselves into believing that they have surfaced, are likely to end up on the governor's stringer or to live on with the scar tissue after they spit out the lure" (194). As Kyle makes clear, the dominant image and the language used to describe that image ("The Good Life in Minnesota") operate on the surface. Until quite recently, the surface images have been taken as objective reality in Minnesota and other upper midwestern states. The existence of other worlds beneath the surface is ignored if acknowledged at all. While the process of surfacing may be necessary to force acknowledgement of alternative narratives, Kyle's analogy graphically depicts the threat of violence inherent in such attempts.

The autobiographies and memoirs examined here describe "the buried coming to the surface," as Michael M. J. Fischer characterizes the phenomenon in his article "Ethnicity and the Post-Modern Arts of Memory." In coming to the surface, then, these autobiographies expose the cracks in the dominant mythology. Fischer assesses the "florescence of ethnic autobiography and the academic fascination with textual theories of deferred, hidden, or occulted meaning . . . in order to ask whether they can revitalize our ways of thinking about how culture operates." Autobiographies may offer, Fischer suggests, explorations of a pluralist society by discussing ethnicity as more than quaint customs and faded memories passed on from generation to generation. Ethnicity, he believes, is "something dynamic, often unsuccessfully repressed or avoided." [16] In other words, it can surface. While Fischer uses "ethnicity" in the context of discrete racial, religious, or cultural groups, his ideas also provide a fruitful way for thinking about any group that has been pushed below the surface of the dominant culture.

Articulation of these voices has long been a function of oral and written personal narratives in American literature. The tradition is particularly strong in women's literature as it is in African-American and Native American letters. Part of the power inherent in autobiographical writing is its ability to "unmask" differences in a seemingly coherent community. Autobiographical writing in the form of daily diaries fulfilled this function in the *Minneapolis Star Tribune*'s 12-day series on *Issues of Race* in June 1990. The *Star Tribune*'s decision to print personal narratives challenged the newspaper's presumed mission as the transmitter of "objective news." The diaries wove subjective perspectives into a discussion of race that could easily have lapsed into sociological, detached reportage. Not surprisingly, the diaries generated intense reader response, creating a heated public dialogue in the paper's Op-Ed section. As executive editor Joel Kramer put it, the letters demonstrated the reactions of a "community that was coping—not always well—with diversity and change." [17]

These personal narratives, published in a very public space, chronicled project members' responses to race as it surfaced in their daily lives. Two general themes arose in the narratives of white and black female staff members. For the white women, issues of race in the Twin Cities became conflated with personal safety. In the black women's entries, images of rootlessness and displacement dominated their assessment of race issues. Susie Eaton Hopper, a white senior graphics and photo editor, wrote: "After a summer of walking to the Government Center at noon and being hit on by black guys who were leaning up against the buildings there, I turned into one of those 'make no eye contact, put that purse strap around your neck' white women. It used to make me furious that sometimes someone would walk by and say rude, insulting, sexual things to me. And I started judging black men in general on the actions of a few jerks." [18]

In her final entry, Rosalind Bentley, a black fashion and feature reporter-whose diary generated the most response, evoked the frustration of "looking for answers to questions asked for years in this country. . . . I heard my co-workers tell me my diary entries were depressing, stand-offish, devoid of a conciliatory tone. But before you write me off as a young, hot-headed Black nationalist, do this for me. Imagine how you would feel if you had to point to a huge region of a continent and say, 'My people came from somewhere in here.' . . . If my diary is depressing, I make no apologies. The wounds are deep, the assault has been long." [19] Unlike most Minnesotans with European roots, Bentley cannot even point to a definitive homeland on a map. Furthermore, she finds herself restricted from full participation in the place in which she now resides.

The last articles of the series focused upon the future of race relations in the Twin Cities. Understandably, Hispanics, African-Americans, Native Americans, and Asian-Americans were not as optimistic as their white counterparts in thinking that relations would improve over the next decade. The series also consistently challenged Minnesota's reputed liberalism: "'Minnesota was a very liberal place as long as there were only 10,000 [members of] minorities here,'" said Rafael Ortega, who manages a social service agency in the Twin Cities. Participants in a forum sponsored by the *Star Tribune* agreed that racism in the Twin Cities was subtle, "hiding under a coat of liberal ideas and good intentions." [20]

As a metaphor, the image of "hiding" describes the role language plays in the negotiations surrounding current calls for cultural diversity. A month before the series appeared, an ad campaign for the Minnesota state lottery was scrapped because it played upon the assumption that "Norwegian" correlated directly to "Minnesotan," a connection reinforced by the Lake Wobegon myth. The lottery ad posited *Uff da* (translated variously from the Norwegian as "wow," "oh no," or "my goodness") as the quintessential Minnesotan reaction to winning the lottery. "Typical Minnesota style," the ad called it. The *Star Tribune* demurred. "*Uff da* as a bid to win the hearts and wallets of Minnesota's communities of color? In the Asian, Hispanic and Indian newspapers? Doesn't the lottery know Minnesota? Apparently not." [21]

Healthy cultural diversity does not exist, Minnesotans have slowly come to realize, when the knotty mess of racism remains cloaked and hidden. In the 13 August 1973 issue of *Time* magazine discussed by Toyse Kyle, Minnesota is described as having a "comparatively open and serene population a decade or two behind the rest of the U.S. The place lacks the fire, urgency and self-accusation of states with massive urban centers and problems. . . . Blacks rioted in Minneapolis in 1966 and 1967, but with only 1% of the state's population, they have not yet forced *Minnesotans* into any serious racial confrontation. Or at least, not an apocalyptic confrontation" (emphasis mine).[22]

Again, the rhetoric betrays any attempt at fruitful confrontation or understanding. As long as "Minnesotan" is equated directly with "white," challenges to the dominant regional identity remain simply "them" against "us." While the current situation in Minnesota is hardly apocalyptic, those folks who identified with Governor Wendell Anderson rather than with the fish on the stringer are slowly becoming conscious of the mythology of place they helped construct. As the saying goes, a fish doesn't think about water until it's out of it. Perhaps the state is two decades behind the rest of the nation, but Minnesota is slowly identifying with the fish, and it's slowly coming out of the water.

Such identification can be troublesome when it leads to uninformed romanticism. When Americans of European heritage see their past as "lost, smudged," according to Patricia Hampl, that sense of loss can lead artists to appropriate other cultures, such as the American Indian, who "knew how to live here." Our awareness that "our presence on the continent has made it less beautiful," Hampl argues persuasively, does not allow European-descended artists to use their pasts easily. The relationship between artists, the past, and folk culture is further confused, she writes, "because the 'folk' have often not been an indigenous peasantry, but an oppressed minority (and have not been '*us*,' but black or Indian)" (121–22; emphasis mine).[23] By contrast, the image of "us" promoted by civic boosterism and Lake Wobegon can obscure the existence of groups sharing the same geographic region while promoting a regional shorthand that seems right and natural to one group while distant and superficial to another.

As Hampl and others have indicated, ethnic revivals of the past thirty years have at times created isolated groups. This fragmentation, based on the supposed homogeneity of ethnicity, she writes, "tends to make people romantic about the peasantry and about the past." But the history of voluntary and involuntary migration to the United States challenges attempts at following lines of descent, as Hampl and Rosalind Bentley make clear. Despite such difficulties, the impulse to uncover one's origins remains compelling. In Hampl's words, this impulse may explain "why Americans are suddenly, after generations of doing the opposite, digging up their roots (if they can be found) to look at them. And then to . . . but that's part of the problem. What *do* you do with your roots? Aren't they supposed to be buried? Isn't that where they belong?" (122).

The impulse arises to answer yes. Roots need to be grounded for nourishment. But if the ground (or place or environment) is not supportive, then it seems necessary that the answer be no. If roots are buried, the past is hidden and history is lost. There may be a connection between the present and the past, but that connection remains largely hidden.

The question about roots also implies that simply finding them may not be sufficient. Perhaps the focus should be on an earlier part of the question: What does one do with roots? What is their function? A possible answer resonates in the related theme of fragmentation. To draw upon Werner Sollers's argument, the tendency to see ethnic and racial groups as autonomous "homogeneous units" obscures the complex interactions that exist in regional and cultural identities. In isolation, roots may be only a nostalgic trip down memory lane. But roots can also form an important part of one's identity with a particular place.[24]

In an especially eloquent article, Yi-Fu Tuan also attempts to explain contemporary preoccupation with roots and sense of place in American culture. While the two terms have been used interchangeably, Tuan argues that they are "opposed." "Rootedness," he writes, "implies being at home in an unself-conscious way. Sense of place, on the other hand, implies a certain distance between self and place. For modern and self-conscious Americans, rootedness is perhaps an irretrievable Eden, but developing a sense of place—like prior efforts to reach some kind of utopia—is within the realm of the possible. Memory and a sense of history must also be developed before roots can be traced, but through "speech, gesture, and the making of things" place can be consciously created. The search for one's past arises when "wealth and status are unevenly distributed, and people within a group or in rival groups begin to make rival claims." Tuan calls this situation "the problem of legitimacy," whereby "length of gene-alogy confers prestige on an individual, . . . length of history confers pres-tige on a nation."[25]

What is autobiography but primarily a claim to legitimacy through, among other things, genealogy? Autobiography is reflective, consciously drawing connections and laying claim to one's own story. It takes some digging to find connections, and the process of bringing roots to the surface helps the autobiographer challenge cultural assumptions about her rightful place; it shows how one individual's mental map of her situation may or may not correspond to what is presented as a universal reality.

In light of the personal narratives considered here, the opposition be-tween rootedness and sense of place as Tuan draws it appears elusive. When this distinction is applied to the experiences of place discussed ear-lier in the autobiographies, only Brenda Ueland is unreflectively secure and comfortable, as Tuan might say, in her Minnesota home. While this distinc-tion provides a useful clarification, the word "roots" as used in the auto-biographies discussed here moves beyond the notion of rootedness as unreflective at-homeness to an understanding of origins as a source of strength. For many women, roots are less a means of Edenic return than a place from which to *begin*.

Patricia Hampl's question about roots speaks on several levels to wom-en's experiences of rootedness and displacement.[26] In a genre that osten-sibly elevates the individual, women's autobiographies use memory and retrospection to voice alternative visions of connectedness and community in their critique of narratives that displace them physically or psychologi-cally from the larger cultural context. The narrative strategies in the auto-biographies discussed here explore the connections between the individual and her environment. In varying ways, Hampl, Ueland, and Kyle focus on community as a means by which they explore these connections between themselves and this expanded sense of place. These explorations result in different maps of the same geographic location. For Hampl, developing roots or community involves giving voice to her grandmother's silence. Hampl needs to understand her ancestral history, the "echo of something" that precedes her life in Minnesota. Ueland, while a daughter of an immi-grant, apparently has none of the immigrant's desire to return to the old country. Her roots are in a vision of Minnesota that corresponds rather closely to the image depicted on the cover of *Time* magazine, but she also struggles to negotiate the space between cultural expectations of women and her desire to work as a serious artist. Community, for Ueland, encompasses a strong sense of self within a supportive ring of friends, family, and place. Kyle's memoir shatters the illusion of community sustained by a region that pretends to have no race problems. Her piece functions to resurrect the past, for "those early pains can never be forgotten. They must be remembered. I now arm myself quite proudly with my differentness. In doing this I find myself less vulnerable and more able to cope with objective reality" (198).

Both Toyse Kyle and geographer Robin Haynes use the term "objective reality," but in startlingly different ways. As I stated earlier, Haynes writes that what "matters is not objective reality, but how it is perceived." Within the context of Haynes's field of study, this distinction stresses the difference between cartographically "correct" maps and maps that capture individuals' perceptions of the place in which they live. For Kyle, however, "objective reality" *is* her perception. Objective reality is the thing she needs to perceive and understand. She has to see the "northern utopia" as a delusion before she can survive on the surface.

Personal narratives offer a means by which this delusion can be understood. When Toyse Kyle recognizes the deception as a product of the dominant regional mythology, she can arm herself "quite proudly with . . . differentness"—a positive and strategic tactic. Hampl, on the other hand, sees the current emphasis on difference as akin to fragmentation. What's missing, she writes, is "some kind of authentic *relation*" between "isolated enclaves" (122).

Fragmentation is not necessarily negative, since recognizing difference does not necessarily result in absolute isolation. Ignoring difference, on the other hand, can amount to assimilation, rather than *relation* between what appear to be distinct groups and experiences. It is all too easy to explain away stories that run counter to expected patterns. The reception of Evelyn Fairbanks's memoir *The Days of Rondo* provides an appropriate example.[27] Her memoir about growing up in Rondo, St. Paul's largest black neighborhood in the 1930s and 1940s, depicts a happy childhood surrounded by women and men who were not victims. "I wanted people to know that we don't go home every night and talk about the struggles. We have joy in our lives, and I wanted people to know that," she said. Fairbanks wrote "Being Black in Minnesota," chapter 16 of *The Days of Rondo*, at her editor's suggestion. The editor felt the memoir was "not realistic otherwise."

While Fairbanks is proud that some readers believe her memoir describes "everybody's childhood" (an aspect some reviewers mistrusted and found naive), Fairbanks as author and as narrator is well aware that the forces that destroyed Rondo selected the path of least resistance. Dissected and largely obliterated by the construction of Interstate 94 in the 1960s, the thriving, vibrant neighborhood exists only in the memories of people who lived there. In this sense, *The Days of Rondo* is truly a mental map of a lost place and way of life. Nearly thirty years later, Fairbanks refuses to take Interstate 94 to St. Paul from her current home in Minneapolis. "It was not built for me," she says.[28]

Fairbanks's memoir offers a unique perspective on the Minnesota myth because it refuses to follow expectations. In this case, *The Days of Rondo* strives consciously to avoid the correlation that to be black in Minnesota is necessarily to be blue. From another perspective on the regional myth, the self-confessed fiction, nostalgia, and sentimentality of Lake Wobegon have been emphasized at the expense of Garrison Keillor's often explicit irony. Members of the "Prairie Home Companion" audience who find that Keillor's monologue expresses parts of their personal histories are regarded as naive, adopting "a passive and uncritical approach toward community life."[29]

Scholarly methodology tends to flatten evidence that varies too widely from established patterns. As Yi-Fu Tuan points out in his essay in this book, our desire to create coherent wholes runs counter to our simultaneous awareness of human separateness. In light of this awareness, he asks, do we use place and culture to mask the individual in favor of community? Or do we do the difficult and acknowledge the individuals who exist? It is useful at this point to remember that autobiographies also involve biographies. The personal narrative may set the individual apart, but it is nonetheless an individual in relation to others. Tuan encourages us to do both, to see separateness *and* connection. Just as the autobiographies discussed here resist simplistic presuppositions about women's experiences of place, as scholars we must learn to consider narratives that might throw the most carefully crafted "coherent whole" off-kilter.

NOTES

1. My essay takes a polyvocal approach to a distinct urban setting—the Twin Cities of Minneapolis–St. Paul, Minnesota—within a geographic region variously labeled the Upper Great Lakes or the Upper Midwest. This essay is part of a larger interdisciplinary study that follows an ethnographic approach to the study of place and regionalism. For Yi-Fu Tuan's point, see his essay in this volume.

2. I use the word "narrative" in its widest sense in order to include discussions of cultural phenomena like advertisements and regional mythologies. I also use it in referring to literary works. In both usages, I rely upon the idea of narrative as created story.

3. Toyse Kyle, "Minnesota Black, Minnesota Blue," in *Growing Up in Minnesota: Ten Writers Remember Their Childhoods*, ed. Chester G. Anderson (Minneapolis: University of Minnesota Press, 1976), 194 (hereafter cited in the text).

4. I do not intend to imply that my research constitutes a lone voice in the field. Definitions of place and regionalism abound in a variety of disciplines, but communication between them has been sporadic. My larger study attempts to bring these strands together while clarifying the need to understand place as a psychological and cultural construction as well as in its more readily understood geographical meaning.

The absence of gender-based research is particularly evident in geography. In "Regional Patterns of Female Status in the U.S.," D. Lee and R. Schultz write: "Women have been ignored in most geographic research, which has traditionally treated humanity as being homogeneous. We hope . . . that our findings may encourage others to [include] disaggregate groups, male and female. Though many papers now show an awareness of sex differences, geographical exploration of the world of women so far has mapped only some general features of the periphery; more detail is needed" (*Professional Geographer* 34 [1982]: 32–41).

In American studies, Annette Kolodny's *The Lay of the Land: Metaphor as Experience and History in American Life and Letters* (Chapel Hill: University of North Carolina Press, 1975) and *The Land before Her: Fantasy and Experience of the American Frontiers, 1630–1860* (Chapel Hill: University of North Carolina Press, 1984) both provide a view of American history and environment from the perspective of women. Kolodny's emphasis on language and metaphor in *The Lay of the Land* spurred my work in that area.

Regionalism continues to be a viable form of classification in literary studies, but the label "regional literature" continues to carry emotional and often detrimental weight, especially when applied to women's literature. *Regionalism and the Female Imagination: A Collection of Essays*, ed. Emily Toth (New York: Human Sciences

Press, 1985), chronicles an impressive array of women writers, but lacks a critical assessment of regionalism.

A substantial body of work exists from historians working with women and southwestern regionalism. *Western Women: Their Land, Their Lives*, ed. Lillian Schlissel, Vicki L. Ruiz, and Janice Monk (Albuquerque: University of New Mexico Press, 1988), is a particularly impressive collection of essays that provides a much-needed overview of the field, while discussing and experimenting with new methodologies. Other influential work by Janice Monk includes her "Approaches to the Study of Women and Landscape," *Environmental Review* 8 (1984): 23–33.

Scholars working in architecture have provided the most comprehensive work to date on women's sense of place and space. Delores Hayden's *Redesigning the American Dream: The Future of Housing, Work, and Family Life* (New York: W. W. Norton, 1984) provides an impressive critique of mythologies of place as they apply to women's lives. See also Hayden's *Seven American Utopias: The Architecture of Communitarian Socialism, 1780–1975* (Cambridge, Mass.: MIT Press, 1976), and *The Grand Domestic Revolution: A History of Feminist Designs for American Homes, Neighborhoods, and Cities* (Cambridge, Mass.: MIT Press, 1981). *Women in American Architecture: A Historic and Contemporary Perspective* (New York: Watson-Guptill Publications, Whitney Library of Design, 1977), ed. Susana Torre, provides a necessary and thoroughly readable overview of women's contributions to the field of architecture.

Two excellent collections combine perspectives from women's studies and public policy (among other fields) to illuminate women's experiences of both the home and urban settings: *New Space for Women*, ed. Gerda R. Wekerle, Rebecca Peterson, and David Morley (Boulder, Colo.: Westview Press, 1980); and *Women and the American City*, ed. Catharine R. Stimpson et al. (Chicago: University of Chicago Press, 1981). The articles in *Women and the American City* originally appeared as a supplement to *Signs: Journal of Women in Culture and Society* 5 (1980).

5. Robin M. Haynes, *Geographical Images and Mental Maps* (London: Macmillan, 1981), 1. For a perspective that links geography with literature, see Douglas C. D. Pocock, ed., *Humanistic Geography and Literature: Essays on the Experience of Place* (London: Croom Helm, 1981).

6. Clarence Mondale, "Concepts and Trends in Regional Studies," *American Studies International* 27 (1989): 16.

7. See my discussion of Garrison Keillor's "A Prairie Home Companion." See also Yi-Fu Tuan, "Rootedness versus Sense of Place," *Landscape* 24 (1980): 6.

8. Judith Yaross Lee, *Garrison Keillor: A Voice of America* (Jackson: University Press of Mississippi, 1991), 19. For another perspective on the relationship between Keillor, his monologues, and the "Prairie Home Companion" audience,

see Charles U. Larsen and Christine Oravec, "A Prairie Home Companion and the Fabrication of Community," *Critical Studies of Mass Communication* 4 (1987): 221–44. Larsen and Oravec overstate their argument that "Lake Wobegon stories ultimately encourage a passive, accepting attitude toward Lake Wobegon as it is and contemporary American life as it has become" (224). They also lack perspective on Keillor's stance as a storyteller. Lee's study, in contrast, develops this theme.

9. Walter F. Mondale, commentary included in "Thanks for the Memories: Words of Appreciation from a Few Folks You Might Have Heard Of," *Minnesota Monthly*, June 1987, 31.

10. This emphasis on the Norwegian population is especially interesting since Germans actually constitute the largest ethnic group in Minnesota.

11. Werner Sollers, *Beyond Ethnicity: Consent and Descent in American Culture* (New York: Oxford University Press, 1986), 175–76, 186, 194.

12. Ibid., 207.

13. Patricia Hampl, *A Romantic Education* (Boston: Houghton Mifflin, 1981), 52, 23, 52 (hereafter cited in the text).

14. Brenda Ueland, *Me* (1938; St. Paul: North Central, 1983), 328 (hereafter cited in the text).

15. Carolyn G. Heilbrun, *Writing a Woman's Life* (New York: Norton, 1988), 18.

16. Michael M. J. Fischer, "Ethnicity and the Post-Modern Arts of Memory," in *Writing Culture: The Poetics and Politics of Ethnography*, ed. James Clifford and George E. Marcus (Berkeley: University of California Press, 1986), 195–96.

17. Joel Kramer, ed., *Issues of Race* (reprint), *Minneapolis Star Tribune*, 10–24 June 1990, 1. In his preface to the *Issues of Race* series, executive editor Kramer outlined the history of the project. Its roots, he wrote, were in a 1988 article about an unwed black teenage mother. The piece "aroused the anger of many black readers. Her story, said the critics, reinforced negative stereotypes." The complaint was taken to the Minnesota New Council, whose white members found the story not to be racist. The discussion, however, continued at the *Star Tribune* and culminated in the series.

18. Susan Eaton Hopper, *Issues of Race*, 13.

19. Rosalind Bentley, *Issues of Race*, 62.

20. See *Issues of Race*, 36, 63.

21. Editorial, "How Not to Advertise to Typical Minnesotans," *Star Tribune*, 7 May 1990.

22. "Minnesota: A State That Works," *Time*, 13 August 1973, 24–35.

23. Carla Bianco offers a related perspective in "Ethnicism and Culturology: The

Cultural Identity of Regional and Immigrant Groups," *Sociologia Ruralis* 20 (1980): 151–64.

24. Bianco (ibid.) criticizes current ethnic revivals that lack "political consciousness" (155). For white ethnics, she argues, emphasis on roots can mean "recapturing a lost innocence from ancestral memories and using it as an alternative to an artificial modern society" (155), which can lead to isolated groups. She suggests instead "a systematic effort towards a scientific interpretation of the many factors of peripheral, regional, or ethnic culture, abandoning the Romantic flirtation with the ideas of roots, origin, and natural culture. Among other things, a responsible effort in this sense would help the 'peripheries' to avoid yet further exclusion" (161). While Bianco's point about taking into consideration all the variables is well-taken, and relates to Sollers's attempt to avoid dualistic constructions of both ethnicity and region, her rather arbitrary distinction between romantic and scientific interpretations excludes much of the evidence found in so-called subjective personal narratives.

25. Tuan, "Rootedness versus Sense of Place," 4, 6, 7.

26. I am not arguing that all experiences of place are gender-specific. Autobiographies by men, particularly men of color, also document the disparity between dominant mythologies and personal experience.

27. Evelyn Fairbanks, *The Days of Rondo* (St. Paul: Minnesota Historical Society Press, 1990).

28. Evelyn Fairbanks, remarks made before public reading of *The Days of Rondo*, Minnesota Museum of Art, St. Paul, 14 February 1991.

29. Larsen and Oravec, "Fabrication of Community," 221.

Topographies

The Built Environment and

Modern American Culture

Beyond the Sacred and the Profane: Cultural Landscape Photography in America, 1930–1990

TIMOTHY DAVIS

This essay provides an overview of the ways in which a number of prominent photographers have dealt with the problem of interpreting the American cultural landscape. The diversity of twentieth-century landscape photography reveals more than varying personal interests and private aesthetic preferences; the different ways in which photographers have represented the relationships among place, culture, and individuals reflect larger cultural transformations, both in the appearance and concerns of American society and in the intellectual community's conception of the nature and function of cultural analysis.

I have divided the history of mid–twentieth century cultural landscape photography into three more or less distinct and successive phases: a "sacred" period typified by Walker Evans's and the Farm Security Administration's canonization of the vernacular landscape of 1930s America; an iconoclastic interlude inspired by Robert Frank's challenging of photographic conventions and mainstream American values in the 1950s; and a "profane" period, dubbed the "New Topographics" and characterized by Robert Adams's and Lewis Baltz's depictions of the modern American landscape as a wasteland of banality and self-imposed isolation.

The essay relates these photographic viewpoints to changes in American society and to changing conceptions of the role of the cultural observer and of the nature of cultural interpretation. It goes on to examine the work of several important contemporary photographers who are experimenting with concepts that echo postmodern anthropology's belief in the emergent and indeterminate nature of cultural meaning. These photographers use a variety of techniques designed to challenge the perception of a single "correct" interpretation of any place or cultural situation. Both photographers and ethnographers frequently employ these strategies in attempts to empower the inhabitant's perspective on cultural values, places, and processes.

THE SACRED

It is difficult to say whether Walker Evans created the vocabulary, grammar, and ethics of seeing that still shape our vision of the cultural landscape of 1930s America or whether the near perfection of his vision simply confirmed sentiments that had been in the air since Walt Whitman urged Americans to sing the praises of everyday life in the United States. Both Paul Strand and Eugene Atget preceded Evans as explicators of the cultural significance of ordinary landscapes, yet Evans's photographs, through their influence on other photographers working for the Farm Security Administration's photography division and through the prestige they garnered from the support of the Museum of Modern Art, became iconic images symbolizing the noble simplicity, folkloric charm, redeemable errors, and stoic determination they located in the cultural landscape of

Depression-era America. Evans's photographs suggested that beauty and significance could be found in small town streetscapes, storefronts, cemeteries, gas stations, rooming houses, country churches, and the newly evolving automobile landscape—many of the subjects, in fact, that still occupy the concerns of professional historians of the vernacular landscape.

Evans's photographs reflected the view that the cultural landscape was a complex symbolic text. According to this perception—which still has many adherents—a landscape's significance and its inherent beauty or tragedy were latent qualities that could be revealed by a perceptive, informed, and suitably empowered interpreter. While Evans would likely have compared himself to contemporary modernists in his construction of multilayered and often enigmatic artistic statements, he was also a visual anthropologist with an essentially semiotic view of culture. He used his camera to engage in the process of "Thick Description" later advocated by Clifford Geertz in the 1960s and 1970s. As conceived by Geertz, "Thick Description" involves "sorting out the structures of signification" by closely studying a culture until one is able to "draw large conclusions from small, but very densely textured facts."[1] This cultural sleuthing resembles the virtuoso intuitive process through which literary analysts explicate complex modernist texts. Evans was a master at visually articulating the cultural significance he discerned in landscapes and objects that most observers routinely disregarded as minor or disconnected social detritus. Virtually every Walker Evans photograph appears to be a densely textured "fact" from which several generations of scholars and photographers have continued to draw conclusions.

Photographs like "Graveyard, Houses, and Steel Mill, Bethlehem, Pennsylvania, November 1935," "Billboards and Frame Houses, Atlanta, Georgia, March 1936," and "Louisiana Plantation House, 1935" take everyday situations and, through studied isolation and precise structuring, transform them into richly symbolic social commentary. In many cases, the act of photography itself enabled Evans to confer symbolic importance on such seemingly innocuous subjects as junkyards, gas stations, and movie posters. For most people, junked cars or rundown houses were hardly worth a second glance. If they paused to consider such scenes at all, it would most likely have been to criticize them as aesthetic affronts or as straightforward evidence of the moral lassitude of their creators, not to analyze them as complex cultural statements. But when photographs of junked cars or sharecroppers' shacks appeared on the wall of a prestigious museum, or in

Walker Evans, "Graveyard, Houses, and Steel Mill, Bethlehem, Pennsylvania, November 1935." Library of Congress.

important publications, the altered context encouraged viewers to reflect on both the photographs and their subjects as significant cultural texts containing valuable information about American society.

. In the midst of the Depression, America was looking for answers to basic questions about where the nation had come from and where it was going. The country needed icons to rally around, whether they were symbols of problems to be overcome or emblems of basic American virtues that had not been corrupted. Although Evans later disavowed the existence of any political intent behind his images, the New Deal mandate to rediscover the sources of America's faltering strength clearly provided an interpretive framework for his personal exploration of the vernacular landscape.

Depending on which of the two one cares to believe, Roy Stryker either developed or adopted Evans's fascination with the social implications of the American landscape. As director of the photographic arm of the New Deal's Resettlement Administration, the Farm Security Administration, and, after World War II, the Standard Oil of New Jersey Photography Project, Stryker was able to exert unparalleled control over the influential image of the American landscape that these enterprises created.[2] The FSA photographers extended Evans's exploration of the symbolic potential of the American cultural landscape. As the Depression dragged on and war broke out in Europe, these photographers shifted their attention from documenting Dustbowl casualties to canonizing rural and small town landscapes. In the process of recording the struggles and triumphs of rural America, they codified a vocabulary of landscape expression and created photographic "documents" that reified a powerful vision of a sacred American landscape, where *Saturday Evening Post* cover homilies had not yet succumbed to the social and visual transformations of post–World War II corporate and consumer culture. Even the tragic images of Dustbowl suffering reflected an optimistic faith in human progress through increased knowledge and efficiency, which subsequent social critics found difficult to sustain. While academic analysts have grown skeptical of the objectivity, motives, and effectiveness of photojournalistic activism, the FSA vision continues to exert considerable influence on the ways that past and present American landscapes are seen and interpreted.

For modern analysts, the photography of Walker Evans and his contemporaries presents two major problems. First, the dominance of the Walker Evans/FSA vision in characterizing American society between the two world wars means that our primary images of the period reflect the prejudices and concerns of half-a-dozen or so well-educated white males, two white women, and, belatedly, one black man.[3] Other valuable perspectives that might contribute to our knowledge of the symbolic and experiential nature of the mid–twentieth century landscape are far less accessible. One wonders, for instance, how the Okies and migrant workers viewed their own landscapes. Their views of their own homes might be expected to differ considerably from those of photographers whose explicit mission was to present images of hardship that would justify New Deal policies. Did Oklahoma and the journey west appear as bleak to the subjects of the FSA photographs as it did to Dorothea Lange and Arthur Rothstein, or were there pockets of contentment and hope in the Dustbowl and images of

Walker Evans, "Billboards and Frame Houses, Atlanta, Georgia, March 1936." Library of Congress.

excitement and adventure along Route 66? How might the landscape of South Dakota have appeared to the fiercely proud farmers who were outraged by Rothstein's staging of the infamous skull pictures?[4] What about the personal landscapes of blacks, Hispanics, Native Americans, and the nonpoor, nonrural people who rarely appear in the more widely disseminated FSA images? These important perspectives on the American cultural landscape find little expression in the body of work that has been promoted by its creators and many later analysts as the period's premier visual document. The more widely disseminated FSA images, meanwhile, present and promote numerous cultural stereotypes such as the sleepy Hispanic village, the beaten, bewildered Okie, and the poverty-stricken southern hillbilly, while reducing the African-American experience to cotton-culture pastorals and scenes of unremitting squalor in crowded northern slums.[5]

The second question is the degree to which Evans and his contemporaries invented the cultural significance of the situations they represented as social facts.[6] Like the Geertzian anthropologist narrating incidents of "Deep Play," in which ordinary experiences theoretically served as ritualized expressions of hidden social values, Evans lifted landscapes out of their everyday context and raised them to the status of symbolic texts. The Walker Evans photograph was the visual equivalent of Geertz's celebrated Balinese cockfight: the figurative portrayal by an outside observer of a complex system of cultural values that may or may not have existed in the minds of its subjects.[7] The intellectual community's acceptance of Evans's interpretations as trenchant evocations of contemporary American life reflected the long-held view that cultural meaning revealed itself in a series of symbolic performances that could be identified and analyzed by qualified experts, rather than as a series of specific events whose primary significance lay in the meanings they had for the people who experienced them. Who knows what the residents of Bethlehem, Pennsylvania, or Hale County, Alabama, thought about the landscapes that they lived in but that Evans's pictures defined for the rest of the world?

In his role as the "expert outsider," structuring the visual facts of everyday life to support his reading of the scenes he witnessed, Evans embodied a long-established trend of cultural analysis. Historically, the self-appointed interpreters of culture have generally held positions of unequal power in relation to their subjects, who seldom saw and were rarely able to contest the conclusions of the ensuing texts. As scientific treatises or artistic masterpieces, most photographs and ethnographies have been presented as authoritative documents about the practices and beliefs of people who generally had limited ability to present their own conceptions of their cultural experiences and values.[8]

Evans's formal brilliance contributed to the apparent authority of his perceptions. With evident confidence in the legitimacy of their visions, both Evans and his Nebraska contemporary Wright Morris structured their photographs with a classical precision that sought to convince the viewer that the scenes they presented were perfectly and properly articulated; to move the lens a foot or two to the right or left would not only ruin the picture,

Wright Morris, "Abandoned Farm with Windmill and House, Western Nebraska, 1941."

but would also undermine the credibility of the interpretive statement.[9] This notion that authority rests in virtuosity has long served to validate literary works as well as to authenticate more "objective" forms of cultural analysis. The seductive appeal of authorial majesty can be seen in the intellectual community's embrace of modernist literature and in the renown accorded to the grand theories of master anthropologists who claim to be capable of discerning a tribe's entire cultural system in the confusion of a chicken fight or of constructing universal systems of human behavior based on a scattering of secondhand accounts of the workings of a few "savage" minds.

In *Reading American Photographs: Images as History, Mathew Brady to Walker Evans*, Alan Trachtenberg has suggested that Evans, in his 1938 book *American Photographs*, deliberately rejected the role of authoritative cultural interpreter. Trachtenberg asserts that *American Photographs* is open-ended and ambiguous; that it presents a multidimensioned and deliberately indeterminate cultural landscape of the sort that postmodern narrators might try to evoke. In his eagerness to extend the current critical emphasis on privileging the receiver's role in negotiating the meaning of cultural productions, Trachtenberg exaggerates the degree to which Evans's photographs were designed to foster ambiguity and encourage alternative readings. He claims that *American Photographs* is "not a finished thesis but a continuous process" of interaction between autonomous viewers and "a series of acts and gestures toward the making of a place." But to suggest that the book, and Evans's photographs in general, "[propose] no immanent whole named America" is to deny the context of the work's conception and initial reception and to credit Evans with the insights and motives of a much later generation of critical theorists and artists.[10]

This sort of hindsight is attractive, and Trachtenberg makes no attempt to disguise the fact that he is viewing historical works through contemporary filters. But it seems more accurate to assume that Evans was influenced by the then-current modernist literary credo that an author was the creator of a complex literary conundrum, in which various narrative twists that initially appeared ambiguous or arbitrary combined to form a precise and laboriously articulated message, which skillful and informed readers could eventually ascertain. Without taking anything away from Trachtenberg's thoughtful analysis of the complexity and sophistication of *American Photographs*, a review of contemporary critical responses to the book—and Evans's own statements—may argue for the more logical conclusion that Evans and his viewers believed that the photographs did, in fact, propose to define American culture as a large, loose, inherently confusing yet ultimately definable whole.

Recent critics revel in disclosing the incomplete and highly opinionated nature of photographic interpretation, but the 1930s and 1940s were the heyday of the naive view of photography as a transparent documentary medium. While we tend to view Walker Evans's images as more sophisticated than those of many of his contemporaries, it is probably wrong to assume that Evans's photographs were interpreted in a radically different manner from other contemporary "documentary" images. As even Trachtenberg himself admits, reviews in the period of the book's initial release addressed the images as insightful social facts, whose distinction lay in their spare formal qualities and the incisiveness of their vision, rather than in the indeterminate messages and existential ambiguity that later critics have ascribed to them. Evans's general reticence, his disavowal of personal political agendas, and the numerous instances Trachtenberg has identified in which his images self-consciously comment upon the discursive practices of photographic seeing might lead some critics to pronounce him a prescient postmodernist. This studied diffidence was an essential component of the myth of the modern-artist-as-intuitive-genius, however, a role Evans seemed to relish. In later years, Evans was less modest. In 1971, he told Museum of Modern Art curator John Szarkowski that he hoped his photographs would go down in history as "authorative [*sic*], transcendent" images of the period.[11]

Lincoln Kirstein, whose accompanying essay explained Evans's work to the readers of *American Photographs*, stressed the book's unity of conception and touted the authenticity of Evans's images. For Kirstein, it was absolutely clear that Evans had created the definitive photographic document of their time. As one turns the pages of *American Photographs*, he advised, "the facts pile up with the prints." While current critics discount the possibility of "objective" social inquiry, in 1938, even as sophisticated an observer as Kirstein could assert that Evans's photographs were "social documents" that testified to American social conditions. Kirstein lauded Evans's dispassionately "clinical" (and thus scientifically objective) vision as a corrective to the "sensational truth" of contemporary photojournalism, which, according to Kirstein, "drugs the eye into believing that it has witnessed a significant fact when it has only caught a flicker." Despite their pretensions to sociological validity, Kirstein saw photojournalists as mere "stamp collectors of unrelated moments," whose "anarchic, naive, and superficial" approach precluded meaningful social analysis. Thanks to Evans's sweeping and supposedly objective gaze, *American Photographs* heralded a restoration of photographic veracity, presenting the "facts of our homes and times, shown surgically, without the intrusion of the poet's or painter's necessary distortions." Kirstein compared Evans's photographs to the comprehensive photographic surveys of Mathew Brady and Eugene Atget. According to Kirstein, the straightforward style of those two men prefigured Evans's own. While other photographers created idiosyncratic artistic expressions of little historical relevance, Evans was one of those unique artists whose photographs comprised a "catalog of the facts of their epoch." [12]

Kirstein presented Evans as the model for a new type of photographer whose task was "to fix and to show the whole aspect of our society." Unlike the sensational photojournalists, Evans "fixed" contemporary American society in photographs that preserved otherwise inchoate impressions as enduring cultural icons. Kirstein applauded Evans's skill in "elevating the casual, the everyday, the literal into specific, permanent symbols." His compositional skill and literary mind "managed to elevate fortuitous accidents into ordained designs." [13]

Poststructuralist critical theory does not look kindly on cultural analysts who attempt to "fix" society into "ordained designs." If culture is only a series of discursive moments situated in the immediate context of their performance, then it is clear that the notion of "elevating the casual, the everyday, the literal into specific, permanent symbols" becomes epistemologically, politically, and ethically suspect. While postmodern photographers and other cultural analysts may have returned to the anarchic stamp-collecting of unrelated moments, Evans's unapologetic authorial control answered the need of his time to fix a symbolic order amidst the flux and disillusionment of Depression-era America.

The meticulously structured symbolic landscape photographs of the 1930s and 1940s reflected the contemporary view that wise and well-intentioned individuals could reshape society into agreed-upon ideal constructions. The pursuit of social and political ideals provided the driving force for much of the FSA photography, while Evans and Morris sought a more abstract and aesthetic form of perfection and clarity. Less self-consciously artistic and more politically overt than Evans, Roy Stryker and his FSA photographers believed that they were documenting the American landscape in order to introduce their audience to the need for limited social reform. In typical New Deal spirit, their best-known photographs reflected a hopeful attitude about America and an underlying faith in social and material progress. While they frequently pointed out America's weaknesses, they generally reaffirmed the strength of its human resources. Documenting the problems facing American society was not a fundamental attack on American values, it was simply the first step in eliminating temporary setbacks and ensuring a return to a cherished way of life, which it simultane-

Wright Morris, "Grain Elevator and Lamp Post, Nebraska, 1940."

ously helped define. The cultural landscape photographers of the 1930s and 1940s called attention to the rising influence of mass communications, consumer capitalism, and automobiles, but much of their imagery was tinged with nostalgia, memorializing the familiar virtues of rural and small town life at a time of rapid social upheaval and economic change. Stryker's belief in the sociological validity of documentary photography was apparent in the title of his governmental division: the "Historical Section" epitomized contemporary faith in the ability of the photographic image to serve as an objective historical record.

ICONOCLASM

The next generation of photographers to explore the American landscape chronicled the effects of the cultural transformations hinted at by their predecessors and sharply questioned the American dream of unlimited material and social progress. They also exploded the myth of documentary veracity, producing highly stylized images that underscored the photographer's subjective interpretation of society. Led by Robert Frank and his influential book *The Americans* (1959), the photographers of the 1950s and 1960s rejected Evans's restrained classicism in favor of a bold, iconoclastic, and essentially romantic reinterpretation of the American cultural landscape.[14] Evans had experimented with small cameras and candid photography, but the photographs of Robert Frank and his followers replaced the calm finality of Evans's more famous classically structured images with a continual flux of ever-changing perspectives, appearances, and values. Photographers influenced by Frank and Henri Cartier-Bresson increasingly reveled in the ways in which split-second timing and clever juxtapositions could imply significant relationships among gestures, forms, and symbols. As with the contemporary trend of abstract expressionist painting, the results of snap-decisions, reflexive gestures, and lucky accidents often appeared to replace carefully conceived and executed compositions.

The spontaneity and visual promiscuity afforded by the popularization of the compact camera combined with the general iconoclasm of the Beat Generation to challenge the primacy of such hallowed photographic criteria as the "correct" technique and the "proper" composition. At the same time, the diminished optical resolution of 35mm film refocused attention from the precise description and extended tonal gradations of large-format fine prints to the symbolic recognition of social relationships or psychological states. These perceptions often found expression in grainy, contrasty, and even blurry photographs that earlier photographers would have considered technically inferior. Photographs were no longer meant to be solemn artistic masterpieces; they rarely tried to be "beautiful" in the conventional fine-art sense. Instead they were supposed to express their author's opinions and emotions—to shout, cry, laugh, whisper, brood, or howl about whatever caught the photographer's attentions. Photographers like Garry Winogrand, who shot hundreds of frames of film for every image he printed, were liable to the photographic variant of Truman Capote's famous criticism of Jack Kerouac.[15] But the appeal of both writer and photographer was the same: one was not concerned so much with Kerouac's or Winogrand's ability to mimic conventional modes of artistic expression, but with how they as individuals responded to their surroundings, and with their ability to transform ordinary scenes to critique mainstream American values. Feelings and flashes of insight, not carefully reasoned facts, were the order of the day.

Taken altogether, these developments led to an era in cultural landscape photography in which dreamlike imagery, odd camera angles, shots to and from moving cars, and an ironic fascination with the ephemeral quality of American symbols and kitsch consumer products replaced the previous generation's quietly dignified enshrinements of the American vernacular landscape. Prominent photographers like Robert Frank, Lee Friedlander, and Garry Winogrand detailed ironies and odd juxtapositions presented in the interaction between people and their landscapes. All sorts of cherished American symbols, from the flag and the ubiquitous automobile to emblems of corporate America and monuments to civic, military, and spiritual virtue, were held up to iconoclastic scrutiny. While Frank created a dark, surreally cinematic vision of a journey across the mid-fifties American landscape, Lee Friedlander used mirrors, reflections, and obstructing elements to fragment America into a barely controlled collage of images and associations. Friedlander's literally iconoclastic work *The American Monument* challenged, parodied, and deconstructed the intended meaning of public monuments throughout the American landscape.[16] Like a number of academic landscape analysts and sociologists during the 1960s, many photographers of the period concentrated on the users of social spaces, regarding the cultural landscape less as a heroic construction or immutable emblem of cultural achievement than as a stage where cultural processes and private and public lives were enacted.[17] Some of Winogrand's most famous series focused on specific environments such as zoos, rodeos, or public demonstrations, but the actual imagery was often more concerned with human relations within a common type of space than with the physical landscape as a separate symbolic entity.

THE PROFANE

By the mid-1970s, the built environment had retaken center stage, though restraint replaced romanticism as the ruling aesthetic of cultural landscape photography. In an attempt to reinvest photography with the documentary illusion of unfiltered transcription, landscape photographers such as Lewis Baltz, Robert Adams, and Joe Deal attempted to reduce the artist's visible imprint by pursuing a detached and supposedly democratic vision. This new aesthetic, dubbed the "New Topographics" for its concern with the precise rendition of appearances and for its self-conscious invocation of nineteenth-century western landscape photographers as models of supposedly objective photographic practice, professed that the ultimate value of the photographic process lay in its ability to record appearances with a minimum amount of interpretation by the photographer.[18] The photographer was expected to forego an egotistical stance as heroic creator of form and significance and serve as a dispassionate witness to mundane scenes and events. According to Lewis Baltz, one of the leading theorists of the movement, "The ideal photographic document would appear to be without author or art."[19]

The New Topographics photographers' landscapes were antidramatic in form, content, and tonality. If the tightly structured symbolic landscapes of Evans and Morris recalled the carefully controlled perspectives and complex iconography of sixteenth-century Italian landscape painters, the New Topographics photographers recalled the detached, all-encompassing gaze of the Flemish realists. In contrast to the meticulously constructed photographs of Evans or the precisely timed juxtapositions of Friedlander or Winogrand, the New Topographics landscapes often appear indifferent to spatial or temporal variation. The timeless, almost haphazard appearance

Robert Adams, "Colorado Springs, Colorado, 1968."

of many New Topographics landscapes diminished the individual photographer's apparent input and cast the photograph as the objective transcription of social and physical facts. Superficially, at least, the photographs appeared to be the dispassionate results of autonomous photomechanical processes rather than the visual polemics of self-interested authors. Once again, changes in the technical process of making photographs reinforced shifts in aesthetic and conceptual concerns. As optical precision and finely graded tonal rendition supplanted maneuverability and split-second timing, hulking eight-by-ten-inch Deardorff cameras replaced tiny Leicas as the badge of the photographic elite.

In addition to minimizing the formal drama and individual visual impact of their photographs, many of the leading New Topographics photographers sought out the most mundane subject matter in their self-proclaimed effort to deny the iconographic significance of their images. Joe Deal, whose photographs appeared in the original New Topographics exhibit, claimed that he was committed to "denying the uniqueness of the subject matter . . . in the belief that the most extraordinary image might be the most prosaic, with a minimum of interference from the photographer."[20]

In practice, most of the New Topographics photographers gravitated toward a specific sort of subject matter: the new industrial spaces and tract housing developments of the West and Southwest, whose visual monotony mirrored the mind-numbing repetitiveness and calculated banality of their images. In both style and subject matter, the reticent vision of the New Topographics appeared to bear witness to the growing contention on the part of geographers, designers, and critics that deadening uniformity and rampant environmental degradation had become the primary characteristics of the modern American landscape. Baltz's photographs of the development of Park City, Utah, and of nameless industrial parks near Irvine, California, looked as if they could have been taken in practically any newly suburbanized region of the country.[21] In Baltz's prefabricated America, Lewis Hine's heroic testimonials to America's industrial vigor gave way to muted confirmations of mass-produced apathy. In hundreds of bland, uninspiring photographs, Baltz and Colorado photographer Robert Adams created an image of America as a land of bland, new, uninspiring spaces.[22] As step-by-step documents of development processes, the photographs of Baltz and Adams were unmatched; as art for general consumption they were as unsatisfying as the environments they claimed to represent: intellectually estimable perhaps, but emotionally unapproachable. Nevertheless, the New Topographics aesthetic dominated "serious" landscape photography throughout the 1970s and 1980s. While some aficionados of minimalist art undoubtedly approved of their spare formal qualities, the primary reason for the dominance of New Topographics was that many critics be-

Robert Adams, "Aurora, Colorado, 1974."

lieved that their sterile, alienated images served not only as accurate reflections of the contemporary American landscape, but also as chilling metaphors for the fate of humankind in the late twentieth century.

If the cultural landscape photography of the 1930s exhibited the contemporary determination to define a sacred American landscape and Frank's photographs reflected the reckless iconoclasm of the Beat Generation, the New Topographics offered an appropriate testimony to late-modern apathy and alienation. While Evans, Morris, and the FSA consecrated and Frank and Friedlander questioned, the New Topographics photographers quietly observed that the American cultural landscape had degenerated into a morass of bankrupt dreams, existential despair, and environmental despoilment. The cultural landscape of the 1930s proclaimed confidence in the possibility of exercising control for higher purposes, whether social or artistic; Frank's generation relied on good fortune and a relentless search for possibilities; the New Topographics philosophy suggested that the possibilities had been exhausted, rejected flashes of individual insight as illusory or self-serving, and embraced an anesthetizing detachment as a refuge from the presumption of control and responsibility. The indiscriminate banality, homogeneity, and sheer ugliness that characterized the New Topographics' vision reflected the photographers' inability or unwillingness to empathize with the modern built environment or its inhabitants.

The writings of many geographers, sociologists, and architectural critics supported the contention that the New Topographics' numbing detachment was not the result of a paucity of authorial vision, but an accurate reflection of the intrinsic inhumanity of the modern landscape.[23] In *Place and Placelessness*, geographer Edward Relph asserted, "The new landscape is characterized not by its profound meaning but by its separation from us." Relph's analysis of the contemporary built environment as a wasteland of spirit-deadening placelessness reads like an explication of a Baltz or Adams photograph. According to Relph, modern development practices had created a landscape in which "rationalism and absurdity undermine commitment to place, everydayness and simplicity promote uniformity [and] proteanism destroys existing places." Like the New Topographics photographers, Relph looked at the modern American landscape and saw "a geography of placelessness, a labyrinth of endless similarities." As the twentieth century drew to a close, Relph maintained, Americans found themselves adrift in "a 'placelessness geography' in which different localities both look and feel alike, and in which distinctive places are experienced only through superficial and stereotyped images."[24]

BEYOND THE SACRED AND THE PROFANE:
PHOTOGRAPHY, POSTMODERN ETHNOGRAPHY,
AND THE SENSE OF PLACE

Swayed by the fervent jeremiads of the philosophers of placelessness, one can scarcely be blamed for viewing the modern landscape as a profane space that cripples human awareness and social activity. After viewing the grim testimonials of the New Topographics, one is tempted to agree with their suggestion that the mass-produced modern environment renders meaningful association with individualized and significant places a lost experience that survives only in a handful of well-designed architectural projects and Black Forest backwaters. This perception can endure, however, only as long as one refuses to recognize that the mass of people are not romantic geographers or alienated photographers, but home owners, apartment dwellers, family members, neighborhood residents, and explorative children. Banal and featureless as they may have appeared when held up to Robert Adams's unsympathetic scrutiny, the tract houses and doublewide trailers along Colorado's Front Range were people's homes. Individuals lived, talked, played, fought, celebrated birthdays, made love, grew old, and entertained grandchildren in them—though one could scarcely imagine this from Adams's grim depictions.

Before condemning a considerable portion of the modern landscape—and, by implication, its inhabitants—to such a subhuman status of deprivation and despair, it is important to remember that the dismal interpretations provided by a few prominent critics are just that: interpretations. In the words of anthropologist James Clifford, they represent not "*the* story, but a story among other stories"[25]—and stories provided not by the inhabitants of the landscapes in question, but by outside observers, each with their own personal agendas. What Relph or Baltz chose to portray as undifferentiated wastelands and insubstantial structures might have existed for their inhabitants as "the house we moved into after we got married," "the place we used to play baseball," or "the parking lot where I first kissed Betty Lou."

Contemporary photographers and a group of ethnographers who refer to themselves as "Postmodern Anthropologists" have begun to explore a variety of investigative strategies and representational techniques designed to give greater emphasis to the insider's interpretation of cultural significance. One of the primary tasks of postmodern anthropology is to dislodge the semiotic paradigm which casts the ethnographer as interpreter of culture-as-text with a discursive paradigm that encourages the anthropologist to present cultural events as specific incidents whose meaning is negotiated by the individuals who experience them. By challenging the authority of the autonomous photographer or critic to define the nature of cultural experience, these photographers and ethnographers privilege the perception of the cultural insider over the "official" interpretations of scholars and other outside "experts." By viewing the cultural landscape as a composition to be analyzed in literary or aesthetic terms rather than as an environment for living and working, "expert" critics have often overlooked the ways in which places function and gain significance for their everyday inhabitants.

Unlike the seemingly authoritative interpretations supplied by the New Topographics photographers or by their more optimistic New Deal predecessors, the postmodern anthropologists don't profess to decode culture as if it were some sort of obscure text or to penetrate to some internal logic of structure or universal essence. Instead, they try to evoke the multiplicity of meanings and perspectives inherent in any cultural situation. Acknowledging that the perfect, all-inclusive interpretation is an impossible and ethically suspect goal, postmodern anthropology is content to be discursive rather than definitive. The postmodern ethnography, therefore, like the work of several recent "documentary" photographers, aspires to be evocative rather than analytic, fragmentary rather than complete, authored rather than authoritative, a dialogue rather than a monologue, collaborative rather than condescending, and allegorical rather than representational.

While anthropologists have explored these concepts in relation to a wide array of subjects, several recent photographers have employed postmodern narrative techniques such as polyvocality, collaborative authorship, pastiche, and situated discourse in order to call attention to the varieties of environmental experience. Consider, for example, the ways in which photographers Joel Sternfeld and Bill Owens have portrayed the modern American suburb. By encouraging us to view the suburban landscape through the impressions of its inhabitants, these two photographers present the supposedly profane, undifferentiated spaces of contemporary suburbia as a collection of meaningful and individualized places.

Joel Sternfeld reverses the traditional definition of the environmental portrait. Conventional environmental portraiture as practiced by Helmut Newton and Arnold Newman employed the subject's physical environment as the means of evoking character. Sternfeld's environmental portraits present individuals as the key to understanding the personality of the landscapes that they inhabit. In this way, Sternfeld encourages the viewer to consider such routinely criticized landscapes as trailer parks, retirement condominiums, amusement parks, and suburbs through the experience of the people who live and work in them and thus invest them with meaning on a daily basis.[26]

Joel Sternfeld, "Page, Arizona, August 1983."

It is easy to criticize trailer parks. But when Sternfeld confronts us with an image like "Page, Arizona, August 1983" he asks the viewer to respond to trailer parks as the everyday home environment of a normal-looking woman who doesn't appear appreciably degraded or dehumanized by her supposedly insubstantial physical surroundings. By situating the abstract evil of trailer park life in the context of a specific and apparently content human life, Sternfeld reminds his audience that environments that generalizing critics tend to dismiss out of hand can be invested with considerable individuality and significance by the people who inhabit them. Many of Sternfeld's photographs demonstrate the ways in which inhabitants have personalized their supposedly undifferentiated environments. "Buckingham, Pennsylvania, August 1978" demonstrates the ability of children to make place out of space by creating a fantasy landscape of their own. "Near

Joel Sternfeld, "The Bronx, New York (Sculpture by John Ahearn and Rigoberto Torres), November 1982."

Lake Powell, Arizona, August 1979" shows how a basketball hoop serves to differentiate place from abstract space on the border between built and natural wastelands. "The Bronx, New York (Sculpture by John Ahearn and Rigoberto Torres), November 1982" provides evidence of the willingness and ability of local communities to create environmental identity and cultural pride in the midst of landscapes long ago written off by the professional design community.

Sternfeld's suburban portraits also demonstrate the postmodern anthropologists' concern with polyvocality and the multiplicity of meanings. "Canyon County, California, June 1983," "Beverly Hills, California, May 1979," and "Domestic Workers Waiting for a Bus, Atlanta, Georgia, April 1983" present divergent views of the meaning of suburban America. "Can-

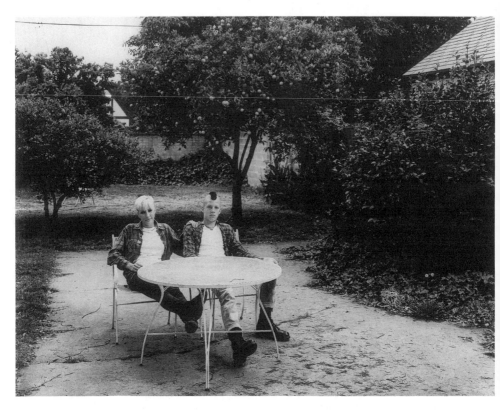

Joel Sternfeld, "Studio City, California, July 1983."

yon County" presents the classic image of suburban America as the idealized landscape of wealthy white men and their perfect blonde daughters. "Beverly Hills" portrays the suburb as a Garden of Eden for its hot tub–ensconced inhabitants. "Domestic Workers" gives the viewer a contrasting perspective on the suburbs. Sternfeld's photograph presents the suburban landscape through the eyes of three black maids who are shut off from its attractions, forced to stand in the middle of the road waiting for a bus amidst the three-car garages of an affluent subdivision.

Bill Owens's *Suburbia* goes beyond Sternfeld's implicit suggestion of the inhabitants' points of view to provide actual commentaries from the subjects of his photographs. Owens mediates criticism of the suburban lifestyle by combining photographs of suburban landscapes with quotations that he claims reflect "what the people feel about themselves."[27] The highly specific nature of many of the comments suggests that Owens showed the photographs to his subjects and asked them to supply their own interpretations. This strategy shifts the tone of the book from a photographer's assessment of suburban life to a kind of suburban confessional, in which Owens serves as a mediator between the people of Livermore, California, and the book's audience. Obviously, Owens has carefully edited his selections; some of the quotations seem almost too good to be true. But assuming the selections are genuine, Owens's approach enables his suburbanites to participate in conveying the meaning of their environment to the readers of *Suburbia*.

Many of Owens's subjects take this opportunity to explain the appeal of middle-class activities and mass-produced environments that the outsider might perceive as superficial or banal. Even when the comments seem as clichéd as the lifestyle they describe, they provide personal testimony to the attractions of the often-criticized suburban dream. In one example, an unexceptional couple stands in a modern kitchen spooning creamed corn into the mouth of an alert-looking baby. "We're really happy. Our kids are healthy, we eat good food and we have a really nice home" proclaims the accompanying quote. They are both a bit overweight, the plastic fruit provides a subtle jibe at their middle-class sensibilities, and a high voltage relay station fills the view through their sliding glass patio door. But what right has the outside observer to suggest that their environment or lifestyle prevents them from being happy, when they assert that they are?[28]

One of the most significant advantages of coupling photographs and insiders' interpretations in this manner is that the subjects' comments can help combat the reader's tendency to project his or her own prejudices into the photographs. When photographs of the cultural landscape appear without any indication of what the scenes mean to their inhabitants, they serve as Rorschach blots awaiting the unrestrained projection of the viewer's prejudices. While the reader's bias can never be totally eliminated, Owens's approach transforms his subjects from passive anthropological specimens to active participants in the construction of their cultural significance. Of course, printed subjects' comments can be used to reinforce cultural stereotypes. At first glance, in fact, Owens's ironic humor makes it easy to mistake *Suburbia* for a condescending manipulation of both verbal and visual imagery compiled to belittle his subjects' experiences. Owens's suburbanites often say things that display their bourgeois values and underscore the tawdriness of their environments. But Owens's book is more subtle and so-

Bill Owens, Suburbia, *1973. Caption reads, "We're really happy. Our kids are healthy, we eat good food and we have a really nice home."*

phisticated than it initially appears: while it attracts and disarms readers by playing into many antisuburban stereotypes, it subversively empowers its "victims" by allowing them to speak up as proud and opinionated individuals.

Many of Owens's photographs are potentially tragicomic images that initially seem to be straightforward indictments of the banality of suburban life. But Owens allows the subjects to defend themselves by explaining the significance and attraction that the scenes hold for them. One photograph depicts an elderly couple posed in the bedroom of their mobile home. The comment accompanying the image states, "We've been married for 35 years and for the last five we have lived in the trailer park. We love it because everything is so convenient and the neighbors watch out for each other."

Bill Owens, Suburbia, *1973. Caption reads, "I get a lot of compliments on the front room wall. I like Italian Syrocco floral designs over the mantel. It goes well with the Palos Verde rock fireplace."*

Another image shows a woman sitting at an electric organ with a man seated behind her at a desk. The man in the photograph proclaims, "We really enjoy living in a mobile home. My hobby is collecting coins and my wife plays her Wurlitzer for entertainment." In similar fashion, though sophisticated designers and advocates of authenticity in the built environment would undoubtedly cringe at the suggestion, an obviously proud matron sits in front of her fireplace and proclaims, "I get a lot of compliments on the front room wall. I like Italian Syrocco floral designs over the mantel. It goes well with the Palos Verde rock fireplace."

Several comments clearly express the subject's playful participation in shaping the humorous messages of certain photographs. A harried-looking woman writing a check at a kitchen table piled high with bills grins at the camera: "If Bank of America only knew the truth. . . ." Another housewife makes fun of her gigantic hair curlers, and two obviously inebriated men seated at a tiny corner bar joke about their drinking. Owens's approach allows the subjects to acknowledge and participate in the humor of such images. They become not so much the objects of the joke but its perpetrators. When photographer, subject, and viewer are all privy to the same conversation, the interpretation of culture becomes an empathetic act rather than a predatory incursion. In such cases the subject, photographer, and viewer are united by shared understanding rather than divided by exploitative condescension.

While Owens and his subjects counter elitist critics by demonstrating that such things as community pride, civic spirit, and aesthetic awareness exist in the suburbs, they also voice their awareness that suburban life is far from perfect, that it does have social, economic, and architectural shortcomings. Owens presents several images that suggest the problems that suburbs pose for minorities. A black woman complains about the problem of maintaining a sense of cultural identity, while a Chinese family speaks of their inability to purchase familiar food. An interview with a garbage man provides a skillful critique of the wastefulness of the affluent suburban lifestyle. Criticism of the shortsightedness of suburban builders appears in a photograph of a family sitting in lawn chairs in front of their garage. "Our house is built with the living room in the back," explains the caption, "so in the evenings we sit out front of the garage and watch the traffic go by."

One of the last photographs in the book portrays the inexorable march of suburbanization, situating the faceless generalizations of the New Topographics in specific human terms. "They cut down our tree forts to put in some new houses," protest two boys on stingray bicycles. "We don't want houses. We want our trees back. They paid us five dollars to keep people back while they cut up the trees, but we're not going to keep anybody out." This image and its accompanying text criticize the development process while underscoring the ability of individuals to invest seemingly undifferentiated spaces with significant attachments. While their protest may be in vain, the boys refuse to sit by as passive victims while the developers destroy the hideouts they had created in the kind of vacant lot that the New Topographics photographers categorically dismissed as unredeemable wastelands.

Meridel Rubenstein's photographs explore another approach to evoking the human experience of place. In order to suggest the complex nature of environmental experience, Rubenstein makes collages with various combinations of portraits, landscape photographs (often of the same site seen

Bill Owens, Suburbia, *1973. Caption reads, "Our house is built with the living room in the back, so in the evenings we sit out front of the garage and watch the traffic go by."*

from several different perspectives), found objects, poems, letters, and pieces of fiction. According to Rubenstein, these constructions allow her to suggest the way that such intangible qualities as the relationship between the past, present, and future contribute to the experience of the places she photographs.[29] In "Past and Present Owners of 'The Macario Torres Place,' Progresso, 1982–83," for example, she combines a portrait of the current owners with a handwritten list of the former owners, along with a photograph of the land itself. The aim is to evoke the ways in which the identity of a place is constituted not just by its current appearance and inhabitants, but also by the human history that has transpired there.

In "Fred and Maria Luna, 1982–83," Rubenstein places a photograph of

Meridel Rubenstein, "Fred and Maria Luna, 1982–83."

the couple in the center of four separate images depicting a house, a road, a view through a window, and a tree. While it is unclear whether or not these photographs represent actual elements of the Lunas' environmental experience, the effect of the collage is to suggest the many elements and experiences that constitute geographical perception. The collage reminds the viewer that the Lunas and their place are inexorably bound together: each is a constituent of the other and should not be dissected into abstract analytical entities. Rubenstein's image asserts that the Lunas' place is not just the house they live in and the land they own, but a complex association of places and experiences that includes the Lunas, their relationship to each other, their religion, the drive to their house, the view from their window, and the natural environment and ranch activities that provide their livelihood. In addition to asserting the complexity of environmental perceptions, Rubenstein's use of multiple imagery allows her to counter the tendency of the single heroic photograph to assert the primacy of one particular viewpoint as the "correct" perspective of a subject in either a formal or symbolic sense.

Meridel Rubenstein, "Delpha Graham and Son, 'All my dreams are of this place,' Progresso, 1982–83."

Another Rubenstein construction, "Delpha Graham and Son, 'All my dreams are of this place,' Progresso, 1982–83," consists of a photograph of a mother and son that is framed in an oval of natural wood and suspended in front of a collage containing a large photograph of a tree and three smaller photographs of an adobe house. This collage's combination of simple, snapshotlike images of a home and images of family, generational change, and rootedness, together with the suggestion of spiritual significance provided by the title, epitomizes the "humanist placemaking" advocated by Edward Relph. Relph urges geographers to develop an approach to the study of places that is "responsive to local structures of meaning and experience, to particular situations, and to the variety of levels of place." One need not be a convert to the more mystical aspects of phenomenology in order to admire the evocative power with which an image like "Delpha Graham and Son . . ." fulfills Relph's request for an approach to the built environment that "takes its inspiration from the existential significance of place, the need many people have for a profound attachment to places, and the ontological principles of dwelling and shaping identified by Heidegger."[30]

Some critics might complain that Rubenstein's approach artificially fragments the environments she depicts, isolating and juxtaposing elements in a way that never occurs in the real world, and thereby creates a fictive world that reflects the author's perception more than it captures any shared ethnographic reality. The same could be said of the landscape photographs of Thomas Barrow and Allan Sekula, who also work with multiple imagery as a means of suggesting relationships between a variety of objects and concepts in the cultural landscape.[31] But, like the postmodern anthropologists, these photographers aim to suggest the varieties of meaning in any given cultural experience, rather than to attempt to represent observable facts or to provide one single authoritative statement. Anthropologist Stephen Tyler's description of the allegorical function of the postmodern ethnography provides an apt summary of the sort of poetic recognition that these photographers attempt to awaken in their audience. According to Tyler, postmodern ethnography "defamiliarizes common sense reality in a bracketed context of performance, evokes a fantasy whole abducted from fragments, and then returns the participants to the world of common sense—transformed, renewed, and sacralized."[32]

The use of representational strategies such as multiple voices, fragmentary perceptions, divergent points of view, and verbal and visual pastiche reinforces the contention that the ethnographer's perspective provides just one interpretation among many possible options. The unconventional form of postmodern ethnographic texts and much recent cultural landscape photography reflects a self-conscious effort to make the reader aware that the photograph or text is a subjective interpretation. These radical representational techniques may not always reflect the inhabitants' points of view, but they serve a valuable function by encouraging reflection on the nature of cultural experience and on the process of cultural interpretation.[33]

The viewer knows that a Rubenstein collage is as much a personal fiction created by the artist as a reflection of the New Mexico landscape. Rubenstein makes no pretense of conventional ethnographic representation. Her collages could be entirely fictional; the implicit relationships among the landscape, people, poems, and artifacts may not exist in these specific forms anywhere but in the minds of the collage's creator and viewers. But this does not detract from the work's status as valid and insightful reflection on the relationship between place and culture. After viewing a Rubenstein exhibition, the amateur or professional landscape analyst may view the cultural landscape with a new appreciation of the many ways in which it functions as a place for symbolic interaction, for personal experience, and for the storing and sharing of cultural and spiritual values.

While some critics may object to the fragmentary and incomplete nature of such presentations, anthropologist George Marcus argues for "a sustained tolerance of incompleteness and indeterminateness," since this corresponds, in his view, both to the actual state of the world and to any individual's ability to make sense of it.[34] Stephen Tyler agrees with this assessment, asserting that "a Post-Modern anthropology is fragmentary because it cannot be otherwise." This is true, Tyler claims, because "life in the field is itself fragmentary, not at all organized around familiar ethnological terms such as kinship, economy, and religion."[35]

To represent culture otherwise would be misleading and inaccurate, a submission to the misguided methodologies of conventional cultural analysis. Such an approach would also contradict the postmodern anthropologist's commitment to the emergent nature of cultural meaning. By preserving the fragmentation, incompleteness, confusion, and multiple perspectives inherent in any cultural situation, postmodern ethnography and the photography of Rubenstein, Barrow, Sekula, and Donigan Cummings encourage the reader to participate in the search for meaning and order among the evidence presented in their texts and exhibitions. Whereas the conventional cultural analyst treats the reader as a passive consumer of prepackaged cultural theory, the author of the postmodern ethnography forces the reader to become an active participant in the dialogic negotiation of cultural meaning and significance. Of course, even the postmodern anthropologist excludes, censors, exaggerates, and otherwise shapes the material presented in the text. While polyvocal texts can be just as controlled as other forms of cultural interpretation, the postmodern ethnographer's attempt to stress the indeterminate nature of cultural meaning and empower diverse voices represents an acute awareness of this problem as well as a desire to distribute ethnographic authority more equitably.

Postmodern anthropology's commitment to collaboration in the construction of cultural meaning can also encourage a sense of partnership between scholars and informants in the cooperative search for meaning. Genuinely collaborative projects can contribute to community pride and self-awareness.[36] The widespread currency of the photographic image can be a valuable asset in the attempt to bring the results of scholarly inquiry to a broader, nonacademic audience. Unlike much scholarly prose, most photographs transmit their observations in a manner that remains intelligible to a wide variety of audiences, including, more often than not, the inhabitants of the observed places themselves. This is particularly significant in the realm of intercultural research, where subjects and observers are likely to have different modes of discourse and divergent agendas. Such ethical concerns further unite photography with the phenomenological approach to the study of environmental experience. "One of the first aims of a phenomenology of geography," writes phenomenologist Edward Relph, "should be to retrieve these experiences from the academic netherworld and return them to everyone by reawakening a sense of wonder about the earth and its places."[37]

CONCLUSION

This essay has traced the development of several important trends in twentieth-century cultural landscape photography, locating their interpretive strategies in the intellectual concerns of their times. As a number of prominent American studies scholars have recently demonstrated, photographers have long been among the most insightful interpreters of the relationship between place, landscape, and culture.[38] The insightful cultural analysis provided by these photographers suggests that the active practice of cultural landscape photography could have an important role to play in future American studies scholarship. While the subject matter, point of view, and representational strategies employed by various photographers reflect their individual proclivities and unique moments in history, recent critical debates have emphasized that similar forces temper the writings of professional historians.

Scholars of the relationships between place and American culture have much to gain by exploring the potential synthesis between their aims and recent developments in anthropology and creative photography. The academic community should not simply report on, but actively embrace, more widespread and innovative experimentation with interdisciplinary approaches that combine photography and text as a means of analyzing the relationships between landscapes and cultures. As the geographer D. W. Meinig has emphatically stated, the time is right for "a greater openness, a clearing away of pedantic barriers, for a toleration of geographic creativity wherever it may lead."[39]

Unfortunately, traditional boundaries between the arts, sciences, and humanities still hold sway. The American studies community still finds it proper to critique photographs rather than create them, and ethnography is only gradually making headway in academic American studies practice. Is it unreasonable, though, to suggest that American studies scholars might combine the efforts of anthropologists and contemporary landscape photographers, taking camera and tape recorder in hand to interpret the evolving landscapes, places, and cultures of modern America? The interdisciplinary nature of American studies can only profit by exploring a synthesis between its aims and the conceptual issues, representational techniques, and ethical stances evolving in postmodern anthropology and landscape photography. Further development of a cooperatively evolved, inhabitant-based paradigm that presents and preserves cultural differences and multiple voices through various combinations of verbal and visual imagery offers unsurpassed potential as a highly evocative and ethically desirable approach to studying the human experience of place.

NOTES

1. Clifford Geertz, *The Interpretation of Cultures* (New York: Basic Books, 1973), 9, 28. While this comparison might initially seem anachronistic, Thick Description was an essentially modernist enterprise that owed a large debt to the New Criticism.

Its popularity in anthropological circles in the 1960s and 1970s suggests the varying rates at which ideas move through different academic disciplines.

2. See F. Jack Hurley, *Portrait of a Decade: Roy Stryker and the Development of Documentary Photography in the Thirties* (Baton Rouge: Louisiana University Press, 1972); and Roy Stryker and Nancy Wood, *In This Promised Land: America 1935–1943 as Seen in the FSA Photographs* (New York: Gallahad Books, 1973), for general accounts of the FSA photography project. Stephen Plattner's *Roy Stryker, U.S.A., 1943–1950, The Standard Oil of New Jersey Photographic Project* (Austin: University of Texas Press, 1983) chronicles the continuation of Stryker's efforts to create a photographic record of America after the government stopped funding his project.

3. As the project continued under the Office of War Information, Stryker hired a few more women photographers. In *Let Us Now Praise Famous Women: Women Photographers of the U.S. Government 1935–1945* (London and New York: Pandora Press, 1987) Andrea Fisher details the activities of the government's female photographers and suggests that their photographs exhibited a distinctly feminine sensibility.

4. A number of historians have described this incident. While photographing drought conditions in South Dakota in 1936, Rothstein moved a bleached cattle skull around to get photographs against several backgrounds. When newspapers demonstrated Rothstein's multiple images, westerners who felt that the FSA was unfairly criticizing their region used the incident to denounce the FSA photographic project in general as fabricated New Deal propaganda. See Hurley, *Portrait of a Decade*, 86–90.

5. Richard Wright, in his *Twelve Million Black Voices: A Folk History of the Negro in the United States* (New York: Viking Press, 1941), assembled photographs taken primarily by white FSA photographers to illustrate his impassioned portrayal of African-American culture and landscapes. *Documenting America: 1935–1945* (Berkeley: University of California Press, 1988), edited by Carl Fleischer and Beverly Brannan, with essays by Alan Trachtenberg and Lawrence Levine, addresses the bias of the Farm Security Administration's photographic "documentation" of American life, and provides a glimpse of some of the FSA/OWI photographs of blacks, Hispanics, Asians, urbanites, and socialites that have rarely appeared in published sources. The fact that these photographs have languished in the files for years underscores the degree to which Stryker and subsequent interpreters of the FSA/OWI images have used these "documents" to reify a highly selective view of the period (and also of the history of photography).

6. Scholars have been debunking the myth of the objective documentary photograph for several decades, and this essay need not recount the argument that even the most self-avowedly "documentary" photographs are highly subjective opinions

rather than the authoritative facts that some early practitioners and writers have claimed. Two of the best books on the cultural bias of documentary photography are William Stott's *Documentary Photography in Thirties America* (1973; Chicago: University of Chicago Press, 1986), and Alan Trachtenberg's *Reading American Photographs: Images as History, Mathew Brady to Walker Evans* (New York: Hill and Wang, 1989). James Curtis's *Mind's Eye/Mind's Truth: FSA Photography Reconsidered* (Philadelphia: Temple University Press, 1989) provides a blow-by-blow account of the numerous manipulations Evans and his contemporaries performed in order to produce images that would "document" their personal interpretations of Depression life.

7. For a discussion of the shortcomings of the Geertzian semiotic approach's reliance on "Deep Play" situations that present culture as "a sort of ideal, a Platonic performance," see Vincent Crapanzano, "Hermes' Dilemma: The Masking of Subversion in Ethnographic Description," in *Writing Culture: The Poetics and Politics of Ethnography*, ed. James Clifford and George Marcus (Berkeley: University of California Press, 1986), 55–76.

8. See Talal Asad, "The Concept of Cultural Translation in British Sociology," in *Writing Culture*, 141–64.

9. In *The Inhabitants* (1946; New York: De Capo Press, 1971) and *The Home Place* (1948; Lincoln: University of Nebraska Press, 1975) Morris evoked the landscape and sense of place of his Nebraska home with a three-part harmony of photographs, dialogue, and observation. In narrative terms, these books serve as valuable precedents for contemporary efforts to evoke the multiple dimensions of the human experience of place. Morris's multiple voices were all products of a single refined intelligence, however. Contemporary photographers and ethnographers often try to include the perceptions of the actual inhabitants in their work.

10. Trachtenberg, *Reading American Photographs*, 284.

11. Quoted in *Walker Evans*, with an introduction by John Szarkowski (New York: Museum of Modern Art, 1971), 13. Szarkowski advised: "It is difficult to know now with certainty whether Evans recorded the America of his youth or invented it." At the same time, he acknowledged that "the accepted myth of our recent past is in some measure the creation of this photographer." More people have probably seen Evans's work in collections like this retrospective or as individual "greatest hits" images in larger photographic compendiums than in the more varied and subtly structured *American Photographs* (New York: Museum of Modern Art, 1938). Viewing Evans's photographs as individual statements in this manner would tend to promote the reading of his photographs as attempts to present masterful and complete cultural texts, rather than as ambiguous elements in an open-ended literary construction.

12. Evans, *American Photographs*, 191–97.

13. Ibid., 192–97.

14. Robert Frank, *The Americans* (1959; Millertown, N.Y.: Aperture, 1969).

15. Winogrand rose to prominence through numerous exhibitions in the 1960s. He continued more or less in the same mold until his death in 1984. For examples of his work, see Garry Winogrand, *The Animals* (New York: Museum of Modern Art, 1969), *Public Relations* (New York: Museum of Modern Art, 1977), *Stock Photographs* (Austin: University of Texas Press, 1980), and the posthumous retrospective *Figments from the New World* (New York: Museum of Modern Art, 1988).

16. Friedlander gained recognition at the same time as Winogrand, but his work has developed in a number of different directions since the 1960s. See Lee Friedlander, *The American Monument* (New York: Eakins, 1976). *Like a One-Eyed Cat: Photographs by Lee Friedlander* (New York: Harry N. Abrams, 1989) provides an overview of the artist's work.

17. Writers like J. B. Jackson, Jane Jacobs, and William Whyte were contesting the conventional emphasis on the built environment as an aesthetic entity that should be comprehensively designed by powerful experts. They called attention to the users of ordinary landscapes and attempted to validate the experiences and concerns of people who inhabited landscaspes that didn't conform to the upper-middle-class norms of urban planners. Environmental psychologists and sociologists teamed with architects and planners to study the ways in which people used and perceived urban spaces.

18. See *The New Topographics: Photographs of the Man-Altered Landscape* (Rochester, N.Y.: International Museum of Photography, 1975). Ironically, a number of scholars and photographers were soon to demonstrate that many of the most prominent nineteenth-century western landscape photographers had carefully framed and manipulated their images to reflect various aesthetic, economic, and political concerns. See Rick Dingus, *The Photographic Artifacts of Timothy O'Sullivan* (Albuquerque: University of New Mexico Press, 1982); John Szarkowski, *American Landscapes: Photographs from the Collection of the Museum of Modern Art* (New York: Museum of Modern Art, 1981); and Peter Hales, *William Henry Jackson and the Transformation of the American Landscape* (Philadelphia: Temple University Press, 1988).

19. Lewis Baltz quoted in Thomas Barrow, Shelley Armitage, and William Tydeman, *Reading into Photography: Selected Essays 1959–1980* (Albuquerque: University of New Mexico Press, 1982), 57.

20. Joe Deal quoted in ibid., 94.

21. See Lewis Baltz, *The New Industrial Parks near Irvine California* (New York: Light Impressions, 1974), and *Park City* (Millerton, N.Y.: Aperture, 1980).

22. While other members of the New Topographics have feigned indifference toward the social implications of their imagery, Adams has been more forthright and articulate about the cultural polemics of his photographs. A recent retrospective, *To Make It Home: Photographs of the American West* (New York: Aperture, 1989), includes an extended discussion of his motivations. Two of his earlier books, *Denver* (Boulder: Colorado Associated University Press, 1972) and *The New West: Photographs along the Colorado Front Range* (Boulder: Colorado Associated University Press, 1974), contain brief explanations of his desire to use photography to critique the modern American landscape.

23. Lewis Mumford wrote early and often on the negative effects of modernization on American landscapes and society. Peter Blake's *God's Own Junkyard* (New York: Holt, Rinehart, and Winston, 1964), Ian Nairn's *The American Landscape: A Critical View* (New York: Random House, 1965), and Christopher Tunnard's *Manmade America: Chaos or Control?* (New Haven: Yale University Press, 1963) provided outspoken critiques of the perceived deterioration of the American landscape. Blake's book is notable for its heavy reliance on the persuasive power of landscape photography. Phenomenologist geographers and architects have recently been among the most vociferous critics of the modern built environment. Edward Relph's *Place and Placelessness* (London: Pion Limited, 1976), *Rational Landscapes and Humanistic Geography* (London: Croom Helm, 1981), and *The Modern Urban Landscape* (Baltimore: Johns Hopkins University Press, 1986) and Christian Norberg-Schulz's *Genius Loci: The Phenomenology of Architecture* (New York: Rizzoli, 1980) and *The Concept of Dwelling: On the Way to Figurative Architecture* (New York: Rizzoli, 1985) contain numerous diatribes against the modern landscape that parallel the New Topographics photographers' visual polemics.

24. Relph, *Place and Placelessness*, 139–40, 118.

25. James Clifford, "On Ethnographic Allegory," in Clifford and Marcus, *Writing Culture*, 109.

26. Joel Sternfeld, *American Prospects* (New York: Random House, 1987).

27. Bill Owens, *Suburbia* (San Francisco: Straight Arrow Press, 1973), n.p. Jim Goldberg's *Rich and Poor* (New York: Random House, 1985) and Donigan Cummings's 1986 exhibition "Reality and Motive in Documentary Photography" provide more recent and elaborate examples of this technique, but Owens's book deals more directly with the American landscape. Goldberg presents a series of portraits on which the subjects have written their comments about their lives, as well as their feelings toward the photographs and the photographer. Cummings used photographs, letters, and tape recordings to create an exhibition about a group of people he photographed and interviewed in their homes and workplaces.

28. Owens, *Suburbia*, n.p.

29. See J. B. Jackson, *The Essential Landscape: The New Mexico Photographic Survey* (Albuquerque: University of New Mexico Press, 1985), 132.

30. Relph, *Place and Placelessness*, 147.

31. Portfolios by Meridel Rubenstein and Thomas Barrow can be found in Jackson, *The Essential Landscape.*

32. Stephen Tyler, "Post-Modern Ethnography: From Document of the Occult to Occult Document," in Clifford and Marcus, *Writing Culture*, 122–46 (quotation on 126).

33. See George Marcus, "Contemporary Problems of Ethnography in the Modern World System," in ibid., 165–93.

34. Ibid., 192.

35. Tyler, "Post-Modern Ethnography," 131.

36. This issue is discussed in detail in Michael J. Fischer's "Ethnicity and the Post-Modern Arts of Memory," in ibid., 194–233.
The success of public sector folklife projects such as the Pinelands Folklife Project provides evidence of the local popularity of collaborative efforts to combine the insider's experience of geographic places with the professional scholar's organizational skills and resources, though too few academics pay attention to developments in this area. See Mary Hafford, *One Space, Many Places: Folklife and Land Use in New Jersey's Pinelands National Reserve* (Washington, D.C.: Library of Congress, Publications of the Folklife Center, no. 15, 1986). *Neighborhood: A State of Mind* by Linda Rich, Joan Clark Netherwood, and Elinor Cahn (Baltimore: Johns Hopkins University Press, 1981) provides an excellent example of a collaborative community portrait based on photography and oral history. Community residents posed for pictures, provided historical photographs and information, and were very satisfied with the resulting exhibition.

37. Edward Relph, "Geographical Experiences and Being-in-the World: The Phenomenological Origins of Geography," in *Dwelling, Place and Environment: Towards a Phenomenology of Person and World,* ed. David Seamon and Robert Mugerauer (Dordrecht: Martinus Nijhoff, 1985), 16.

38. Photography scholarship is experiencing a rapid growth in both quality and quantity. For treatments of landscape-related issues, see Trachtenberg, *Reading American Photographs*; Hales, *William Henry Jackson and the Transformation of the American Landscape* and *Silver Cities: The Photography of American Urbanization* (Philadelphia: Temple University Press, 1984); Esthelle Jussim and Barbara Lindquist-Cock, *Landscape as Photograph* (New Haven: Yale University Press, 1985); and Tim Davis, "Photography and Landscape Studies," *Landscape Journal* 8 (1989): 1–12.

39. D. W. Meinig, "Geography as an Art," *Transactions of the Institute of British Geographers* (1983): 314–28 (quotation on 325).

The Formal Garden in the Age of
Consumer Culture: A Reading of the
Twentieth-Century Shopping Mall

RICHARD KELLER SIMON

The contemporary American shopping mall is the formal garden of late twentieth century culture, a commodified version of the great garden styles of Western history with which it shares fundamental characteristics. Set apart from the rest of the world as a place of earthly delight like the medieval walled garden; filled with fountains, statuary, and ingeniously devised machinery like the Italian Renaissance garden; designed on grandiose and symmetrical principles like the seventeenth-century French garden; made up of the fragments of cultural and architectural history like the eighteenth-century irregular English garden; and set aside for the public like the nineteenth-century American park, the mall is the next phase of this garden history, a synthesis of all these styles that have come before. But it is now joined with the shopping street, or at least a sanitized and standardized version of one, something that never before has been allowed within the garden.

A garden, the Jesuit author Henry Hawkins wrote in *Parthenia Sacra* in 1633, is "a Monopolie of al the pleasure and delights that are on the earth, amassed together . . . a world of sweets."[1] "A garden," Derek Clifford has written more recently, "is man's idealized view of the world, and because most men are representative of the society of which they are a part, it follows that fashionable gardens of any community and any period betray the dream world which is the period's ideal."[2] Garden styles, as others have noted, are attempts to replicate what Kenneth Clark has called "the most enchanting dream which has ever consoled mankind, the myth of a Golden Age in which man lived on the fruits of the earth, peacefully, piously, and with primitive simplicity."[3] In this latest version of the earthly paradise, then, people live on the goods of the consumer economy, peacefully, pleasurably, even with some kind of sophisticated complexity, for although their pleasure comes from buying and everything is set up to facilitate that pleasure, the garden itself is no simple place. "Commodity fetishism is a specific problem of our age, the age of modern capitalism," Georg Lukács argues in *History and Class Consciousness*. "Reification requires that a society should learn to satisfy all its needs in terms of commodity exchange."[4] Certainly the mall confirms Lukács, and yet, seductively, subverts his warning by presenting the specific problem of our age in terms of the pastoral tradition of earlier ages, the Golden Age, and Paradise, "the most enchanting dream which has ever consoled mankind." There have been dangers, temptations, of course, in the very first garden, and the delights dangled before us have been equally powerful. We have moved from the knowledge of good and evil to a Marxist reification.

In his essay on "The Function of the Work of Art in the Age of Mechanical Reproduction," Walter Benjamin argues that with the rise of mass culture, "the technique of reproduction detaches the reproduced object from the domain of tradition." And again, "The uniqueness of a work of art is inseparable from its being imbedded in the fabric of tradition."[5] What Benjamin's essay suggests for a study of the artifacts of mass culture is the possibility of placing them back into the fabric of the tradition from which they have been removed in order to see their meanings more clearly. It follows, then, that once we can recognize the essential similarity of the shopping mall to the formal garden we have a standard against which to judge its structures and a new tool for reading and understanding its spaces. After all, beyond being a grouping of stores surrounded by parking lots, the mall is a carefully designed aesthetic space that has only rarely been read or studied in any careful critical way, in spite of its importance. In "Shopping for Pleasure," John Fiske argues that "shopping malls and the cultural practices, the variety of shoppings that take place within them, are key areas of struggle, at both economic and ideological levels, between those with the power of ideological practice . . . and those whose construction as subjects in ideology is never complete. . . ." "Shopping is the crisis of consumerism: it is where the art and tricks of the weak can inflict the most damage on, and exert the most power over, the strategic interests of the powerful."[6] Applying ideas that have their origin in the work of Michel DeCerteau, Fiske properly initiates the cultural study of the mall, but his interest is less in the formal aspects of the space itself (indeed any shopping area would do) than in the activity that takes place within it. But it is the formal characteristics of the space itself that must be understood first, before the activities that take place within it can be properly considered.

Visitors learn the meanings of a consumer society at the mall, not only in the choices they make in their purchases, but also in the symbol systems they walk through, just as visitors to those earlier gardens were invited to learn about the meanings of their own times from their experiences of the space and from the pastoral adventures presented to them. "Remember ever the garden and the groves within," the Earl of Shaftesbury wrote in *The Moralists* in the eighteenth century: "There build, there erect what statues, what virtues, what ornament or orders of architecture thou thinkest noblest. There walk at leisure and in peace; contemplate, regulate, dispose. . . ."[7] In his reading of "The Poetic Garden" of the eighteenth century, Ronald Paulson explains that "the visitor, sometimes supplied with a bench to sit on, saw a carefully-arranged scene, something between a stage set and a landscape painting, with statues, temples, and other objects of a high degree of denotation arranged to express a topos on which he could meditate or converse." The visitor to the contemporary shopping mall reads an updated version of this cultural space, and while it appears to be less "poetic" than its predecessor, it is just as rich with meanings. The garden Paulson describes, which is "devoted to the pleasures and temptations of retirement,"[8] has been replaced by the mall, devoted to the pleasures and temptations of consumption, but the objects remain. Jean Baudrillard argues, "Through objects each individual and each group searches out his-her place in an order,"[9] and what the mall presents to us is a great surfeit of objects. "In buying products with certain 'images' we create ourselves, our personality, our qualities, even our past and our future," Judith Williamson argues in her reading of consumer life.[10]

Like the gardens before it, the mall is a construct of promenades, walls, vistas, mounts, labyrinths, fountains, statues, archways, trees, grottoes, theaters, flowering plants and shrubs, trellises, and assorted reproductions from architectural history, all artfully arranged. Some of these features have undergone technological or economic modification, to be sure, such as the mount, which was a standard part of garden design from the Middle Ages to the eighteenth century, the earthworks designed to present a vista of the garden to the visitor and typically reached by path or staircase. This has now been replaced by the escalator, which rises at key points in the enclosed central parts of the mall, where it presents a similar vista of the space to the visitor, who is now lifted dramatically from the floor below by unseen forces without any effort on his or her part. And this, in its turn, is only a modification of a standard feature from Italian Renaissance gardens, the elaborate hydraulic machinery or automata that engineers had devised to move statues about in striking dramatic tableaux. Now, in the mall, it is the visitors who are moved about by the escalators, becoming themselves the actors in the tableau "modern shopping."

Combining the mount with the automata, the mall then encloses this machinery in two or three stories of space, topped with skylights. And this result, something like Houston's Galleria Mall, a massive three-story enclosed mall topped with skylights, is only an updated version of Henry VIII's garden at Hampton Court, where "on top of the mount was the South or Great Round Arbour, three storeys in height, almost all of glass, with a leaden cupola surmounted by the inevitable king's beasts and a great gilded crown."[11] What was once set aside for the king and his guests is now available to everyone willing to embrace the consumer ethic. We have dispensed, therefore, with the beasts and the gilded crown; joggers run on the roof of the Galleria. But, of course, the mount allowed the visitor to look both inside and outside the garden. The escalator within the enclosed mall only allows the visitor to look at the inside space.

Similarly, the labyrinth, the maze of pathways or hedges which confounded the visitor's attempts to find an easy way out and was a favorite device of Renaissance gardens, is now the cleverly laid out pattern of aisles within some department stores which are designed quite successfully to discourage the visitor's easy exit. Shoppers simply cannot find a way out. Bloomingdale's in the Willow Grove Mall in suburban Philadelphia received so many complaints from irate shoppers lost in its mazes that finally small, discrete exit signs were posted. What "may have had . . . [its] origins in the penitential mazes of the Christian Church" on the model of the paths "laid out in stone or tiles" on which "the penitent performed the journey on his knees, saying particular prayers at particular points," and was then moved out into the garden where it was secularized, has now become thoroughly commodified, a journey in which purchases have replaced prayers. Buy enough and we will let you out. Played against the maze and labyrinth in the Renaissance garden were the axial and radial avenues, which began as extensions of the hallways of the palace and ended in suitably grand natural vistas, a structuring device which allowed house and garden to become "a single unit."[12] Played against the department store maze in the mall are the axial and radial avenues, which begin as extensions of hallways of one anchor department store and end in the grand vistas of the entrances to others.

The kitchen garden, that area of the formal garden closest to the house and set aside for the production of food, has become the food court, that area of the mall set aside for the consumption of food. The statues, assorted imitations of Greek and Roman models, portraits of contemporary royalty, or stylized representations of the ancient virtues, now decked out in fashionable clothing, have become the mannequins, the generalized imitations of consumers in their most beautiful, heroic, and changeable poses, portraits of contemporary anonymous life that we should see as stylized representations of the modern virtues: poise, flexibility, nubility, interchangeability, emotional absence. The generalized faces on the statues are now the empty faces of the mannequins.

And the various architectural antiquities which became a feature of eighteenth-century English irregular gardens—the miscellaneous copies of Greek temples, Gothic ruins, Japanese pagodas, Roman triumphal arches, and Italian grottoes—are now represented not so much by the miscellaneous architectural reproductions that appear seasonally in the mall, as in the Easter Bunny's cottage or Santa's Workshop, but much more profoundly by many of the stores themselves, which present idealized versions of architectural and cultural history to the consumer: the Victorian lingerie shop, the high modernist fur salon, the nineteenth-century western goods store, the adobe Mexican restaurant, the barnlike country store, the dark grottolike bar. Also present in smaller details such as the grand staircase, the wall of mirrors, the plush carpeting, and the man playing the white grand piano are echoes of the 1930s movie set; in the merry-go-round, the popcorn cart, and the clown with balloons, the echoes of funland. The eighteenth-century garden included such historical reproductions in an effort to make sense of its past and to accommodate its cultural inheritances to new situations. One can say the same about the mall's inclusion of historical recollections. If we judge this to be playful and parodic, following Linda Hutcheon in *A Poetics of Postmodernism*, then we can call the space postmodern, but if it is only a nostalgic recovery of history, we cannot. And this can be a tricky thing. "The collective weight of parodic practice," Hutcheon writes, "suggests a redefinition of parody as repetition with critical distance that allows ironic signalling of difference at the very heart of similarity."[13] Thus, the mall's appropriation of history into idealized spaces of consumption can be nostalgia or parody, or both at the same time.

The Stanford Shopping Center in Palo Alto presents such a parodic and nostalgic *bricolage* of cultural and architectural history: Crabtree and Evelyn with its images of eighteenth-century life, Laura Ashley with its images of romantic and early Victorian life, Victoria's Secret (the late Victorian bordello with overtones of French fashion), Banana Republic (the late Victorian colonial outfitter), the Disney Store with its images of 1940s art, and nearby the Nature Company, closest to the sixteenth century and the rise of science, since it is full of simple instruments and simple observations of nature. (Not present at this mall, but at others are stores like the Sharper Image, with its images of the twenty-first century.) One walks through history, then, or, to be more precise, through the images of history, just as one did in the formal garden, but now it can be appropriated by the act of consuming. One buys images, but learns "history." It is a clean, neat, and middle-class version of history without the homeless of downtown San Francisco and thus a retreat from the frenzy of contemporary urban life, which is exactly what the formal garden was also designed to be. To one side is an alley devoted to food, a lavishly idealized greengrocer, a pseudo-Italian coffee bar, and Max's Opera Cafe, a reproduction of a grand nineteenth-century cafe in Vienna—but what one finds when one wanders inside is not real or ersatz Vienna, but a glorified deli. Here the history of central Europe is rewritten as it might have been. (And down El Camino Real, not in the mall at all, is a ruined health spa, ruined as far back as I can remember, sometimes covered with cheap reproductions of the statuary of antiquity, more recently bare. The eighteenth-century formal garden built such ruins.) In the Renaissance garden of the Villa d'Este at Tivoli "a grotto of Venus, symbol of voluptuous pleasure," was juxtaposed to "one of Diana, symbol of virtuous pleasure and chastity. Groupings of such oppositions as these made the visitor himself experience the choice of Hercules," the myth around which the entire garden was constructed.[14] Viscount Cobham in the 1730s devised a plan for his English garden that would feature "the river Styx and beyond, the Elysian Fields to which the busts of his 'British Worthies' would be transferred. Near to the pure and graceful form of . . . the Temple of Ancient Virtue, there was to be a contrasting ruined temple, satirically dedicated to Modern Virtue, and containing a headless statue representing the fate of vanity. . . ."[15] In a similar manner the visitor to the modern garden at Stanford is presented with choices between Victoria's Secret, the shop of voluptuous pleasure, and Westminster Lace, the shop of virtuous pleasure and chastity, but does not have to choose between the Temple of Modern Virtue, the modern shopping center itself, or the Temple of Ancient Virtue, the remnants of the gardens of the past, because the mall artfully combines both.

We are almost at an end of our catalogue of garden elements. In fact the only standard feature of garden design not present in the modern mall, either in original or in modified form, is the hermitage, a favorite eighteenth-century architectural ruin designed to allow the visitor to pretend to be a hermit, to be alone and meditate. There are only two places you can be alone in the mall: in the toilet and in the clothing store changing room, although even there one can find surveillance cameras. Meditation and isolation are not virtues encouraged by the modern garden, because, interestingly enough, given the opportunity, too many of these consumers will not meditate there at all, buy try to steal whatever they can. It is, of course, quite an imperfect paradise, although here it is not so much something that can be blamed on the garden as on the shopping street it has come to assimilate. Shoplifting, it turns out, was first noted as a problem with the rise of the great nineteenth-century department stores.[16] According to one contemporary account of shoplifting at the Bon Marché, "Women find there a milieu where whatever they possess in the way of moral staying power can no longer protect them, whereas they defend themselves successfully in all other settings."[17] The desire to consume, apparently, is strong enough to overthrow the usual trappings of morality. "Consumerism is often represented as a supremely individualistic act—yet it is also very social," Judith Williamson writes. "Shopping is a socially endorsed event, a form of social cement. It makes you feel normal. Most people find it cheers them up—even window shopping. The extent to which shoplifting is done where there is no material need (most items stolen are incredibly trivial) reveals the extent to which people's wants and needs are translated into the form of consumption."[18]

There is finally the matter of nature within the garden. It is true that there are very few trees in these postmodern gardens, and those that do show up are typically confined in antipastoral concrete planters, but such subordination of nature has always occurred in garden history. In *The Renaissance Garden in England*, Roy Strong notes that "the [Renaissance] garden evolved into a series of separate yet interconnected intellectual and physical experiences which required the mental and physical cooperation of the visitor as he moved through them. Strange as it may seem to us, plants became almost incidental, apart from their contribution towards achieving a symbolic effect." Later, after quoting from a contemporary visitor's account of an ornate Italian Renaissance garden filled with grottoes, fountains, and automata, he remarks, "For those who see a garden in terms of trees, plants, and flowers, . . . [this] eulogy of what amounts to a series of hydraulic tableaux vivants might seem somewhat extraordinary. This in itself is an important fact. For . . . [the visitor], as he experiences the gardens of late Renaissance Italy, they have become a setting first and foremost for sudden and miraculous mechanical metamorphoses."[19]

By bringing the mundane world of commerce into the garden, along with its attendant ills, the mall appears to be inverting the fundamental purposes of many of those earlier gardens as places of repose and contemplation, of escape from the mundane world. Conspicuous consumption has replaced quiet repose. But many of the great styles of garden history have been practical, if not precisely in this way—for example, the *ferme ornée* or ornamented working farm designed in the eighteenth century with its fields, kitchen gardens, orchards, and pastures placed beside the more decorative and formal elements of the garden. "Fields of Corn make a pleasant Prospect, and if the Walks were a little taken care of that lie between them, if the natural Embroidery of the Meadows were helpt and improved by some small Addition of Art, and the several Rows of Hedges set off by Trees and Flowers, that the Soil was capable of receiving, a Man might make a pretty Landskip of his own Possessions" Addison wrote in *The Spectator*.[20] And Addison, one of the central figures of the development of the eighteenth-century irregular garden, described his dream of the ideal garden in *The Tatler* as "dominated by the goddess of Liberty" and assisted by "two other dependent Goddesses. . . . The First of them was seated upon an Hill, that had every Plant growing out of it. . . . The other was seated in a little island, that was covered with Groves of Spices, Olives, and Orange-Trees; and in a World, with the Products of every Foreign Clime. The Name of the First was Plenty; of the Second Commerce. . . ."[21] Leo Marx has noted that "the formal style of garden which . . . [Addison] rejects embodies a purely aristocratic, leisure-class ideal of conspicuous waste. It separates beauty from utility and work." "In effect Addison is building a theoretical bridge between the ideal of the old pastoral, the imaginary landscape of reconciliation, and a new attitude toward the environment more congenial to a scientific and commercial age."[22]

But granting that the mall is a far more commercial place than even Addison could have imagined, the shift has not destroyed the garden—for most of history a space set aside for the rich—only adapted it to new social and economic realities, and it is thus the appropriate garden for a consumer-oriented middle-class culture. In the formal gardens of the past, where nature was rearranged to fit the aesthetic taste of the period, one walked through the landscape contemplating the vistas and approaching the beautiful. In the mall, where nature is similarly rearranged to fit the commercial needs of the period, one walks through the landscape, now contemplating not the vistas of nature, which have been completely blocked out, but the vistas represented by the entrances to the anchor department stores, and now not approaching the beautiful, but contemplating the commodities by which one can become the beautiful. These are practical times. The earlier aristocratic citizen who walked down the path of the garden admired the flowers and smelled their scents; the twentieth-century middle-class citizen who walks down the path of the shopping mall buys the flower scents in bottles and then smells like the flower or the musk ox. The focus has shifted, from the individual in reverie facing an artificial version of nature, to the individual in excitement facing a garden of consumer products. In the eighteenth century, Stephen Switzer wrote in his preface to *The Nobleman, Gentleman, and Gardener's Recreation*, ". . . tis from the Admiration of these [rural delights] that the Soul is elevated to unlimited heights above and modell'd and prepar'd for the sweet Reception and happy Enjoyment of Felicities, the durablest as well as happiest that Omniscience has created."[23] It is unlikely that the visitor to the modern mall has a comparable experience, although there are plenty of individuals who love to shop, but Switzer, certainly, can also be accused of enthusiastic overstatement. The pleasures of a consumer society are quite different.

IF THE MALL can be understood as a garden, then, against the standard elements of garden design, it can also be understood as a special moment within the larger history of gardens. Garden design from the Middle Ages to the nineteenth century shows a shift from enclosed to open space and, from the seventeenth century on, a shift from the symbols of state power to symbols of individuality and liberty. Walls gave way to grand natural views, and symmetrical landscapes that communicated the power of the monarch gave way to irregular and "natural" spaces set aside for individual contemplation. As thinking shifted from theology to science, the garden gradually changed from "a series of emblems telling of virtues and vices. . ." to "a series of botanical specimens."[24] As philosophy shifted from rationalism to empiricism, the garden changed from a place of geometrical form and shaped shrubs to a representation of a "naturally" occurring landscape. And as political systems shifted from regal and authoritarian to mercantile and democratic, the garden changed from an allegory of state power to one of individual freedom. "The palace or great garden begins with Henry VIII's Hampton Court," Strong argues, ". . . in which the garden is made the symbol of the new monarchy's power and prestige," adding that "the Medici were among the first to use the garden as a means of intertwining the natural world with a dynastic apotheosis. As a result of this gardens began to assume an increasingly symbolic function." He concludes that "pleasure gardens are seen to pertain to the king and the court as outward signs of regal magnificence. The English Renaissance garden from the start is strongly cast as a vehicle for symbolic display."[25]

This is in sharp contrast to the eighteenth-century view. Addison in *The Tatler* has a dream of the garden in the Alps as a place of "LIBERTY": ". . . this happy Region was inhabited by the Goddess of Liberty; whose Presence softened the Rigours of the Climate, enriched the Barrenness of the Soil; and more than supplied the Absence of the Sun. The Place was covered with a wonderful Profusion of Flowers, that, without being disposed into regular Borders and Parterres, grew promiscuously, and had a greater Beauty in their natural Luxuriancy and Disorder. . . ."[26]

But the mall marks a return to enclosure, symmetry, and control, to space even more confined than the medieval walled garden, and just as authoritarian as Renaissance and seventeenth-century design. About the gradual shift to more open space in the late Middle Ages, Clifford writes that "the association of man-made hills with gardens" was "a sign that the Middle Ages were trying to look beyond the protective walls behind which physically, spiritually, and intellectually, the Christian West had succeeded in preserving itself alive. Once the protective walls were down the Middle Ages were at an end and the sensual world without limit stretched out invitingly. The fortress slowly became a villa; the view become more important than the wall."[27] But the mall now encloses this sensual world once again, not simply with walls, but with grandiose displays of consumer goods. Barton Creek Square, built on a hill above Austin, Texas, and resembling a fortress, has one of the finest views available of the city and of the Texas Hill Country beyond and is immediately adjacent to a major creek, greenbelt, and recreation area. But all the views are from the parking lots, since the mall, like so many others, is completely enclosed; there are vistas inside the mall, to be sure, of the grand entrances to the anchor department stores, the front doors of Sears and its competitors. Where once practical buildings were blocked from sight and vistas created, by the selective planting of trees and shrubs and by the creation or relocation of hillsides, as in the eighteenth-century garden, now the vista is blocked from view, to produce the sight of the practical building. And, of course, where once the vista was of the grandeur of nature, it is now of the grandeur of manufactured commodities, the second "nature" of capitalist economy.

The medieval garden may be the most important model for the mall. Read against that garden of earthly delight and erotic dalliance, the mall is immediately a very recognizable space, the place of earthly delight sealed off from the cares of the mundane world, and for many of its visitors a place of "courtly dalliance, le jardin d'amour."[28] The teenagers who prowl the malls after school hours, preening and flirting, are making an essentially medieval use of the space. In the medieval *Romance of the Rose*, an allegory of behavior, the poet-hero comes upon a walled garden owned by Pleasure to which he is admitted by a sexy, young, rich, and powerful woman, Idleness, who spends her time grooming and amusing herself. Hate, Treachery, Infamy, Covetousness, Greed, Envy, Sadness, Old Age, Hypocrisy, and Poverty are excluded from the garden by Pleasure, but within Pleasure relaxes with his chosen companions, Youth, Beauty, Riches, Candour, Courtesy, Liberality, and the God of Love himself. The poet-hero wanders off to explore the garden, peers into the fountain of Self-Love, and sees there a perfect rose in the reflection, the symbol of his true love. When he is shot by one of Cupid's arrows, he knows "he must possess the object of his unreasonable passion despite all obstacles and arguments against it."[29]

With only minor modification, we have an allegorical interpretation of our shopping mall, into which the visitor is admitted by Idleness, guided by Pleasure, victimized by Self-Love, and then overtaken by Unreasonable Passion—not for a true love this time so much as for the endless objects of consumption which litter the place. And while the visitor may leave Hate, Treachery, Infamy, Sadness, Old Age, Hypocrisy, and Poverty behind, Covetousness, Greed, and Envy seem to have gained entrance to the garden, where they have joined Youth, Beauty, and Riches, while Candour, Courtesy, and Liberality appear to have disappeared altogether. We have built for ourselves, with some significant modification, the stage set upon which, everyday, we ourselves enact the *Romance of the Rose*.

But if the mall repeats the medieval garden, it is the exact inversion of the eighteenth-century garden. Addison wrote in *The Spectator*, "You must know, Sir, that I look upon the Pleasure which we take in a Garden, as one of the most innocent Delights in Humane Life. A Garden was the Habitation of our first Parents before the Fall. It is naturally apt to fill the Mind with Calmness and Tranquility, and to lay all its turbulent Passions at Rest. It gives us a great Insight into the Contrivance and Wisdom of Providence, and suggests innumerable Subjects for Meditation. I cannot but think the very Complacency and Satisfaction which a Man takes in these Works of Nature, to be a laudable, if not a virtuous Habit of Mind."[30] Read against the eighteenth-century English garden, the mall reveals more political aspects of its character. The garden of that period, Maynard Mack has written, "arranged itself in 'scenes' to remind the traveler and virtuoso of Rome, Arcadia, and Elysium; of Praeneste, Daphne, and Tempe." "Altogether, landscape and garden . . . serve as aids to reflection—or to recollection, introspection, and worship. . . . They present themselves to be read as epitomes of recent history, or psychological states, or human life in general . . . or of politics and the relationship of social classes . . . or of the concordia discors that ties the universe together. . . ."[31] One notable example was the design by Aaron Hill for an elaborate garden in which

> A Temple of Happiness was to stand on a mount without the cloister and be visible over the outer wall of the cloister from all parts of the garden. The mount was to be surrounded by an idyllic pastoral scene comprising cornfields, meadows and a cottage, and which was to be extended by frescoes on the inner wall of the cloister. In order to reach the temple, one had to choose the correct path through one of 12 grottoes outside the cloister. The four largest grottoes were dedicated to Power, Riches, Honour, and Learning, but all ended in disappointment. It was only by taking a small pathway between statues dedicated to Reason and Innocence, and passing through the Grotto of Independence, that access to the cornfields could be discovered. The whole design was, therefore, merely a laboured and highly allegorical way for Hill to illustrate his controversial view that Man is essentially good, and that all he requires for happiness is the gift of reason.[32]

The visitor to the contemporary shopping mall faces no less intricate choices. Our mall can be seen as following this pattern, arranging itself into stores to remind the visitor, not now of Rome or Arcadia or Elysium, but of life on the farm, or in the American West, or in the Victorian bordello, or in a Parisian cafe. History, psychological states, human life in general (stores for children, for adolescents, for pregnant women, for adults, for the elderly) all appear in this set of scenic arrangements, and the eighteenth-century concordia discors that ties the universe together is now quite clearly the demonstration of the twentieth-century economic system in operation. And although politics and the relationship of social classes are issues which are rarely made explicit in such ideological space, class relationships are always present in the ways in which stores aimed at different economic markets are separated from each other in the mall. Mack argues that the eighteenth-century garden was designed as an aid to reflection—recollection, introspection, worship—but, after all, it was quite consciously created as an elaboration of the pleasures of individual liberty, with vistas of open space, places to make choices, and secluded bowers to be alone. In contrast, the mall was quite consciously created as an elaboration of the pleasures of consumption, with enclosed space, places to make economic choices, but no bowers to be alone. Introspection and reflection are discouraged, but education, nevertheless, is constantly taking place, for visitors to the mall are constantly confronted with information about the meanings of the space and their role within it.

The transition from such a conception of the garden as a free and open space, an aid to reflection and individuality, to the enclosed authoritarian shopping mall is supplied by the nineteenth-century park. With that public park, the garden was opened for the first time to great masses of ordinary people; but if the benefits of freedom and liberty were hereby extended to all, the garden needed to be changed accordingly. Frederick Law Olmsted designed New York's Central Park to be "a distinctly harmonizing and refining influence upon the most unfortunate and most lawless classes of the city—an influence favorable to courtesy, self-control, and temperance." In 1873, Lawrence Levine writes, "his Park-Keepers were informed that 'every foot of the Park's surface, every tree and bush, as well as every arch, roadway and walk had been fixed where it is *with a purpose*.' The park, they were reminded, 'is not simply a pleasure-ground' but a place meant to improve those who came to it. An observer noted in 1869 that under the influence of the park 'rude, noisy fellows . . . became hushed, moderate, and careful.'" This is the classic ethic of the garden, extended now to the immigrant masses of New York who are to be socialized to dominant WASP values. To do this Olmsted had to create what he called "a class of opposite conditions" from the city. "We want the greatest possible contrast with the streets and shops and the rooms of the town which will be consistent with convenience and the preservation of good order and neatness. We want . . . to completely shut out the city from our landscapes."[33] The first generation of European immigrants learned American culture in the special garden that was set aside for them. Their grandchildren and great-grandchildren do the same at the mall.

But at the same time that parks were being built for ordinary people, especially in urban areas, new commercial space was similarly being devised, the great department stores of the nineteenth century. The mall is an artful conflation of these two spaces. The shops and streets of the town enter the park, but the disorderly world of which they are a part does not. The courtesy, self-control, and temperance of the park are extended to the commercial aspects of the town, but this can only work if new kinds of rules are enforced, which essentially sanitize and standardize the street.

The relationship of the mall to the grandiose urban department stores of the late nineteenth and early twentieth centuries is obvious enough, but it is important to note a paradigm shift between those spaces and the contemporary mall: from work and seriousness to fun and play. The semi-Gothic, cathedral-like John Wanamaker Department Store in downtown Philadelphia, for example, which still stands, was built around an interior Grand Court, several stories high, at the center of which is a gigantic bronze statue of a resting eagle around which shoppers are invited to gather, rest, and experience the space. An equally monumental organ complete with a wall of organ pipes occupies one of the sides of the court on its upper floors and regularly fills the space with classical organ music, to which people are invited to listen while shopping. This is sacred space being appropriated by the marketplace, the nineteenth-century model. In his study of the Bon Marché department store in Paris, Michael Miller describes its space as "part opera, part theatre, part museum," but he notes other contemporary critics who saw it as a church, Emile Zola among them.[34]

But while some Philadelphians still shop at Wanamaker's, most have abandoned it for the suburban malls. Nowhere can the paradigm shift be seen more clearly than at one of the fanciest of these spaces, Willow Grove Mall, built on the site of Willow Grove Park, at one time the region's major amusement park. Some of its walls are covered with large photographs of the amusement park in its glory days—the rides, concerts, and visitors. Reproductions of carousel horses and of other amusement park artifacts hang from the ceilings. One walks through such a space, then, being constantly reminded of the individuals who had walked there before, one form of amusement having been replaced by another. Every space refers back, self-consciously, to the space it replaces and mimics. Where visitors once paid out money to shoot guns at plates, they now pay out money to buy plates; where they once drove kiddie cars and tried to keep them on the tracks, they now park grownup cars; and where they once got lost in the fun house, they now get lost in Bloomingdale's. In the Gothic department store, shoppers were asked to see themselves in sacred, religious space. Shopping was worship. In the mall, shoppers are asked to see themselves in funland. Shopping is play. We are out of the church and into the garden. But the garden comes to us from the nineteenth-century public park, Olmsted's oasis that must shut the city out of its landscapes. "Developing along with the great cities," Susan Porter Benson writes, "the department store expressed their spirit much as the meetinghouse embodied that of the seventeenth-century New England town. The congestion, the liveliness, the anonymity, the grand scale, the material promise, and the class divisions of the city were all distilled into the great stores."[35] Certainly, then, the same can be said for the mall, developing along with the great suburbs (where city and countryside come together) and illuminating the way in which the serious work ethic of the nineteenth century, with its religious reinforcement, has dissolved into the play ethic of the twentieth century. Play, of course, means many things: to Friedrich Schiller it meant the ability to reconcile that which otherwise could not be reconciled, the real and the ideal, the finite and the infinite, the emotional and the rational. And this, certainly, the mall does. To Clifford Geertz, play, now called "deep play," means the ways in which the members of a culture, in their leisure, learn the meanings of their culture. This too the mall does. Funland is a place in which serious activities take place.

William Kent, the foremost English landscape designer of the early eighteenth century, "decorated the interior of the Temple of Venus at Stowe with scenes" from Edmund Spenser's *Faerie Queen*, attempting in this fashion to remind visitors to the garden of the earlier garden allegory.[36] The visitors to Kent's garden at Stowe got to envision themselves as knights crossing allegorical fields of play. There is a fundamental difference from the contemporary shopping mall like Willow Grove worth noting here: where eighteenth-century citizens were reminded of their heroic past, contemporary shoppers are reminded of their past in funland. These are, as others have noted before, not very heroic times. In 1586, Francesco de Vieri praised the garden of Pratolino as "the earthly paradise, as an expression of princely magnificence, and as a means whereby philosophers were able to express the truths of the universe."[37] Today we must praise the mall as our own earthly paradise, as an expression of the magnificence of commodification, and as a means whereby ordinary people learn the truths of their universe.

In "Some Motifs in Baudelaire," his assessment of street life, Walter Benjamin wrote that "Baudelaire saw fit to equate the man of the crowd . . . with the flâneur." But, Benjamin continues, "it is hard to accept this view. The man of the crowd is no flâneur. In him, composure has given way to manic behavior. . . . There was the pedestrian who would let himself be jostled by the crowd, but there was also the flâneur who demanded elbow room and was unwilling to forgo the life of a gentleman of leisure. Let the many attend to their daily affairs; the man of leisure can indulge in the perambulations of the flâneur only if as such he is already out of place. He is as much out of place in an atmosphere of complete leisure as in the feverish turmoil of the city."[38] But he is not, we must now write as an addendum to Benjamin, out of place in the space that so neatly combines complete leisure with the feverish turmoil of the city. The new flâneur, our new dandy, has turned the city back into a place of play, and if the price for that has been commodification (the devil always demands his due), he or she does not appear to mind. We are waltzing on the ghost of Lukács. "Consumption is the very arena in which culture is fought over and licked into shape," Mary Douglas and Baron Isherwood write.[39] It is, they argue, the activity in which most of the significant decisions we ever make as individuals are made.

Practical then as well as pastoral, ideological as well as utopian, dream as well as reality, tied to the past and yet determined by the present, the mall is an intricate reworking of traditional cultural space. Adapting the pastoral tradition to the demands of mass culture, the mall reconciles the contradictions of our own time and place, the disjunctions between what we think we would like to be and what we are. A generation ago, when Leo Marx studied the clash in American culture between the machine and garden, he wrote, "For more than a century our most gifted writers have dwelt upon the contradiction between rural myth and technological fact." This, he argued, was what always had been resolved by the pastoral. "The desirability of a . . . reconciliation between the animal and rational, natural and civilized, conditions of man always had been implied by the pastoral ideal." This, then, would be our shopping mall. But while Marx believed such a reconciliation was possible in the nineteenth century, he despaired of it happening in the twentieth, ending his study with an analysis of what he called the garden in ashes, the more recent version of this pastoral tradition, ruined by the machine. "The anti-pastoral forces at work in our literature seem indeed to become increasingly violent as we approach our own time." [40] But his final analysis was premature, I would argue, since it has only been in this last generation that the American shopping mall has come into its own, the period of the great enclosure and grandiose magnification of what started out as simply groupings of stores surrounded by parking lots. The garden is not in ashes at all, although it may be covered in a good deal of cement; rather, it is a significant commercial and cultural success, the most important space created by American society in our generation.

Clifford notes in *A History of Garden Design* that "the gardens men make reflect the essential nature of the society to which they belong." [41] "To walk in a Renaissance garden is in fact to walk through the avenues of the Renaissance mind," Strong writes in *The Renaissance Garden.* "Places of pleasure, as Francis Bacon only almost dismissively called them, is a term which belies the true significance of the great garden as one of the most transitory and miraculous achievements of the civilization of the Renaissance." [42] One might paraphrase Clifford and Strong and argue similarly that to walk in the contemporary place of pleasure, the shopping mall, is to walk through the avenues of the postmodern mentality. What we see, neatly symbolized and codified, are both the promises and problems of commodified life. It is only a matter of learning how to read the meanings of the space.

NOTES

1. Roy Strong, *The Renaissance Garden in England* (London: Thames and Hudson, 1979), 210.

2. Derek Clifford, *A History of Garden Design*, rev. ed. (New York: Praeger, 1966), 15.

3. Kenneth Clark, *Landscape into Art* (London: Penguin Books, 1956), 67.

4. George Lukács, *History and Class Consciousness: Studies in Marxist Dialectics*, trans. Rodney Livingston (Cambridge, Mass.: MIT Press, 1971), 91.

5. Walter Benjamin, "The Function of the Work of Art in the Age of Mechanical

Reproduction," in *Illuminations*, ed. Hannah Arendt (New York: Schocken Books, 1969), 221, 223.

6. John Fiske, "Shopping for Pleasure," in *Reading the Popular* (Boston: Unwin Hyman, 1989), 14.

7. James Turner, *The Politics of Landscape: Rural Scenery and Society in English Poetry, 1630–1660* (Cambridge, Mass.: Harvard University Press, 1979), 247.

8. Ronald Paulson, *Emblem and Expression: Meaning in English Art of the Eighteenth Century* (Cambridge, Mass.: Harvard University Press, 1975), 20, 23.

9. Jean Baudrillard, *For a Critique of the Political Economy of the Sign* (St. Louis: Telos Press, 1981), 38.

10. Judith Williamson, *Decoding Advertisements: Ideology and Meaning in Advertising* (London: Marion Boyars, 1978), 70.

11. Strong, *Renaissance Garden*, 28.

12. Ibid., 10.

13. Linda Hutcheon, *A Poetics of Postmodernism: History, Theory, Fiction* (New York: Routledge, 1988), 26.

14. Strong, *Renaissance Garden*, 28.

15. David Jacques, *Georgian Gardens: The Reign of Nature* (London: Batsford, 1983), 18.

16. See Michael B. Miller, *The Bon Marché: Bourgeois Culture and the Department Store, 1869–1920* (Princeton: Princeton University Press, 1981), 201–5.

17. Ibid., 205.

18. Judith Williamson, "Politics of Consumption," in *Consuming Passions: The Dynamics of Popular Culture* (London: Marion Boyars, 1986), 230.

19. Strong, *Renaissance Garden*, 20, 79.

20. Joseph Addison, *The Spectator*, ed. Donald F. Bond (Oxford: Clarendon Press, 1965), 3:552 (no. 414, 25 June 1712).

21. Joseph Addison, *The Tatler* (no. 161, 18–20 April 1710), in *The Genius of the Place: The English Landscape Garden, 1620–1820*, ed. John Dixon Hunt and Peter Willis (New York: Harper and Row, 1975), 140.

22. Leo Marx, *The Machine in the Garden: Technology and the Pastoral Ideal in America* (New York: Oxford University Press, 1964), 93.

23. Switzer quoted in Maynard Mack, *The Garden in the City: Retirement and Politics in the Later Poetry of Pope, 1731–1743* (Toronto: University of Toronto Press, 1969), 24–25.

24. Strong, *Renaissance Garden*, 11.

25. Ibid., 10, 20, 33.

26. Addison, *The Tatler* (no. 161, 18–20 April 1710), in Hunt and Willis, *Genius*, 140.

27. Clifford, *Garden Design*, 22.

28. Strong, *Renaissance Garden*, 32.

29. Kenneth Woodbridge, *Princely Gardens: The Origins and Development of the French Formal Style* (New York: Rizzoli, 1986), 13.

30. Addison, *The Spectator*, 4:192 (no. 477, 6 September 1710).

31. Mack, *Garden in the City*, 21, 22, 23.

32. Jacques, *Georgian Gardens*, 16–17.

33. Lawrence Levine, *High Brow, Low Brow: The Emergence of Cultural Hierarchy in America* (Cambridge, Mass.: Harvard University Press, 1988), 202.

34. Miller, *Bon Marché*, 168, 177.

35. Susan Porter Benson, *Counter Cultures: Saleswomen, Managers, and Customers in American Department Stores, 1890–1910* (Urbana: University of Illinois Press, 1986), 8.

36. Jacques, *Georgian Gardens*, 34.

37. Strong, *Renaissance Garden*, 82.

38. Benjamin, *Illuminations*, 172, 173.

39. Mary Douglas and Baron Isherwood, *The World of Goods* (New York: Basic Books, 1979), 57.

40. Marx, *Machine*, 354, 102, 26.

41. Clifford, *Garden Design*, 42.

42. Strong, *Renaissance Garden*, 223.

Topographies of Power: The Forced
Spaces of the Manhattan Project

PETER BACON HALES

The story of the Manhattan Project is often recounted. In reminiscences, in official army histories,[1] in Pulitzer-prize-winning works of popular history,[2] in Hollywood films, in the realms of scientific discourse, we are treated to the story, so richly told, so repetitively structured, that we may, I think, safely call it the origin myth of the atomic age and the atomic culture. In this myth, quintessential Americans—immigrants fleeing the dangers of a fetid European civilization—find on these shores the opportunity to convert their abstract knowledge into practical form. With the assistance of a benevolent government—bumbling, perhaps, uncompre-

hending, infuriating, but benevolent—they form a new, utopian community in the fastnesses of the West. And in this new utopia they invent a
product that saves the world from barbarism by transforming Nature into
Culture. In the process, they *become* Americans, and in that transformation, they serve to signify the soon-to-come Americanization of the globe,
the new, postwar Family of Man.

This myth is often retold, and with urgency. The urgency comes, I think,
from what this myth transforms: chaos into order, fear into comfort, peril
into promise and—perhaps most importantly—guilt into vindication. What
we do not have, and what, perhaps, we *may* have, in this uneasy moment
when the Cold War may end or reappear with new force (or a new global
wartime culture may emerge), is a history of the myth of the Manhattan
Project, enfolded within a larger history, of the Manhattan Engineering
District, of the forces and places that produced and were produced in the
metaphorical space of that undertaking.[3]

The organizing framework of this alternative history looks at the Manhattan Engineering District and the Manhattan Project as enterprises of
production. But rather than focusing on the project as productive of weap-
onry in a physical sense, let us expand the field of vision. The project produced more than simply bombs (three of them). It produced radically new
environs, cities, and even—in a peculiar way—American utopias. Those
spaces—their demarcation by boundaries, their organization into urban
centers, their occupation and activation—represented the physical projection of new systems of cultural organization. And in their streets and plans,
their housing patterns, and their relations to nature and the outside society
they were the concrete expressions of complex ideologies.

These systems and ideologies, and the landscapes upon which they were
inscribed, were successful in part because they appropriated and transformed core mythologies of the dominant American culture, in particular
myths about the American relation to the land and its redemptive potential.
By operating under the ethos of these mythologies, the Manhattan Project
was able at the same time to violate core American ideologies—concerning
human and individual rights, freedom and responsibility—contained in
the essential documents of American politics. The result was a network of
spaces, not simply geographical, but *discursive*—systems of coercion and
control, ideologies, and (as I have already pointed out) myths. Appropriating, incorporating, and transforming central elements of the domi-

nant American culture, the Manhattan Project served as the catalyst in the production of a new American culture that would dominate the postwar globe.

TO STRUCTURE the history of the Manhattan Project around its geography seems at first to invite reductionism or its opposite—a wildly metaphoric impulse. But as geographer Yi-Fu Tuan has suggested (albeit obliquely) elsewhere in this collection, the spaces occupied by an enterprise may determine much that will occur within its boundaries. When that enterprise has significant freedom and power to choose the sites it will occupy, and especially when the range of its options is vast, those choices necessarily become invested with significance—for the culture itself and for the historian who wishes to understand that culture. Likewise, the act of occupying and using those spaces, of transforming them, cannot help but serve as the expression of underlying, unspoken, often unspeakable beliefs, values, and structures inherent to that culture.

Once the geographer's enterprise becomes the unveiling of these relationships between the physical and the cultural, geographical practice becomes more than the simple mapping out of spaces and description of what resides within boundaries; it lies beyond even the finding of significance and meaning in the spaces and relations themselves. For focusing our attention on change—particularly controlled, geographical change—we find ourselves presented with an intellectual stage upon which deep questions about cultural destiny, the limits of human enterprise, and the determining effect of environment may be addressed, if only obliquely.

This is the opportunity offered by the strange history of the Manhattan Project. For there we have, in bold relief, a story of incursion, occupation, and transformation in which what might be called cultural *will* is uppermost, and the attempt to impose that will—upon land and climate, upon existing social systems, and upon vast numbers of people—dominates the process.

Here in the Manhattan Project, the stages of that process unfold with an almost preternatural clarity and directness. What follows, then, is a study of these stages, organized around terms used by the Corps of Engineers and the Manhattan Engineering District in describing, planning, and acting out their desires upon the environment. In each case, I hope to suggest how these terms can be expanded to embrace much larger and more subtle fields than originally intended by the corps, without ever straying from the field of meanings implicit in and essential to the district and the culture for which it served as a special case. In the process, I hope, we can recognize a new American geography asserting itself: a topography of power.

ORIGINATION

The Manhattan Engineering District began as a consortium, informal at first, among scientific theorists of the most abstract sort, government and army representatives, and emissaries of the corporate interests to whom, by 1942, the architects of wartime mobilization had already ceded considerable authority. These three forces would, eventually, be joined by a fourth, organized labor. For some of the most powerful and widely based unions made their own bargain: in return for promising assistance in the recruitment, retention, and control of workers, they were guaranteed powers previously denied them and promised an influential place in the managed environments that would result (in the short and the long term) from the project.[4]

The division of power within the district went, roughly, as follows. The government ceded its authority to the military, which then designated the Army Corps of Engineers as the supervising authority. Seeing the project as essentially a manufacturing enterprise, the corps then designated specific corporations experienced in factory construction and management and in chemical and weapons manufacturing, to build and manage the project's production facilities. Oversight, control, and responsibility would, however, ultimately lie in the hands of the corps and its military system. The scientists, for a brief moment the architects and supervisors of the enterprise, rapidly found themselves relegated to the role of nonunionized labor, of pieceworkers. The largest "international" wings of the principal American unions, working with the United States Employment Service, served as recruiters for the skilled labor force and as institutions to negotiate on-the-job conflicts so that minimal time was lost.

For the corps, origination meant location of authority. It was a concept constantly invoked—and as constantly avoided. One looked for the origin of an order, plan, or memorandum to see just how valid was the authority from which it came. One wrote that chain of origination into one's daybook or diary, precisely because it provided evidence from which one could apportion responsibility and blame and protect oneself into the bargain.

But there was another origination, in a strange sense, a preorigination: the spaces themselves. There were three principal sites (though others came and went during the years between 1941 and 1946): the Clinton Engineer Works (CEW) at Harriman, Tennessee; the Hanford Engineer Works at Hanford, Washington; and the small, unnamed site, known formally as Post Office Box 1663, Santa Fe, New Mexico, and more commonly called simply Los Alamos. The selection of each was based on criteria concerning the project's primary concern with "security," its understanding of the need for massive amounts of power, particularly electrical power, and the demands for quickly appropriable land masses of sufficient size to hide the effects of potential devastating accidents within the army's boundaries. But none of these sites was a *tabula rasa*; each was redolent with mythic power drawn from particularly American sources.

Thus, seeing the project as a cultural and geographical entity, our quest for origination leads us back to the three spaces before their appropriation and transformation by the project. Los Alamos was located on a mesa surrounded by the Jemez Mountains of New Mexico. It had undergone multiple occupations by a sequence of cultures; it had come to resemble a sacred site, less for the Native Americans (whose mountains and ceremonial sites were located nearby) than for the expatriate arts, religious, mystical, and psychological cultures clustered around Albuquerque, Taos, and Santa Fe (fig. 1). In its current state it was the site for a boy's school founded loosely on the premise that neurasthenic adolescents of wealthy eastern background could be redeemed and restored by interaction with the windy, arid climate of the region, by hard, open-air work, by contact with wilderness, and by a system of discipline and order based on the Boy Scouts.[5] Each boy arriving at the school received the traditional Boy Scout uniform of shorts, knee socks, sturdy shoes, and neckerchief and wore that outfit year-round. Each boy also received his own horse and the responsibility for keeping it healthy and well-groomed as well as a list of chores and duties for the greater community. The Ranch School combined theories of Deweyian education, Rooseveltian Rough Rider moral models, and a rest-cure program loosely based on Weir Mitchell's mental hygiene theories—boys slept outside winter and summer, as part of a program to promote physical and mental strength.

1. Los Alamos Mesa.

Behind the practices of the school lay a deeper, if unspoken, philosophy concerning the American, the land, and the West. For it depended upon a vision of the West and its redemptive possibilities I have elsewhere called "tourist transcendentalism." Accepting the reality of an urbanized, industrialized America, the Ranch School, and the larger community of expatriates who had escaped to New Mexico over the previous decades, sought a way in which the soul-expanding visionary freedoms of the mythic American West might still redeem the new American citizen (fig. 2). If a properly managed stint in the West might serve as reclamation and even redemption for the damaged urban soul, the region itself might serve as a potent antidote for the newly regimented spaces of the new industrial culture. To settle a scientific-industrial research, development, and manufacturing enterprise in such an environment was to mix the very spheres—redemptive landscape, necessary but soul-damaging industrial urbanism—that expatriates and tourists of the West had sought to keep sequestered, and perhaps to invite conflict between mythologies and the social systems based upon them.[6]

But Los Alamos was only one of three principal sites. The second was a section of wooded Tennessee rising along a ridge up from the Clinch River, spanning Roane and Anderson counties and subsuming a number of small communities, including Wheat, Elza, and Scarboro, Tennessee. On this section, later to be named Oak Ridge, a collection of farmers worked the

2. T. Harmon Parkhurst, Los Alamos Ranch schoolboy. Los Alamos Historical
Society, (R)3174.

land (fig. 3). Some of the farms were prosperous, modern affairs; as one rose from the rich valley up the ridges and into the higher hollows, the land became hardscrabble, the farms smaller and more primitive, the occupants increasingly tenant farmers. Some had occupied the land for generations; others were recent refugees from other land-reclamation projects, including those of the Tennessee Valley Authority (TVA).[7]

Here, too, geographical mythology dominated the thinking of residents and onlookers alike. For more than a century, this region had figured large as a seedbed for the democratic impulse. Settled for the most part in the pattern of the Jeffersonian yeoman farm, it was also a place where Jacksonian democracy had taken on its greatest fervor. The explosion of national interest and concern over the plight of the small farmer that peaked in the 1930s had made these Tennessee hills symbols of a threatened way of life. The popular picturebooks of the 1930s drew from this region too; the Farm Security Administration sent some of its best photographers here, and a spate of books concerning rural southerners included the Tennessee hill-people among its populations. Little of the local life remained free of the symbolic sphere—bare feet, overalls, mules, weathered wood, antiquated tools, and dulcimer music all had come to represent some aspect of the strength of an American heritage.[8]

The third site was Hanford, Washington. Not the emblematic yeoman farm of Oak Ridge or the modern, sanitized, nostalgic western ranch at Los Alamos, it represented a different but equally potent American environment—the Great American Desert tamed and transformed by irrigation. Locacted in the treeless, hostile wastes of eastern Washington state, on the recently tamed Columbia River already made legendary by Woody Guthrie's paid propaganda for the Bonneville and Grand Coulee Power Administrations, Hanford was the site of a cluster of small communities gathered around two small irrigation districts, farming exotic fruits and herbs— apples, pomegranates, mint—making the desert bloom and forging community out of adversity.[9]

While different in its references, Hanford and its people shared basic similarities with the other sites. Its residents saw themselves as symbolic of a vanishing pioneer spirit, inheritors of the mantle of other westerners, defenders of agrarian virtue against the new forces of the agricultural, banking, and development conglomerates that had striven over the last decades to appropriate and control that region. Attracted to the area through a

3. Photographer unknown, possibly Orrin Thacker, "Workstock on Roane County Farm." National Archives.

series of settlement schemes that included Washington state's celebrated Land Settlement Act (which offered lands to soldiers at small start-up payments, with the bulk payable over long-term loans by the state), Hanford-area residents fought hard to keep their small holdings, often against extraordinary obstacles—irrigation district failures, rank inexperience, drought, land-grabs. Those who remained, against the odds, shared a hard-won sense of their place within the western mythologies of land and settlement.[10]

Together these sites tapped three of the great myths of American land-use: of a wilderness Eden; of an agrarian yeoman-farmland; of a desert tamed and reclaimed. To enter these spaces was to be thrust into an arena of mythological significance, in which space, the land, and its occupation were potent issues for more than the small number of citizens who were directly affected. To ignore these myths was perilous, as the district would come to understand.

SELECTION

The district's choice of sites in each case had two components. The first was the set of requirements derived by the army, in consultation with its first major corporate subcontractor, Du Pont. Together they focused their choices around the twin issues of secrecy—"security," they already called it—and power. Assurance that all three sites were isolated was uppermost, and therein lies a revealing paradox. For in each case, the mass incursion by the district onto otherwise silent spaces, and (as we shall see) the style of its condemnation procedure, generated the maximum of disruption and adverse publicity for the district.

The issue of power, likewise, was a confused one. In each case, the leaders of the site-selection teams (drawn from government, scientific, and military communities) agreed on specific requirements for electrical power. But while their sites offered the potential for power, none of them actually had enough of it at hand. Power would have to be negotiated or, more commonly, appropriated, from other sources, often at the expense of secrecy and time—two self-declared priorities. And in each case, the district ignored equally compelling needs—at Los Alamos, for water; at Hanford, for labor; at Oak Ridge, for an easily modified site topography—in the concern with security and power.

At each place, unspoken issues crowded in on the district's illusive ideal of rational, efficient behavior and control. Consider just one site: Los Alamos. There the final location was not on any of the lists of the reconnaissance teams that combed the nation for sites. Instead, the scientist Robert Oppenheimer forced through the choice, not because of its military appropriateness, but because he owned a dude ranch nearby (where he loved to dress up in cowboy costume and boots) and harbored a deep affection for the spectacular vistas and tourist attractions of the surrounding area. From the first, he envisioned his expatriate scientists recapitulating their alpine excursions here in the Jemez Mountains, scurrying up the slopes in lederhosen during weekend jaunts, learning to ride western style, learning to square dance. There they would find, as he had found, "freshness and authenticity"; it would be a place to become "industrious and thoughtful," to ride horses with names like Io, a place that might serve as the intellectual's metaphor for redemptive nature: "the mountains."[11] Everything about the site charmed him, including its limitations. The army wanted a valley that could be ringed by fencing and visible from its perimeter—the usual topography for a high-security facility. Setting Los Alamos high atop a small mesa turned the question of security into one of serene retreat, made the site into a city upon a hill. And, finally, its severe limitations in water, space, and housing reinforced Oppenheimer's vision of a small collective of great minds, minimally hampered by bureaucrats, army people, or support personnel. Oppenheimer called this visionary utopia "Shangri-La." In this, as in so much else where the scientists' conception confronted the military-industrial system, he profoundly underestimated the strength of his adversaries, to the ultimate destruction not only of his vision, but of his scientific community itself. Rather than discouraging growth and bureaucratization, the site's limitations simply guaranteed that the building of this system would occur in the most violent and disruptive of ways, as the ultimate built environment testifies.[12]

CONDEMNATION

Once the sites were selected, the lands themselves had to be acquired, and the process of that acquisition not only exemplified the channels of power the project constructed, but in some ways served as testing grounds for the alliances of forces within the district.

At each location, the district's controlling figures applied similar techniques. At the onset, they used the military/government powers of condemnation to acquire the land; they combined this with an aura of secrecy ensuring that the notifications of condemnation occurred virtually without warning and with little or no information about the greater good to which this disruption was aimed or about the compensation for lost land.[13]

The reasoning behind this abrupt process was dual. First was the ubiquitous necessity for haste that permeated every aspect of the district's activities. Without any clear idea of what might be produced out of the still unfinished scientific enterprise, with no notion of what schedule might be imposed by the war itself, the Army Corps of Engineers struck with maximum speed and efficiency in all areas where it had some measure of control. Land acquisition was one of these areas. Second, district officials believed that a preemptive strike and quick eviction would keep comment and publicity, and resistance as well, to a minimum.

But there was a third, inadvertent contributor to the process: the already developed bureaucracy that the Army Corps of Engineers represented. Since the Manhattan Engineering District was a division of the corps, the district's commanding officer, General Leslie R. Groves, was obligated to follow standard corps procedure. This dictated that land acquisition be controlled by a local corps subsidiary of its Real Estate Division. Once the district put in its order for land, Real Estate took over; synchronizing its activities with the larger goals of the district was not at issue.[14]

Rather than secrecy, the result was immediate hostility and opposition. Through a series of land-acquisition reforms instituted during the years immediately preceding the war, the corps had developed a procedure in which legal condemnation of the land came before negotiation; as a result, both the corps' intentions and estimates of the appraisals of property values became public knowledge. And each further step in the district's standard operating procedure further inflamed the local population, enticing them to call upon their supporters and make the battle public.

Appraisals were the most inflammatory documents. Despite the urgings of some of the early site-selection officials that "it would be well to have appraisers who are familiar and sympathetic with the people in this area,"[15] the corps hired hard-nosed appraisers, many from far outside the area, with little initial concern for the effects of their choices. At each site, the valuations were far below what owners expected. At Los Alamos, the land was efficiently acquired, because the principal landowner was already the federal government, because the school had sufficient influence and power to affect changes in the valuation, because the power to resist the army's steady, implacable advance had been fractured by the complexities of the legal situation, and because the other affected landowners were almost entirely Indian or Hispanic sheepherders with little money and less influence.[16] But at the other sites, the actions of individual appraisers infuriated landowners—appraisers and negotiators insulted the land and grounds, offending the deep allegiances of landholders who had been at Hanford since before World War I, at Oak Ridge, in some cases, for generations. Hanford's appraisers were largely drawn from a pool of Land Bank officials from the Pacific coastline; most had small understanding of the blank, largely treeless landscape of southeastern Washington, with its shrunken, misshapen fruit trees and its farmyards where most buildings were made from scavenged wood due to the shortage of lumber in the region. In addition, none of them, it appears, could understand the complexities of irrigation farming or the byzantine financing that bonded the tangible farm to an intangible water system. As a result, they rarely assessed the farms according to yields or capital costs and routinely categorized them as "abandoned," "dilapidated," or "run-down."[17]

At Oak Ridge, the case was even more spectacular. There a number of the farmers, possibly the majority, were relatively recent settlers. They had been moved to the region when the TVA flooded the fertile lower valleys. A number had even been evicted twice, first from the Great Smokies National Park sometime in the 1920s, and then from the TVA's flooding in the 1930s. Bitter memories of searching unsuccessfully for better land and forced migration from fertile to less fertile to nearly sterile lands were fresh in the minds of these farmers. The others, many of them residents since the revolution, were even more recalcitrant; they were the ones who most powerfully retained their allegiance to the Jeffersonian ideal of a fixed yeoman population, anchoring the land and providing continuity for the national identity.[18]

The presence of the TVA fostered that resistance, because its policies of amicable relocation and integration with the community provided a fresh contrast to the army's program of rapid condemnation and tightfisted recompense. The army's procedure involved a legal declaration of condemnation and a "certificate of taking," followed by eviction, often before negotiations were completed. Because of the rush to build and the rule of secrecy, most evicted farmers found they were competing for land and housing with the vast numbers of laborers arriving or soon to arrive to work on plant construction. As the army itself put it, "asking prices within a radius of many miles increased greatly overnight,"[19] and most farmers were forced far away, off the land to cities like Chicago—or into the labor pool at Oak Ridge itself, a double irony, for they became tenants on their own lands, working for those who had evicted them—yeoman farmers turned into indentured servants.[20] And little or nothing is known of the fate of the 1,500 or so tenant farm families who received no recompense, no moving money, no relocation assistance, nothing but the eviction notice.[21]

By comparison, the TVA's strategy had always involved supportive, negotiated land transfers; during the five-month period in which the Manhattan Engineering District condemned and acquired the Oak Ridge site, the TVA acquired an even larger stretch of land, but did so with 97 percent of the properties acquired by voluntary sales. The TVA offered up to $300 an acre; the MDH offered at most $125 an acre, and as little as $9 an acre.[22] And TVA negotiators worked hard to promote its activities by pointing out the ways it would directly benefit those it relocated. Not so with the Manhattan Engineer District. As witnesses at a congressional subcommittee hearing in Knoxville reported, district negotiators "weren't negotiators;

they were persuaders. They had no power to negotiate; only to talk the owner into accepting the price set by the appraisers."[23] Thus, the process of land acquisition served as a testing ground for ways in which the district would interact with the world outside its boundaries throughout the war and beyond.

But the TVA's history on the land had another effect—despite its strenuous efforts to remain on a friendly basis with everyone, the TVA had created a vocal minority of landholders, lawyers, and government officials trained to oppose the will of the government. Embittered by earlier indignities, experienced in strategies of resistance—one division consultant called it "a technique of complaining"[24]—these farmers, lawyers, senators, and congressmen not only delayed land acquisition, but eventually managed to force the district into substantial increases in purchase prices.

But for most of the farmers, this was a matter of too little, too late: the longer they waited for money, the less the money was worth; as land values inflated, their isolation from the land became more and more permanent. And while corps officials described the eviction process as "really child's play,"[25] they were brusquely angry that the farmers did not go willingly, using their resistance to justify further coercive action. By mid-1943, the standoff was complete; the district had committed itself to acting only in its own behalf and without concessions, while the residents of the region had come to believe—as one man wrote in an appeal to his senator—that "we had misjudged the honesty and fairmindedness of the directing officials" of the district.[26] Still, the best the district's opponents could hope for was, in the words of U.S. Representative John Jennings, that "those men who have been mistreating these people will repent in the sight of God and man."[27]

CONSTRUCTION

The building of these three spaces began as early as the site selection. Actual construction was a haphazard affair, in which constant engineering changes mixed with equally constant expansions in the scale of the projects, to generate a continuous process of building and rebuilding; in which a highway might be completed just in time to be closed to be rebuilt; in which housing opened and was occupied just in time for the occupants to be moved to newer (usually more substandard) housing; in which more and more newly arrived upper-level management officials evicted longtime workers, be they scientists at Los Alamos or construction workers at Hanford Engineer Works.[28]

Beneath this seeming chaos, however, lay very different building programs and visions for each site. Los Alamos, as we know, was to be a scientific version of Oppenheimer's much dreamed-of combination of dude ranch and Tibetan monks' colony. That, at least, was the fantasy of the scientific community, persuaded by Oppenheimer's eloquent descriptions and charismatic presence. What Oppenheimer got, however, was a vast expanse of army-base architecture and urban planning, which involved wholesale demolition of all natural site elements, destruction of previous buildings where they interfered with "rational" planning, and, most generally, the inscription of a military plan on the existing environment despite the complaints and even the protest activities of residents and workers. For the scientist-residents, this was an unconscionable violation of a compact—Oppenheimer had promised them one thing and now presided over something uncomfortably close to the prison camps the expatriates had striven to escape by emigrating to America. But in reality, the Los Alamos site plan reflected the standard building practices of the Army Corps of Engineers, and the resulting landscape lay well within the parameters of the prototypical wartime army base. Oppenheimer's betrayal was more precisely a matter of misjudgment on his part.

Eleanor Jette's first glimpse of Los Alamos provides a graphic picture of the site in 1944:

We stopped at the first guard house about half an hour after we crossed the Rio Grande. It stood just east of the fence which was a seven-foot chain link affair with three strands of barbed wire at the top of it. It was liberally festooned with signs which read:

U.S. Government Property
DANGER! *PELIGRO!*
Keep out

The MPs in battle helmets who manned the guardhouse were a formidable looking bunch of young men. . . . After we left the gate, the road wound through thickets of piñon and juniper for a couple of miles. The sun sank behind the Jemez Mountains. The umbrella of black smoke ahead marked the town site. As we approached it, the thickets gave way to an open field. Green construction workers' huts stood disconsolately on the right. There was a barracks area on the left. The whole scene was as raw as a new scar. . . . The fresh snow was covered with soot. . . . The apartment buildings looked like hell. The green barracks-type structures sat jauntily in a sea of mud.[29]

At the Hanford Engineer Works in Washington, the combination of corps and corporation made for a clearer vision of what ideal community should be built upon the ruins of the old. The result was less chaotic and more authoritarian than at Los Alamos. At HEW, two cities were planned from the beginning: one (Hanford Camp) a temporary workers' shanty-town; the other (Richland Village) a more permanent managerial suburb, safely separated from the dangers of the workplace. Because Hanford Camp was built on land the district had already determined would be scorched earth once the atomic piles and the far more hazardous chemical separation facilities began their work, efficiency and cheapness were the prime planning factors. Existing buildings might remain if they could be used more cheaply than razed; trees might remain if their fruit could be harvested and sold. Otherwise, nothing was to stay.[30]

Hanford Camp was almost entirely planned and constructed by the Army Corps of Engineers, with little or no input from Du Pont. But planning is, perhaps, too thoughtful a term for the process. Because it was constructed before the district fully understood the production rigors necessary for the making of plutonium, its size, like the size of Los Alamos, constantly expanded, reaching a peak of more than 45,000 workers in 1944. Defined as a temporary installation and designed and built by a bureaucracy for whom the only true precedent was the army base, Hanford Camp bore only a cursory resemblance to a town or community. Economics drove the plan—the economics of paucity, for each expenditure had to be defended before the penurious General Groves. Theaters, community halls, cafes, shoe repair facilities: these appeared at Hanford Camp after major conflicts, and only after the district's aggressive labor recruitment programs failed to attract specialized workers, and officials could persuade Groves that livability had to be given some consideration.[31]

The result was a vast treeless wasteland of Quonset huts (fig. 4), punc-

4. Hanford Camp from the air, ca. 1944. National Archives.

tuated by huge, faceless production facilities topped by chimneys designed to disperse radioactive poisons to the highest atmospheric region so as to minimize their parts-per-million factor (fig. 5). Virtually without natural topographical definition, defined instead by the neat rectilinear boxes of Quonset huts and barracks facilities, it resembled nothing so much as the perfect company town or prison camp.[32]

Richland, however, was an entirely different matter. Designed for Du Pont managerial staff, army decisionmakers, and corps engineers, its goal was to attract unwilling middle-class dwellers and keep them satisfied. From the first, the corporation developed its own city plan, employing its Wilmington-based architects and engineers for the prosaic matters of infrastructure and the like, but depending on the Spokane firm of G. A. Pehrson to adapt and apply the lessons of other ideal cities and towns of the twentieth century, in the design of everything from houses to recreation areas.

The housing designs, supervised by Pehrson and worked on by the Du Pont design staff in the makeshift headquarters at Pasco High School, were part of a much more elaborate city plan. Housing plans were designed for

5. Chemical separation plant from the air, ca. 1944. National Archives.

each "type" of Richland occupant, from executive to transient. Du Pont had worked out the average number of people per family and family type expected and from that extrapolated building types and numbers of each. But Du Pont also designed the village and its housing units around certain prototypically American ideals of community-building—that is to say, Richland was to be a model town, even a utopia.

Arguing for his designs in an official "Report" in 1943, G. Albin Pehrson was eloquent on this topic. Richland's planners, Pehrson said, "had a definitely democratic attitude in the planning of the houses. Since the whole venture is a use of public monies, such an attitude is relevant to a high degree and should interest the public. . . . [Thus] the building types are . . . as similar . . . as could be planned so that no one might feel himself slighted in the quality of housing. The smallest house has a proportionate share of the things considered vital to good living."[33]

Pehrson/Du Pont's ideals ranged beyond simply providing egalitarian housing. They also saw the building of a community as an essential part of what was necessary to generate the production efficiency the district and Du Pont demanded. The design team's goal was to produce a town that drew upon the aura of the New England village or midwestern farm town celebrated in American mythology—in Thornton Wilder's *Our Town* or the numberless picture essays in *Life* and *Look* both before and during the war that suggested such communities were the locus of the American values for which we were fighting.[34]

In this respect, their work bore a close resemblance to the rationale and plans for Oak Ridge. There, too, the army turned to a respected architectural firm to augment the work of a major corporation (in this case the army-affiliated engineering firm of Stone & Webster) in producing a city that could attract and keep middle-class corporate managerial workers for the vast interlocking network of companies operating the Oak Ridge facilities.[35]

At Oak Ridge, the choice of an architect reflected the district officers' desire to produce a satisfactory antidote to army-base architecture. And their decision to turn first to the John B. Pierce Foundation, and then to the affiliated architectural firm of Skidmore, Owings, Merrill (SOM), emphasized the dual nature of the goals they sought for their atomic utopia. On the one hand was the desire for a new, up-to-date, even futuristic model for this invented town—a desire that found expression in everything from the location of railroad sidings to the type of building materials to be used. This desire drove the district to the Pierce Foundation, a future-oriented think-tank funded by building material firms like Celotex. And Pierce's proposals, for modular buildings of all types based upon repeatable variations of "pods" made from new low-cost materials like Cemesto, resonated with utopian plans that had surfaced in the building and architectural literature of the 1920s and 1930s.[36]

Within a few months after the architectural firm had gone to work, this utopian direction of Oak Ridge had become clear. SOM was more than familiar with the so-called Greenbelt towns planned and built in the 1930s and early 1940s and marked out the turf accordingly. Oak Ridge was to be "self-contained, with no dependence on outside facilities. . . ." Its clientele was to be elite, and "the preponderance of experimental units . . . is reflected in the higher number of top bracket family and bachelor units."[37] Pehrson had planned Richland as an exercise in democratic ideals; SOM paid lip service to the concept but in the end promoted a far different goal. The utopianism lay in the engineering, planning, design, and economic aspects of the town; their social engineering was entirely conservative, even *retardataire.* As partner Nathaniel Owings reported, the goal was to attract and retain an essential conservative middle-class male managerial or scientific-technical employee of supervising firms like Tennessee Eastman, and the town was designed "to keep him and his family contented while he works eight to ten hours a day. . . ."[38]

"Our scientist and his family . . . and his baker and his mortician . . . were to be our clients," Owings reported. But to ensure "their health and their welfare and their happiness," the architects looked not to the future but to the past. The model was, as at Richland, the nostalgic vision of the American small town: architect Owings boasted later that "we hinted at satellite towns, talked of concentric systems of planning, ribbon-type cities as developed by foreign-named people like Hilberscheimer. . . . We would have submitted to torture rather than admit that all we wanted was a series of homely little American villages."[39]

More than underlying structure reflected this conservative outlook. The actual apportionment of resources, the location of houses, and the construction of communities also bore this imprint. At Richland the goal was a rigid egalitarianism, with family size determining the type of house one received. But this seeming attack on American class distinctions could occur only because the community had been conceived from the start as entirely middle-class in its constituency. Oak Ridge was a heterogeneous community; there an attempt to equalize would have been far more radical. SOM did not take that option. Instead, there were modest homes, unattractive homes, homes by the tracks, as well as "ideal homesites . . . lovely building sites tucked away in inaccessible areas." The former went to workers; the latter were the spaces reserved for the elite, corporate executives, and military officers with clout. "When an Army officer began to treat us kindly, Nathaniel Owings remarked, we knew [what] he was looking for. . . . The word went out: See John Merrill."[40] At Hanford, worker housing remained (at least hypothetically) the province of the Hanford Camp. At Oak Ridge, the necessity of large numbers of on-site workers was built into the requirements of the city plan. And the result was to institutionalize the ghetto, the shantytown, and the southern institution of "the tracks."

This was not the original order of things. At Oak Ridge, as at Richland, the earliest plan had been to house a significant number of workers, particularly construction workers, laborers, and blacks, offsite, in "nearby towns with adequate transportation." But by September 1943, this plan had proved glaringly inoperable. Vast expansions in the scale of the projects swamped the region with workers, and district officials looked belatedly at the surrounding regions and discovered them to be almost completely without surplus housing. If the program was to be maintained at speed, a far larger community would have to be built.

The hiring of SOM in the first place reflected an earlier stage in this realization. Calls to the architects to expand their original plan significantly brought real protests, but to no avail. Time was short, population was bulging, plans would be remade. The result was phase-II, whose effect was to set up, in even bolder relief, a multitiered community, in which the utopian housing in clustered "villages" was relegated to the managerial class (fig. 6), while shantytowns of prefab structures and trailer camps served the worker populace (fig. 7). A plan for a cluster village identical to the others, designated the "Negro Village," was proposed (in part as a result of pressure from the black community), then surreptitiously scrapped, and black housing was kept, wherever possible, off-site and, where necessary, separated into particularly rudimentary facilities called "hutments."[41]

This separation by class and race was also locked into the economics of housing. Whereas at Los Alamos and indeed at nearly all army facilities housing cost was determined as a percentage of income rather than as a matter of facilities, the Oak Ridge city manager successfully appealed to abandon the procedure on the grounds that it was "unfair inasmuch as the greater percentage of employees living in the town will be employed by private firms." The resulting rates were "scaled in accordance with the type of quarters furnished rather than the employee's salary"—that is, the bigger the house, the more expensive the rent. In addition, sections of the townsite itself rapidly were assigned on the basis of class—elite "villages" on the rolling hillsides, lower-class communities in the "hollows" and muddy valleys.[42]

What resulted, then, from the continuous period of construction on the district as a whole was a set of three different compressed urbanizations. Hanford became a company town masquerading as a boom town; Oak Ridge, a utopian planned community minus the social utopianism of a classless, povertyless society; Los Alamos, a philosophers' or artists' colony converted by the unspoken demands of military production into something closer to a prison camp. The interaction between social space and landscape, between each city and its surroundings, remained a potent but

6. Cemesto house.

largely unspoken aspect of the project's productions in each of these places. But this matter lies, perhaps, more firmly in our next term.

COMPARTMENTALIZATION

Compartmentalization was the military's system for assuring security in the workplace. Its model was straightforward, simple, elegant. Two workers stand at a laboratory table. They may not speak to each other, only to their immediate superiors. These superiors may only speak to their superiors who may . . . and so on up the line, until finally the two superiors turn out to be the same person. In this way, information within the district moved only vertically; this prevented anyone from assembling the pieces of the giant puzzle that was atomic warfare (though Klaus Fuchs and others proved the ineffectiveness of that notion).

But the system was perfect for the military for other reasons that had little to do with the actual program for producing an atomic weapon. The

7. Demountable housing, Oak Ridge, ca. 1945. National Archives.

system of compartmentalization clustered influence increasingly at the top, reinforcing the army's hierarchical maps of power (fig. 8) and rewarding those locked within the system, rather than those who knew or understood the plan as a whole. In addition, the system fragmented social and informational networks, isolating individuals in their cells, where they did as they were told. This system was most comforting to the managerial elite at Du Pont and the military elite from the corps. It was perhaps most devastating to the scientific community at Los Alamos.

But compartmentalization was not only a model for the workplace. It was the guiding principle for the entire project; it defined every social relation therein. We find it in a brochure sent to the scientists recruited for Los Alamos. Sent to the scientists, but addressed (covertly) to their wives, the document begins with a self-contradiction. "This is a restricted document," it reads, "within the meaning of the Espionage Act, the contents of this document are not to be discussed with anyone unless he is known to you to be a member of this project. You may discuss them with your wife

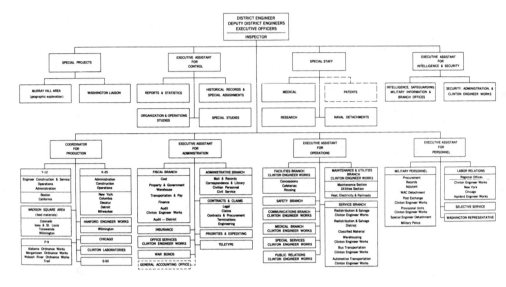

8. Manhattan District organizational chart, January 1945. Manhattan District History.

if she accepts these limitations in all strictness. . . ." Wives, it says, are "members of this project," yet they are not members of this project.

The most telling section, entitled "Security," began by attempting to define the compartmentalization program. The special "precautions" on the MED, "measures which are peculiar to our project . . . are not measures designed primarily against espionage," the pamphlet explained. Rather, they were "designed to make espionage more difficult and to enable us more readily to detect it. *These measures involve essentially breaking the social relationships between the personnel employed at Los Alamos and people not so employed*" (emphasis mine).[43] This plan—"breaking the social relationships"—defined the boundaries between each of these spaces and everything beyond. At Hanford, the corps closed all roads into and out of the works; one of these was the principal road leading from eastern Washington's irrigated farmlands to the marketplace towns. At Oak Ridge, the corps appropriated a series of bridges across the Clinch River, again isolating the community and controlling its boundaries by setting up entranceways with guard houses. One could not pass *through* these sites; one *entered* them if designated a proper security risk.

Every aspect of the plans enforced this rule of separation between the new communities and the old. And within the communities compartmentalization, "breaking the social relationships," dominated. Husbands could not talk of their work to wives or children; the effect was to marginalize and disempower women, who had traditionally served in the scientific community as highly trained advisors, critics, and colleagues. Eleanor Jette spoke of it most clearly when she described her first months at Los Alamos: her husband Eric came home after his first day, lay on the bed, and "studied the nail holes in the ceiling . . . behind an impenetrable wall of silence" until it was time to go to work again. For Ruth Marshak, writing in 1948, the pain was still fresh. "The Tech Area was a great pit which swallowed our scientist husbands out of sight, almost out of our lives," she wrote. "They worked at night, and often came home at three or four in the morning. Sometimes, they set up Army cots in the laboratories and did not come home at all." In the postwar professional world, this behavior would be common, a badge of honor among corporate lawyers, doctors, advertising agents, industrial chemists, corporate executives. But at this moment it was not. "Few women understood what the men were seeking there" at work, Marshak recalled; "the loneliness and heartache of some scientists' wives during the years before the atomic bomb was born were very real." [44]

This system of social control through forced anomie prevailed at Hanford and Oak Ridge, as well. At the Oak Ridge site, the major corporation, Tennessee Eastman, determined that the ideal operations worker was not a scientifically trained college graduate, but rather a high school–educated female from one of the nearby towns, who would work ignorantly but diligently at her tasks. Similar criteria applied throughout Oak Ridge, and at Hanford too, and they had a deadening effect on the project and on the laborers. One female worker at Hanford reported her experience working at a table pipetting an unknown substance from one test tube to another, day after day, in a sterilized environment, wearing a white uniform. "I remembered that first day when I saw a girl scrubbing one particular area on the floor," she later recalled. "It looked so clean I wondered why she didn't go on to another part of the floor—but no, she stayed in that one spot, over and over. I was sure either she or I was ready for a mental hospital." [45] For the project as a whole, the effect of such disenfranchisement was to guarantee the security of ignorance, by removing from the system of checks and balances anyone who had both the theoretical and the empirical knowledge of the processes involved in atomic technology.

Similar compartmentalizations dominated outside the workplace. The policy of separating laborers from one another dampened chances of large-scale unionization, but also fostered conflict among different crafts and work groups. The district resolved this by refusing to negotiate with worker-constituted union locals, insisting instead on calling in Washington-based "Internationals," with whom they could negotiate over issues of patriotism rather than worker health or safety. When workers resisted, the district resorted to more coercive methods, including bringing in draftees as substitute workers and the threat of drafting recalcitrant workers.[46] Separating housing into neighborhoods defined by class, race, and profession recapitulated the divisions within American culture, even served as steps backward—as at Oak Ridge, where laborer housing was racially segregated and black children were denied schooling, applying a rationale that the army's responsibility lay only in respecting local customs.[47]

Such conflicts between the law of the land and the law of the project underscored the way the project isolated itself from what lay outside its boundaries, creating what might best be called a "forced" culture. With this term I want to suggest two meanings. The building of Hanford, Oak Ridge, and Los Alamos represented an intensified process, out of the natural rhythms of growth and development. In this sense, these cities were forced as a hothouse flower is forced. Because of their isolation from the broader conflicts, currents, and negotiations of American culture, because their aim was a particular streamlined, hierarchical authoritarianism, this "forced" culture concentrated rather than negated authoritarian tendencies. Thus, a crucial component of the development of these cities was the sense in which each was the result of force, of tyrannies of power, impositions upon the land, upon existing communities, upon settled American myths concerning not just landscape in general, but these landscapes in particular. First a new system of cultural power relations was devised within the boundaries; once set in place, it became a model for the postwar environment.

The production of culture, especially the forced production of culture, requires an accompanying new language that must subsume and supplant the existing language if it is to be successful. At least that seems to be a lesson of the Manhattan Project. For this, we turn to the last term.

ENCRYPTION

Encryption was, for the corps, the means by which secrets were coded to prevent their acquisition by an enemy. In this respect, naming the University of Chicago's atomic research facility the Metallurgical Lab and fabricating various code names for uranium, plutonium, etc., are typical of this encryption. But it may also be used to describe something broader, subtler, and more substantial: the appropriation and control of language more generally.

In this area, rich as it is, we may choose two suggestive examples. The first is, quite simply, the name of the project itself. Here we have the appearance of a simple renaming, similar to the district's instructions to call uranium "tenure," an atomic bomb a "topic boat." But its history also reveals the larger issues that lay behind the district's ethos. Once the project moved into the realm of production, under the umbrella of the Army Corps of Engineers, the corps was required by its operating procedure to designate a separate Engineering District for the program, thus drawing unwarranted attention to the project. In addition, the corps' districts were demarcated by geographical region and to generate a new district in the regions where the project was actually at work would be to invite scrutiny of the project sites. There was also the matter of geographical ephemerality; the project subsumed geographical regions—it included rural and urban, West and East, South and North; and it also was dependent on, and derived from, the transgeographical pure-scientific culture of the prewar era, in which German, English, American, and Russian scientists formed a community linked not by geography but by maps of information and transgeographical systems of communication. This pure-scientific culture was, in historian Daniel Boorstin's terms, an "everywhere community," and the project became one too.[48]

And so the Army Corps of Engineers chose to create a new district and name it Manhattan. The decision made a district where there had been none, and where there continued to be none, but where one might logically expect to find one—Manhattan. But this cover location also (perhaps coincidentally) *symbolized* the nature of the project: its polyglot population, its transgeographical identity, its cosmopolitanism, and its modernity. Thus, the process of encryption lied, but it also told the truth. Such was the case with much of the language the project engendered. Calling uranium "tenure" was based on the addition of the atomic weight—$2 + 3 + 5 = 10$, URE = uranium. Almost always ordered and controlled from above, this new language required that project participants wean themselves from communication as they had known it and give allegiance to the new mode, yet it carried within it the very structures and messages it was designed to hide.

Invented nouns formed one part of the new language; connecting these nouns with a project grammar turned codes into codes of behavior. This grammar used passive and expletive sentence structures almost exclusively: "There is a military necessity for the acquisition of land" began the Hanford Condemnation Directive;[49] land appropriation was based on "declarations of taking"—but without mention of who was taking, or what. The result was an aura of permanence, absolutism, and causal insubstantiality that extended from the language into most other areas of cultural production. Residents of Los Alamos never had a home they could call their own—all were, absurdly, crowded into a single rural route box in Santa Fe, New Mexico. For similar reasons, they could not vote: their community was, after all, only a mailbox, without geographical or political reality, and so residents could not register in New Mexico, yet they were no longer legitimately "absentee voters" anywhere else.[50]

The process of appropriating languages extended far beyond simple words or codes, into all regions where language may be seen as a metaphor or an underlying structural system. Take, for example, the question of photography within the district.[51] Photography was the province of the authorities alone. Cameras, even amateur cameras, were hypothetically forbidden to all personnel. But the district did produce "official" photographs which reflected in their authorlessness, in their systematic nature, in their bland facticity, the larger passive grammar of the district.[52]

Neither the language nor the grammar of the Manhattan Project was entirely new; both appropriated existing elements, especially from the military bureaucracies and from the bureaucracies of the increasingly centralized government before and during the war. For example, workers at each site were kept at their jobs by a strategy known as the "certificate of availability" system. Workers who were fired or who quit without permission were not given "certificates of availability"; without them, they were, to quote the corps, "technically prevented . . . from obtaining employment for a period of 60 days."[53] Thus, the project acquired from the War Preparedness legislation a means of preventing workers from leaving their jobs. And this already perilous strategy became even more coercive, because hidden in housing and stores regulations were rules requiring that workers not directly employed on the projects were to be immediately evicted and forbidden to purchase food or other goods from the government stores. At Hanford, to quit without permission meant to be evicted into the desert without the possibility of institutionalized employment for two months.

But encryption, and the development of counterlanguages, also formed a principal means of resistance for project workers. And I will end with a peculiar example, the case of Richard Feynman. Feynman was a young physicist at Los Alamos; like most, he had planned to come with his wife and set up family housekeeping there. But his wife was diagnosed with tuberculosis and forbidden entry into the fenced community of Los Alamos. Instead, she was sequestered in a sanatorium in Albuquerque, and Feynman was periodically allowed to travel to visit her there. In this, the administration made an exception to the general rule that once one arrived at Los Alamos one could not leave for any reason, except to go (under the watchful eye of security forces) to Santa Fe to shop.

District officials thought Feynman should be grateful. He was young, in love, and obstinate. He considered the censorship of his mail a violation of his integrity and found it absurd that he was forced to participate in his own censorship, by writing and rewriting all his letters until the censors accepted the result. So he and his wife developed a series of codes for love letters. Unfortunately, the censors insisted that the couple provide the keys to their codes before the mail could go through. The result was a circumstance in which Feynman could only accept his own participation, accept the presence of the censor, accept even that his playful invention of private languages must be subject to the omniscience of security. Who then won? Feynman, who disturbed and undercut the authority of the censors, forcing their absurdity into the open? Or the authority behind the censors, who, finally, required of Feynman a choice between love and speech, albeit controlled and observed by authority, or isolation and silence?[54]

Without their own language—without freedom to speak, to act, to discuss, argue, or invent new possibilities—the scientific community at Los Alamos, like the worker community at Hanford and the managerial community at Oak Ridge, lapsed first into the stilted language of behavior and communication that was all the project allowed; eventually, the only space of dignity was silence, an admission of impotence.

Counterpoised against this loss of speech was the district's own insistent demand for a substitute language of obedience. Control of language—maintaining silence, preventing "unauthorized" speech, encouraging "proper" and "patriotic" speech—was a feature of the wartime effort in general. From corporate and factory newsletters to official censorship regulations, government representatives waged a vigorous campaign to convince American workers and citizens generally that controlled discourse was an essential part of the wartime effort. In the Manhattan District, the campaign centered on three points: the underlying assumption that dangerous information might inadvertently leak out to enemy agents as a result of uncontrolled discourse; the belief that national morale could be controlled by limiting the type and extent of speech; and the assertion that a common language of patriotism would generate a common national unity, deemphasizing differences and drawing diversity into a harmonious centralized whole.

At its most coercive, the Manhattan District's campaign separated public and private speech. Public speech it controlled through censorship of public institutions (newspapers, elected officials, public union meetings); through the replacement of disparate voices with a single voice; and through propaganda to give that voice a set of uplifting messages. At the private level, the district focused on bringing about voluntary limitations of individual speech, principally through "education" campaigns; on forcing private speech to move through the channels of government and district control; and on embargoing improper or dangerous language. Behind both of these lay a deeper, more complex, and less acknowledged goal: the generation of a new language common to all, but controlled by the authorities.

Possibly the most direct and unabashed of these campaigns for control of speech and language lay within the district's secrecy program. At Oak Ridge and Los Alamos, sites where potent secrets were being worked out by scientists and intellectuals with full grasp of the circumstances, such campaigns made sense. At Hanford, the program took on an aura of fanaticism. There MED Security directed its campaign at construction workers who had no understanding of the project whatsoever—who worked on vast construction programs in which modern methods of subcontracting sequestered them from each other and from other aspects of the site. The district struggled to force a new language of obedience on workers who were already unable to telegraph injurious facts or behave in manners that might alter the power relations within the boundaries of the site. The absurdity of this did not discourage district security forces. Virtually every official utterance included the codas of secrecy and silence: "What You Hear, Keep It Here" or "Caution Leaves No Regrets" or even "MUZZLE UP!!!!" "Let's All HEW to the Line!" was the early, army-invented title of the Hanford house organ, later named the *Sage Sentinel*.[55]

And so silence became both the final act of resistance and the ultimate act of compliance in the topographies of power that formed the cultural geography of the Manhattan Project. Such, I think, was an underlying condition of the community at Alamogordo during the last hours before the first atomic bomb went off. Having, some of them, attempted to persuade their newly installed "superiors" (another example of encryption) that the bomb should be demonstrated at worst, but never used, yet having their petition intercepted and silenced, these scientists found themselves in a peculiar position. Every element of their talk over the past years had concerned the theoretical and practical possibilities that now lay in the bomb itself. Slowly, over the last hours and minutes, they lapsed into silence, a silence not simply of anticipation, but of expatriation. Together yet isolate, each awaited the wash of sound so intense it might be mistaken for silence, the presence so great it might be mistaken for absence.

But this story is not the only account to come from Alamogordo. Another, equally credible, reports a nervous anticipatory chatter, excited activity, suppressed impatience—a bit like Christmas eve. A third presents a portentous discourse on responsibility and implication, among the participants.[56] Thus, this ending is its own myth, one which serves us here, providing closure to a construction never in fact closed. For what of the other response—the response of violence directed by worker at worker, a violence that, scientist Leona Libby reported from Hanford, left bodies in garbage cans on weekend mornings?[57] What of those, like Edward Teller, who embraced the new scientific culture and the new conditions of submission to higher authorities who offered absolution in return for obedience? What, indeed, of the continuation of each of these atomic spaces, the one (Los Alamos) as a living museum of postwar technocracy and managed

*9. Peter Hales, "Plutonium Waste Trench, Hanford Engineer Works,
September, 1990."*

living, another (Oak Ridge) as a virtually unchanged replica of itself, the
third as a ghost-town, a ghost industrial zone, beneath which lies, they tell
us, a lake of radioactive waste fifteen feet deep, the size of Manhattan?[58]

Each of these questions points toward places where the mythological and
the physical shade into one another, where the past, accessible only in part
and never complete, shades into the present, incomplete in a different way.
But we are not, happily, imprisoned within the boundaries of that origin
myth which still remains the dominant image of the Manhattan Project. We
may remake that myth, open it to new endings, and, from these, create new
beginnings.

Today that act will be not simply a social one. It must also be a cultural
one, and as such requires a new geography, physical, mental, and mythical.
Let us end with a picture of one site. Today the Hanford Engineer Works
lies unused, a vast wasteland cut by shallow, open trenches in which sit
rows of drums containing plutonium waste (fig. 9). In a huge pit some miles

10. Peter Hales, "Decommissioned Nuclear Submarine Fleet, Hanford Engineer Works, September, 1990."

away sit the cut-out reactor cores of America's decommissioned nuclear submarine fleet (fig. 10). Nothing can leave; hasty law, politically popular, has guaranteed the impossibility of a rational, feasible restoration of the lands. Close by are the empty, half-completed hulks of nuclear power plants begun by the Washington Public Power System, abandoned now, resembling monuments of a dead civilization (fig. 11).

Here, still, the landscape serves as the effect of decisions based on myths about America's geographical destiny, combined with that other consequential topography of power honed and brought to new heights in the district. We cannot alter the physical topography without transforming the mental one that underlies it, cannot undo the environmental damage without recognizing how fundamentally it is a part of mythologies and belief systems as wide as that lake of radioactive waste and far, far deeper.

But that is another story.

11. Peter Hales, "Power Plant Loop, Hanford Engineer Works, September, 1990."

NOTES

1. Vincent Jones, *Manhattan: The Army and the Atomic Bomb* (Washington, D.C.: Center for Military History [Government Printing Office], 1985).

2. Richard Rhodes, *The Making of the Atomic Bomb* (New York: Simon and Schuster, 1986).

3. Only two books serve as precedents for such a study. One is James W. Kunetka, *City of Fire: Los Alamos and the Birth of the Atomic Age, 1943–1945* (Englewood Cliffs, N.J.: Prentice-Hall, 1978). The second is Charles W. Johnson and Charles O. Jackson, *City behind a Fence: Oak Ridge, Tennessee, 1942–1946* (Knoxville: University of Tennessee Press, 1981). Both of these focus on individual sites; Kunetka's, because it includes the production processes and the scientific discoveries, is necessarily cursory, while Johnson and Jackson's is an exhaustively researched study of social urbanization.

Jones's *Manhattan: The Army and the Atomic Bomb* is still the only study that subsumes the sites. Its sponsorship by the army as part of its "official" series "The United States Army in World War II" makes the work of extremely limited value from a narrative perspective, and the age and limited scope of its primary source research hamper its use as a reference source. Nonetheless, it is still a rich and necessary text.

Most secondary sources (including Jones's) have depended heavily on an early and quite exhaustive compilation of documents and narratives produced between the end of the war and the assumption of control over the district by the Atomic Energy Commission. Titled "The Manhattan District History," it spans some thirteen reels of microfilm and is relatively dispassionate considering its source (see note 19 below).

4. Because of the limitations of this essay, I cannot detail the process by which this transformation of labor policy took place; it is a central part of the larger work *Atomic Spaces*, which this essay presages. Some discussion of the process can be found scattered in chapter 16 of Vincent Jones's army-sponsored *Manhattan: The Army and the Atomic Bomb*. A more rewarding excursion can be made through the diary of Lt. Col. Franklin T. Matthias, who supervised the Hanford Engineer Works throughout its wartime span. A copy of the diary is located in the Library of the Hanford Science Center, a DOE facility in Richland, Washington.

5. The Los Alamos Historical Society has a rich collection of materials concerning the history of the region before its expropriation by the army. It has also published a number of books of interest: one of these is Fermor and Peggy Pond Church, *When Los Alamos Was a Ranch School* (Los Alamos, N.M.: Los Alamos Historical Society, 1974). The society has a large collection of photographs detailing life at the Ranch School as well.

6. I have written about the tourist sensibility in the American West in the later chapters of *William Henry Jackson and the Transformation of the American Landscape* (Philadelphia: Temple University Press, 1988). The literature on the expatriate communities of the Southwest is too rich for a note—Mabel Dodge Luhan alone deserves a multipage bibliography. One particularly appropriate work is Peggy Pond Church's *The House at Otowi Bridge* (Albuquerque: University of New Mexico Press, 1960), a reminiscence by the daughter of the Ranch School's founder which presents the school and its place in the larger expatriate culture with an affecting nostalgia.

7. See the condemnation records for the region, located in the National Archives and Records Administration regional center at East Point, Georgia (henceforth NARA-EP), in N3-326-87-07, boxes 6 and 7. These are eleven notebooks, containing negative photocopies of typescript tract valuation forms, and photographs of all buildings on each tract, minimum one photo per building. The valuation forms

list tract number, beginning with A-1, name of owner, valuation of improvements, replacement less depreciation basis, type of building, size, construction type, roof type, foundation type, condition, value, and salvage value. The photographs are from negatives approximately 2 3/4 × 3 3/4, each of which has a number written on it corresponding to the building listed in the appraisal form (A-1-1, for example, was the farmhouse of the W. B. Thacker family, tract A-1). Photographs and written descriptions of the sites give an excellent picture of each tract. In addition, the district commissioned a detailed appraisal report which treats the region cogently and accurately. Orrin Thacker, Jr., "Gross Appraisal: Proposed Site for Kingston Army Camp, Kingston, Tennessee," done for Ohio River Division of ACE, dated 3 August 1943 in NARA-EP (RG 4nn-326-8505, box 5, file 601.1). It includes a description of "Crops and Special Improvements: Farmers and farm tenants in the area were consulted and the following information was obtained and is believed to be accurate." T. reports that "from 60 to 70% of the farms are owner operated. . . . Farm products consist of corn, sorghum, small grains, lespedeza crimson clover, tobacco, all types of livestock and poultry." "There are approximately 900 tracts within the area containing approximately 1,100 families and with an estimated population of 4,400 inhabitants."

8. See the files of the Farm Security Administration in the Prints and Photographs Division of the Library of Congress; these files are organized by geographical region and afford a rich source for exploring the ways specific regions of the nation were mythologized in the 1930s. On the popular picturebooks concerning the era, I am grateful to have participated in a panel at the 1990 American Studies Association Conference that included a paper by Ralph Bogardus on the Harlan County, Kentucky, photographer Vic Howard, which included valuable contextual information concerning the photography of the South in the period in question; and a second paper by Ruth A. Banes on photographer Bayard Wootten, whose work memorialized in popular picturebook form the ideal of the hardscrabble agrarian South and included a cogent discussion of the portrayal of the Jacksonian southern agrarian as a symbolic figure in the photography books of the period before the war.

9. Hanford's "prehistory" can be traced in the series of continuing oral and written histories comprising the Hanford–White Bluffs History Project, whose materials are currently located in the Hanford Science Center, Richland, Washington. The center also houses a rich archive of movie film made by Harry Anderson, the theater proprietor of White Bluffs, spanning the decade before army occupation. See also two locally published histories: Martha Berry Parker, *Tales of Richland, White Bluffs and Hanford 1805–1943* (Fairfield, Wash.: Ye Galleon Press, 1979); and Mary Powell Harris, *Goodbye, White Bluffs* (1972; Yakima, Wash.: Franklin Press, 1981).

10. See the miscellaneous materials held in files at Hanford Science Center: file marked Hanford History Display; see also Harris, *Goodbye, White Bluffs*; and Parker, *Tales of Richland, White Bluffs, and Hanford, 1805–1943*.

11. Alice Kimball Smith and Charles Weiner, eds., *Robert Oppenheimer: Letters and Recollections* (Cambridge, Mass.: Harvard University Press, 1980), 132, 135. The story of Oppenheimer's "jangling spurs" comes from Edith Warner's recollection of her first experiences with Oppenheimer, in *The House at Otowi Bridge*.

12. John H. Dudley, "Ranch School to Secret City," in Lawrence Badash and H. P. Broida, *Reminiscences of Los Alamos* (New York: D. Reidel, 1980), 4–5.

13. The passive voice was the *voix populaire* of the district, for it could easily combine the imperative without explaining the cause. The standard condemnation letter might start, then, "It has been determined that . . ."—determined by whom and how was the "determination" arrived at?

14. The story of the Real Estate Division's activities is ably, if sympathetically, told in Jones's *Manhattan: The Army and the Atomic Bomb*. Real Estate Division records are held in the various archives for each location; in the case of Hanford, they remain a part of the active files of the Department of Energy.

15. This is Orrin Thacker's recommendation, from his preliminary assessment of the Oak Ridge site. See Thacker, "Gross Appraisal."

16. On the morale of school officials, see the letters that circulated among the various principals of the school, located at the Los Alamos Historical Society. With staff and founding directors scattered, in ill health, or awaiting the draft, the opportunity for any successful resistance quickly passed, and the district's off-the-record hints at appraisal increases eventually evaporated. Little or no research has been done on the many small ranchers who made up the rest of the affected population.

17. Perhaps the most poignant testimony to the experience of condemnation at Hanford is found in the oral histories of the Hanford–White Bluffs History Project, located in the Records Library of the Hanford Science Center.

18. Materials on the condemnation proceedings at Oak Ridge are scattered throughout the hundreds of unprocessed record boxes at the National Archives Federal Records Depository in East Point, Georgia. These include the appraisal notebooks for each of the holdings within the area condemned, as well as site selection reports, acquisition reports, sample condemnation letters, and the like.

19. "Manhattan District History," a multivolume unpublished typescript combining a 1946 narrative with earlier documentary evidence and materials (including photographs, diaries, memoranda, letters, etc.), henceforth MDH. Copies are located at Oak Ridge, Tennessee, and in the National Archives and Records Administration, Washington, D.C., MDH, I, 10, 2.

20. MDH, I, 10, 2, estimates about 60 percent of the residents ended up temporary tenants and construction workers at Clinton, after which they, like all construction workers, were again evicted.

21. See Thacker, "Gross Appraisal."

22. Johnson and Jackson, *City behind a Fence*, 41; MDH, I, 10, appendix 2.

23. *Report of House Military Affairs Subcommittee*, excerpted in *Knoxville News-
Sentinel*, 12 August 1943, clipping in MDH, I, 10, appendix B-2.

24. The phrase comes from the report of Agriculture Department official George
E. Farrell, who served as a consultant to the district when the issue of land values
became particularly hot. See his letter to Real Estate Division head O'Brien, in
MDH, I, 10, appendix B-2-e.

25. Quoted in Johnson and Jackson, *City behind a Fence*, 43.

26. Letter held in MDH, I, 10, appendix B-2-N.

27. Jennings's comment at the subcommittee hearing was included in Fred Mor-
gan's report to the chief engineer, held in MDH, I, 10, appendix B-2-Q.

28. See Eleanor Jette's report on the threatened eviction of tenants from housing
at Los Alamos, in *Inside Box 1663* (orig. written 1949; Los Alamos, N.M.: Los
Alamos Historical Society, 1977).

29. Jette, *Inside Box 1663*, 15.

30. Probably the richest source for information on the Hanford construction
process is Lt. Col. Matthias's diary. No adequate study of the Hanford site has as
yet been written. S. L. Langer, Robert W. Mull, and Robley L. Johnson, *Hanford
and the Bomb: An Oral History of World War II* (Seattle: Living History Press,
1989), a recent oral history of residents at the site during the war, offers some
anecdotal information, but suffers heavily from the effect of nostalgia and changed
attitudes on the part of its informants—it is more accurately a study of the postwar
reorientation of the site than of the wartime years. A short anecdotal history of the
site, made from a compilation of newspaper columns written in the immediate
postwar years, is more rewarding: Ted Van Arsdale, *Hanford: The Big Secret* (Richland, Wash.: Columbia Basin News, 1958).

31. The best source for tracing these conflicts is the Matthias diary.

32. In fact, Hanford had its own prison camp within its boundaries. The district
negotiated an arrangement with Prison Industries, Inc., to transport, house, and
employ prisoners from a Washington federal penitentiary on a variety of tasks from
irrigation to demolition of the camp once production began and the area was
deemed too "hot" for other human occupation. See the relevant passages of the
Matthias diary.

33. "Report on the Hanford Engineer Works Village [Richland, Washington] by
Office of G. Albin Pehrson, Architect Engineer" (Spokane, Washington, Novem-

ber 1943), 42 (single copy held in Hanford Science Center, miscellaneous files in file cabinets of Public Information Officer).

34. Ibid. This report contains everything from detailed plans for each housing type, to rationales for siting of structures, to a detailed defense of the democratic ideals behind the entire program.

35. On Oak Ridge generally, see Johnson and Jackson, *City behind a Fence.* The relevant primary materials are now located at NARA-EP.

36. See, for example, the "Notes on Conference in District Office, 9:45 AM October 26, 1942," in NARA-EP (RG 4NN-326-8505, box 28, file MD337, Meetings and Conferences); Letter Capt. Samuel Baxter to SOM & Andrews, 12 November 1943 in file 624 (RG 4nn-326-8505, box 52); see also the townsite plan itself (RG 4NN-326-8505, file MD 600.18, Town Management Operations).

37. "Memo to Col. Nichols from J. E. Travis—subject: Hanford Engineer Works Townsite," dated 4/19/43 in NARA-EP (RG 4nn-326-8505, box 52, file 624, Housing).

38. Nathaniel Alexander Owings, *Spaces in Between: An Architect's Journey* (Boston: Houghton Mifflin, 1973), 91.

39. Ibid., 94.

40. Ibid., 96.

41. These matters are imbedded in the "Construction Progress Reports" that were presented monthly by SOM and Pierce to the district. They are located in NARA-EP (RG 4nn-326-8505, box 49, file 600.914, JBP Housing).

42. Memo, 13 June 1944, Samuel Baxter to Capt. P. E. O'Meara, "Rental Rates at Clinton Engineer Works," NARA-EP (RG 4nn-326-8505, box 52).

43. Army Corps of Engineers, "Memorandum on the Los Alamos Project," ca. 1943, reproduced in its entirety in Jette, *Inside Box 1663*, 125–28.

44. Jette, *Inside Box 1663*, 24; Ruth Marshak, "Secret City," in *Standing By and Making Do: The Women of Wartime Los Alamos*, ed. Jane S. Wilson and Charlotte Serber (Los Alamos, N.M.: Los Alamos Historical Society, 1988), 10–11.

45. Ted Van Arsdol, *Hanford: The Big Secret*, 69–70.

46. The diary of Lt. Col. Matthias details this process of union control and union-busting—see the entries interspersed throughout the end of 1944 and the early months of 1945.

47. Enoc P. Waters, "Atom Bomb Birthplace City of Paradox: Negro Kids Can't Go to School at Biggest Brain Center," *Chicago Defender*, 29 December 1945, 1.

48. Daniel Boorstin, *The Americans: The Democratic Experience* (New York: Random House, 1973), 1.

49. Hanford Condemnation Directive, 8 February 1943; MDH, IV, 4, appendix A.

50. Alice Kimball Smith, "Law and Order," in *Standing By and Making Do*, 74.

51. Information on photography within the Manhattan District is drawn from the following sources: interviews with the head photographers at both Hanford (Robley Johnson) and Oak Ridge (Ed Westcott); official *Handbooks* for the sites located at the Los Alamos Historical Society, the Hanford Science Center, and the Westcott Room of the Oak Ridge Children's Museum, respectively; and various memoranda and other documents scattered in the archives.

52. I have presented a more elaborate discussion of the photography on the district at the 1990 American Studies Convention and at the "Modes of Inquiry in American City History" symposium at the Chicago Historical Society in 1990.

53. MDH, I, 8, summary S-4.

54. Feynman's story is recounted in his imaginative memoir *Surely You're Joking, Mr. Feynman* (New York: Norton, 1985), 114–17; references to his plight are found in reports closer to the original period as well—in Jane S. Wilson, "Not Quite Eden," from *Standing By and Making Do*, 45–46; and in Jette, *Inside Box 1663*, 34–35.

55. These are all sidebars or captions stuck into the Hanford newspaper, the *Sage Sentinel.*

56. All of these pictures are contained in Badash and Broida, *Reminiscences of Los Alamos*, 59; Kunetka, *City of Fire*, 165–67; and Emilio Segre, *Enrico Fermi, Physicist* (Chicago: University of Chicago Press, 1970), 146; see also the reports incompletely cited in Rhodes, *The Making of the Atomic Bomb*, 661–68.

57. Leona Marshall Libby, *The Uranium People.* (New York: Crane Russak/ Charles Scribner's Sons, 1979), 167.

58. This reference comes from Robert Alvarez, an investigator for the Senate Governmental Affairs Committee, quoted on "The Bomb's Lethal Legacy," a segment of *Nova* aired on PBS in the spring of 1990.

Priesthoods and Power:

Some Thoughts on Diablo Canyon

STEVEN MARX

As soon as I moved to San Luis Obispo from the San Francisco Bay Area, I fell in love with the place—its creekside plaza, its downtown volcanoes, its nearby bluffs and beaches. But after several months of exploring idyllic attractions, I found myself drawn by a different feature of the local landscape: the spot at the center of the map on the Emergency Information brochure I received in the mail; the spot that the siren on my street corner blared about on Saturday morning; the spot that I was reminded of by stickers in the hallways at work that read "Radiation Shelter." I wanted to put myself at ground zero and to experience a direct encounter with the source of energy that heats my shower, runs my computer, and threatens my life. So I called the electric company, PG and E, and signed up for a free tour of the Diablo Canyon Nuclear Power Plant.

Two days later, I parked in front of Sears and climbed into a van along with five other visitors. The guide handed me a security badge, a small brochure with a tasteful brush painting of a nuclear reactor on its cover, and a questionnaire asking me how informed I was on "power plant history, plant construction, wildlife protection, marine biology research, nuclear power production, Chumash archaeological site, public safety" and asking my opinion on whether nuclear power was "generally safe, neutral, somewhat unsafe . . . generally efficient, neutral, somewhat inefficient." I could see I was going to be tested.

On the drive to Avila Beach, the guide, who was also a ranking security officer, recounted the history of the plant's construction as a series of rational calculations in the face of public hysteria and mob violence. After we gained clearance at the first security gate, the barrier went up and we crossed a wide blue line on the road. This, he pointed out, was the border that the demonstrators had tried unsuccessfully for decades to storm, the line at which order had stemmed chaos.

The roadway itself typified the cosmic energies mobilized for the creation of the plant: it was built of reinforced concrete 4 feet thick and 60 feet wide to accommodate the 192-wheeled "transporter" that carried equipment from barges in the bay to the construction site, and its curves were specially unbanked to keep the 400-ton reactor containment vessels from swaying on the way. This road also typified the ultra-advanced technology that made the plant a showpiece of safety and efficiency—a totally computerized facility that runs by "paperless management," fully monitors itself, and constantly "talks to you."

He drove slowly along the unbanked roadway, winding twelve miles through a protective buffer zone of oak-studded hills and flowery pastures overlooking the sea—an 11,000-acre wildlife preserve where we sighted hawk, deer, and a badger. He told us about the environmental study center built on-site and maintained by the company to protect the endangered species of bird and sea life that make it their home and to study the uniquely rich ecosystem that thrives in the heated waters of the bay. He told us about the power company's production of new fish habitats, like the artificial reef along Pecho Rock made from concrete sections of the breakwater destroyed by 1983 storms, and about the salmon enhancement program at the mouth of San Luis Creek. It was an account of a symbiotic co-creation between nature and human artifice nestled in a suitably Edenic setting.

Soon we arrived at another gateway. Our guide explained that before we could pass this second barrier the guard would have to examine our badges. There were two further and more thorough checkpoints that we could not penetrate: the entrance to the actual plant and, within that, the entrance to the reactor area. I was disappointed by this exclusion, but the sense of crossing one threshold after another and the prospect of live nuclear reactions taking place in my presence stimulated my imagination. I was now on a pilgrimage, drawn, in Mircea Eliade's words, by an "ontological thirst . . . to take a stand at the very heart of the real, at the Center of the World—that is, exactly where the cosmos came into existence . . . as it was in the beginning, . . . fresh from the Creator's hands, and . . . where too there is the possibility of communications with the gods." [1]

Once cleared, we rounded a turn in the road and the forbidden valley suddenly came in sight. I felt strangely secured, as if I'd been snapped into a socket and reduced in size by the magnified landscape that surrounded me. The feeling reminded me of my first view of Yosemite Valley at age twelve, and of what a friend once tried to convey about arriving at the Delphic shrine in Greece. A mountain peak soared 1,500 feet above a wide shelf of seaside cliffs. It was flanked by a canyon through which a stream crashed into a perfectly formed cove guarded by majestic headlands and a wave-sculpted island covered with sea lions. In the center, dominating this splendid panorama, stood an immense assemblage of rectangular monoliths, breastlike domes, and delicate webs that throbbed and hummed and crackled. It seemed to me like some vast temple, sucking matter from the unformed waters, reaching for the heavens with its observatorylike towers, and beaming out energy through high tension wires that ran from its heart and disappeared in all directions over the surrounding ridges.

We parked at an overlook above the plant while the guide explained the workings of the reactor: the fissioning uranium heats water to steam which heats other water to steam which runs the turbines that generate the electricity. Enough of it is produced here to supply two million people, 14 percent of the PG and E system, the equivalent of 23 million barrels of oil per year. The fuel is a few tons of uranium; the waste, a few pounds of plutonium. He made it sound matter-of-fact, but to me it was pure magic: the production of limitless quantities of power in a clean, benevolent recycling process. What more appropriate use for such an awesome location?

As we drove around the back of the plant down through the canyon and emerged at its mouth above the cliffs, the guide pointed out a fenced area that surrounds the headland and remains off limits even to PG and E employees. Discovered in the process of excavating for the reactor, it was a major ancient village site and burial ground, containing evidence of nine thousand years of continuous habitation by the Chumash, one of the California Indian tribes whose existence was almost fully extinguished early in this century. He told us that photographs proving that the site has not been disturbed are sent annually to an intertribal religious organization which now uses it occasionally for traditional celebrations of the winter solstice.

As if bombarded by some stray neutrons from inside the plant, my imagination became more excited; I realized that this had been a unique power spot long before PG and E's arrival. I had just been reading a new book on the Chumash, and in the concluding chapter on religion and mythology the author had described just such sacred spaces. The ceremonial ground I was looking at would have been demarcated by woven boughs, feathered banners, and a fence of whale jaws to create a Siliyik or Antap. The *mana* or power concentrated in these spots was viewed as left over from the time of creation, an incorporeal force that allows one to travel out of body, transform the shape of objects, heal illness, make rain. Access to this space and its power was permitted only to priests and priestesses of the Antap cult. Organized as a grid uniting diverse regions and tribes, this priesthood shared ritual and practical knowledge, especially of astronomy and meteorology. One of their primary functions was to help the gods balance the contrary forces controlling nature at times when such equilibrium was threatened. The winter solstice, when their remarkably accurate calendars predicted that the path of the sun would reverse direction, was the most dangerous of such times. Every year in their Siliyiks, they carried out elaborate three-day ceremonies to help pull the sun back from its southward-moving path.[2]

I tried to imagine what the shamans who come back here think as they stand in this place on 21 December in the shadow of the reactor bedecked with Christmas tree lights. Is it that their power has been driven out by an alien power that is destroying their mother earth, or do they sense, as John

Michell has put it, that "strangers may conquer the land, imposing their own gods and cults on the natives, but the sacred places and dates of their festivals remain the same as before, the attributes of the new deities are accommodated to the old, and the invaders become in time subject to the traditions of the country"?[3] I wondered whether the electric company's transformation of the landscape was not similar to what other Native American shamans carried out in Aztec and Mayan cities, in the construction of temples and earthworks and river diversions as massive, impressive, and intrusive on the landscape as this plant. I wondered whether the spiritual power that fuels and structures native societies is not similar to the occult power that fuels and structures ours; I wondered whether the Indian technicians of the sacred and our contemporary sacred technicians perform the identical function of mediating between the rest of us humans and the mysterious, dangerous, and nourishing forces of the universe.

My reflections recalled those of another outsider who described an experience of awe in the face of such power. Henry Adams wrote in 1900:

> The dynamo [or electric generator] became a symbol of infinity . . . a moral force, much as the early Christians felt the cross. . . . Before the end, one began to pray to it; inherited instinct taught the natural expression of man before silent and infinite force. . . . He had entered a supersensual world. . . . Physics [had gone] stark mad in metaphysics. . . . The rays . . . were occult, supersensual, irrational; they were a revelation of mysterious energy . . . they were what, in terms of medieval science, were called immediate modes of the divine substance.[4]

Like Adams at the Paris exposition, here at Diablo Canyon I had received an epiphany.

The final stop on our tour was at the training building, where we were instructed about reactor safety. We entered the simulated control room, a large space filled floor to ceiling with thousands of dials, screens, switches, and blinking lights which exactly replicates the real control room operating the plant from inside the fourth perimeter. Some men were reading printouts, leafing through manuals, talking on the phone, conferring briefly. The guide told us they were either trainees, who study here for up to seven years before becoming licensed, or qualified operators, who spend one out of every five weeks practicing for emergencies. All systems in the plant contain multiple redundancy, so that any foul-ups can be bypassed. Thus, it is unthinkable that a disaster like Three Mile Island or Chernobyl could happen here. The evacuation procedures and sirens are only technicalities required by law.

What could I say? Along with my vision of power came a sense of acceptance and reconciliation with those who controlled it—the priests of PG and E. In the van, on the way back to Sears, I checked off the positive responses on the questionnaire, returned it to the guide, sat back, and left the driving to him.

Six months later, a colleague in the history department handed me a call for papers for an academic conference he was coordinating on "Place in American Culture." Suggested topics included studies of "American sacred places and pilgrimages" and "the 'spirit' and meaning of particular places ... e.g., Diablo Canyon." I took the lure and sent in a proposal outlining the story I have just told. When I received notice of acceptance, I got very nervous and decided to arm myself with a little research. The further I proceeded, the less satisfied I became with my original approach.

First I read some more about the Chumash priests. According to Thomas Blackburn, the power derived from the gods was regarded as less benevolent than I had thought. In most native accounts, "beings with exceptional power are characterized as dangerous or antipathetic to man."[5] According to Lowell J. Bean, those humans who held power were treated with respect and awe, but also with considerable caution, since they were "potentially amoral in their relationships with others. Their allegiance is to power, both the maintenance of power and the acquisition of more power, and thus primarily to other persons of power ... [rather than] the claims of the local social order." One's relation to power determined one's place in an elaborate social hierarchy, a chain of being which guaranteed privilege, wealth, status, and leisure to those in possession of its secrets and exploited those who were excluded. "Priests and shamans ... controlled the principal means of production and distribution of goods, owned monopolies on many goods and services ... possessed the power to levy taxes, fines and establish fees to support institutions, and were able to charge exorbitant interest on loans, thus amassing further wealth."[6] Indeed, a 1978 study postulated that during the early period of European contact Chumash priests willingly entered the missions in search of what they perceived as the Christians' more potent magic and thereby hastened the destruction of their own culture before they discovered that the missionaries were merely leading them on.[7]

This information about Indian priesthoods spurred me to investigate their successors. According to Richard Rudolph and Scott Ridley, utility executives control more assets than any other group of executives in the United States; power is the biggest business in modern America, and half of the income of major investment bankers is estimated to come from financing private power companies.[8] These priests are also regarded with caution and skepticism. Amory Lovins characterized their rule as one of "friendly fascism," while *Fortune* magazine categorized utility officials as "generally unimaginative men, grown complacent on private monopoly and regulated profits."[9]

Studies of the industry concur that the utility priests reached a zenith of prestige and influence during the 1950s, when visions of taming the destructive force of the bomb into atoms for peace proliferated prophecies that electricity would become so abundant it would be "too cheap to meter." Encouraged by the federal government, which was eager to maintain American dominance over the international reactor market, the utilities assumed they could easily control the dangers and uncertainties of nuclear power. Demand for electricity was projected to grow indefinitely at a ravenous 7 percent per year, and liability insurance, which no private carrier would offer, was provided by Congress in form of the Price-Anderson Act, which absolved the companies from any financial responsibility for accidents.

By the late 1970s, however, the vision had dissipated. Fundamental technical problems that should have been dealt with before any plants were built remained unsolved—problems like earthquake safety, what to do with wornout reactors, and the disposal of radioactive wastes. Of the more than 200 nuclear plants ordered by utility companies, 180 had been canceled, while the rest were plagued by construction delays, safety violations, objections of surrounding inhabitants, and financial losses, not to speak of hair-raising accidents. Rather than being reduced, the price of power had tripled, while demand actually shrank. Several companies went bankrupt, while others defaulted on loans or skipped dividends to investors. The overall cost of the miscalculations was estimated as between $100 to $200 billion, to be divided among stockholders, ratepayers, and taxpayers.

Forbes magazine called the nuclear energy program "the largest managerial disaster in business history" (Munson, 7).

My reading revealed that, despite these mammoth setbacks, in 1980 the industry attempted to resurrect itself with a lobbying and public relations initiative dubbed "The Second Coming of Nuclear Power," which had the full support of the new Reagan administration (Rudolph and Ridley, 239). Tax incentives for alternate energy development and conservation were phased out and replaced with government subsidies for the expansion of coal- and nuclear-fired technology. The licensing procedures of the Nuclear Regulatory Commission were speeded up, the public was denied access to them, and the rapidly growing problem of waste disposal was declared solved with a report commissioned by the Department of Energy. Produced by the Battelle Memorial Institute, this report recommended that all waste be transported to a central site called "the nuclear stonehenge." There it would be guarded by

> an "atomic priesthood" which would carry out a "ritual and legend" process to warn generations 10,000 years in the future of the danger of radioactive waste buried . . . three thousand feet down, under a large triangular area bordered by raised mounds. At the center of the site, three twenty-foot tall granite monoliths inscribed with warnings would stand on a concrete mat. . . . Because our language may be incomprehensible three hundred generations from now, the fatal danger located underground would be communicated by stick figure cartoons engraved on the monoliths. Other warnings might include a symbol resembling three sets of malevolent horns facing outward from a circle, or an undying artificial stench which people and animals would avoid. . . . The "atomic priesthood" would reinforce these warnings with oral myths that threatened violators of the site with "some sort of supernatural retribution." (Rudolph and Ridley, 240)

As I marveled at this claptrap, I recognized how close it was to the language and mentality of my treasured epiphany. The equation of electric and spiritual power was not a product of my imagination or of my reading of Henry Adams; it was precisely the way the utility company wanted me to think. At that point, another definition of the word "power" came to mind: political power. I saw the shamans and the utility priests both clad in the vestments of what C. Wright Mills called "The Power Elite." Rather than mediating between the impotent human and omnipotent divine, these priests concentrated power diffused throughout nature and among all people into sacred spaces and private preserves, thereby rendering the rest of the world profane, and the rest of humanity powerless.

I learned that during the last two decades the utility priesthood's drive to centralize power was threatened by the failures of nuclear energy and by the concomitant successes of alternative, independent sources of electricity, including cogeneration, biomass, wind, thermal, and solar. Because government regulations made it illegal for utilities to boycott such sources, they accounted for 40 percent of California's energy generating capacity by the middle 1980s. As a result, a power struggle between the priesthood and its opponents has been taking place all over the country, in federal, state, and local governments and also in the streets and in wilderness areas invaded by transmission lines and saboteurs. The power struggle is between what Langdon Winner has called a "political technology" supported by extremely tight security and authoritarian management that can force citizens to accept irreparable environmental damage and pay the astronomical costs of nuclear plants and those who seek to develop decentralized, autonomous, local sources of power.[10] A sample of that opposing power, in its own way as impressive as the priestly energy that created Diablo Canyon, is the recent spectacle of decommissioning the Shoreham Nuclear Power Plant on Long Island, New York. After twenty years of opposition by local citizens who refused to accept its threat to their lives, their environment, and their solvency, and despite the continuous support of the Reagan and Bush administrations, the $5.5 billion plant was abandoned last June before it ever started up and was sold to the state for one dollar as scrap.[11]

I also discovered that a similar twenty-year power struggle between local citizens and a utility priesthood had taken place in my new home town of San Luis Obispo, but had led to an opposite outcome. In the county museum, documenting that struggle, I found a large archive collected by Mothers for Peace, the group that organized much of the resistance. Once again I saw that the real power was neither spiritual nor electric, but economic and political, that the plant was here against the will of those most affected by it because of the overwhelming money and influence wielded by the utility in Washington and Sacramento.

Among the clippings, I came across a very down-to-earth and local explanation of how the plant arrived at its magical site. Back in the middle

1960s, PG and E wanted to locate it in the Pismo Dunes, but in order to preserve that sensitive area environmental groups agreed to approve an alternate unseen location. The owner of the Diablo property, a rancher named Marre, was eager to develop condos and a hotel on his holdings in Avila beach, so he offered the company a 99-year lease on the 11,000 acres in return for their corporate guarantee of an open line of credit he could use to capitalize his project—the San Luis Bay Inn complex. A few years later, the project went belly up; PG and E sued to take full possession of the land as collateral for his bad debts, and Marre countersued, lending his support to the opponents of the plant. Had the environmentalists not accepted the original deal or had Marre been prevented from pursuing his plans, that sacred spot would have remained a Chumash graveyard.

As I concluded my reading, I came across a quotation by a contemporary of Henry Adams that crystallized my changed perspective on the topic of priesthoods and power. In 1928, the conservationist governor of Pennsylvania, Gifford Pinchot, wrote:

> We need not be surprised that the State and Federal authorities have stood in awe before this gigantic nationwide power monopoly, because beside it, as its creator, financial supporter, and master, stands the concentrated money power of the world. . . . Therefore the electric power monopoly deserves the fullest public attention. The people ought to know what it is and why it is and how it affects them. All the facts about it ought to be publicly available either through government agencies or private effort. The people must learn to judge intelligently of its advantages and its evils. Everything about it should be investigated fearlessly and published fully, because we must learn to regulate and control it before it smothers and enslaves us. (cited by Rudolph and Ridley, 263)

To goad myself into writing the conference paper, I went on another Diablo Canyon tour. This time the meeting place was the "Energy Information Center" near Highway 101, and I joined a group of forty people boarding a lush tour bus. We were led by a pair of very smiling guides, who, it turned out later, could answer few questions that departed from their scripts; they were not PG and E employees but local residents newly hired by a company that contracted to do public relations with the utility. This time as we passed the blue line they said nothing about the hostile demonstrations, but I remembered the picture in the archives of suited professionals, long-haired adolescents, parents with babies in strollers, and sign-carrying seniors facing off at this border with a line of helmeted, masked, and club-bearing police. As we crossed the second perimeter, I noticed the metal cutouts of human figures distributed up and down the hillsides, practice targets for the sharpshooters always on patrol. At the overlook we were told that unit two was shut down for refueling, that plutonium-rich spent fuel was accumulating underwater in the tank directly below us until the government figured out what to do with it, and that the radioactive containment towers would have to remain here permanently sealed after the plant's retirement in twenty or thirty years. At the Indian cemetery I looked backward and realized that layer upon layer of midden was buried under the twenty-acre construction site, and I looked seaward, remembering a recent statement by USGS geologists that the Hosgri Fault a few miles offshore could easily produce an earthquake larger than the 7.5 magnitude that the plant is built to withstand. In the simulated control room of the operator training facility, I fiddled with switches while two men wearing NRC badges joked with a PG and E employee. On the way out of the room, I noticed that the red light was lit on the coffee machine next to the control console. The water had boiled away, leaving a charred and evil-smelling residue of coffee in the bottom of the pot. "Meltdown," the person in front of me quipped. "Human error," someone else replied.

On the bus ride back, one guide spoke briefly of the four levels of possible mishap and the four levels of planned response and then waxed enthusiastic about the future of nuclear power in general. The next generation of reactors, he said, will be smaller, less expensive, decentralized, and safer than Diablo, which was really a white elephant—too big, too expensive, and too dangerous. I crumpled up my questionnaire and held my stomach as the bus swung too fast around the unbanked curves.

NOTES

1. Mircea Eliade, *The Sacred and the Profane: The Nature of Religion* (New York: Harper, 1959), 64–65.

2. Bruce Miller, *Chumash: A Picture of Their World* (Los Osos, Cal.: Sand River Press, 1988), 121–28.

3. John Mitchell, *The Earth Spirit: Its Ways, and Mysteries* (New York: Avon, 1975), 11.

4. Henry Adams, *The Education of Henry Adams*, ed. Ernest Samuels (Boston: Houghton Mifflin, 1973), 380–83.

5. Thomas Blackburn, *December's Child, A Book of Chumash Oral Narratives* (Berkeley: University of California Press, 1975), 69.

6. Lowell John Bean, "Power and Its Application in Native California," *Journal of California Anthropology* 2 (1975): 31.

7. Travis Hudson and Ernest Underhay, *Crystals in the Sky: An Intellectual Odyssey Involving Chumash Astronomy, Cosmology and Rock Art* (Santa Barbara: Ballena Press, 1978), 17–22.

8. Richard Rudolph and Scott Ridley, *Power Struggle: The Hundred Year War over Electricity* (New York: Harper, 1986), xi, 13 (hereafter cited in the text).

9. Quoted in Richard Munson, *The Power Makers: The Inside Story of America's Biggest Business . . . and Its Struggle to Control Tomorrow's Electricity* (Emmaus, Penn.: Rodale Press, 1985), 182 (hereafter cited in the text).

10. Langdon Winner, *The Whale and the Reactor: A Search for Limits in an Age of High Technology* (Chicago: University of Chicago Press, 1986) 175.

11. *New York Times*, 29 June 1989.

NOTES ON CONTRIBUTORS

Ray Allen is a folklore consultant for the World Music Institute and City-lore in New York City and is a guest lecturer in the American Studies Department at Rutgers University. He is the author of *Singing in the Spirit: African-American Sacred Quartets in New York City* (1991).

Timothy Davis, a graduate of the Visual and Environmental Studies Department of Harvard College, is a Ph.D. candidate in American Civilization at the University of Texas at Austin.

Wayne Franklin is professor of English and professor and chair of American Studies at the University of Iowa, author of three books on American verbal and material culture, and editor of the "American Land and Life" series. He currently is writing a book (*Erasing America*) about the verbal and visual representation of the American landscape prior to the Civil War.

Peter Bacon Hales, professor in the History of Architecture and Art Department at the University of Illinois at Chicago, is the author of *Silver Cities: The Photography of American Urbanization, 1839–1915* (1984) and *William Henry Jackson and the Transformation of the American Landscape* (1988). He currently is completing a cultural history of the Manhattan Engineering District, tentatively titled *Atomic Spaces: Geography, Mythology, and the Manhattan Project*.

Steven Marx, associate professor of English at California Polytechnic State University, San Luis Obispo, is the author of *Youth against Age: Generational Strife in Renaissance Poetry* (1985) and is currently working on a book about militarism and pacifism in Shakespeare, Milton, and Blake.

Kinereth Meyer is currently senior lecturer in English and American literature and co-ordinator of the American Studies Program at Bar-Ilan University, Israel. She has published widely on modern poetry and drama and is presently completing a book on American poetry and landscape.

Clarence Mondale is professor of American Civilization at George Washington University and co-author with Michael Steiner of *Region and Regionalism in the United States* (1988).

Don Scheese, who teaches American literature at Santa Clara University, co-edited (with Sherman Paul) a special issue of *North Dakota Quarterly* (Spring 1991) entitled "Nature Writers/Writing" and has published several articles on nature writing and environmental history.

April Schultz, visiting assistant professor in the Department of American Studies at the University of Notre Dame, is currently working on a book about the invention of ethnicity among Norwegian-Americans in the 1920s.

Richard Keller Simon, associate professor of English at California Polytechnic State University, San Luis Obispo, is the author of *The Labyrinth of the Comic: Theory and Practice from Fielding to Freud* (1986). His essay on the mall and the garden is part of a book project on the relationship of contemporary American mass culture to the great art and literature of the past.

Michael Steiner, professor and director of the graduate program in American Studies at California State University, Fullerton, is the co-author with Clarence Mondale of *Region and Regionalism in the United States* (1988) and is writing a history of American regional thought.

Yi-Fu Tuan is John Kirtland Wright and Vilas Professor of Geography at the University of Wisconsin–Madison. His most recent books are *Dominance and Affection* (1984), *The Good Life* (1986), and *Morality and Imagination* (1989).

Kathleen R. Wallace, a doctoral candidate in English at the University of Minnesota, is completing a dissertation on women and place in American culture. Her other research interests include African-American literature, nature writing, and baseball.

INDEX